LIBRARY CATALOGUING

By

Bhagwatiben Govindbhai Prajapati

M.A., B.Lib., M.Lib., B.Ed.

Librarian

Special Education College

Palanpur

(India)

DISCOVERY PUBLISHING HOUSE PVT. LTD.

NEW DELHI-110 002

Published by:
Tilak Wasan

DISCOVERY PUBLISHING HOUSE PVT. LTD.
4383/4B, Ansari Road, Darya Ganj
New Delhi-110 002 (India)
Phone : +91-11-23279245, 43596064-65
Fax : +91-11-23253475
E-mail : discoverypublishinghouse@gmail.com
sales@discoverypublishinggroup.com
web : www.discoverypublishinggroup.com

***First Edition:* 2013**

***Reprinted:* 2017**

ISBN: 978-93-5056-387-8

Library Cataloguing

Printed at:
Infinity Imaging Systems
Delhi

Content

Preface

Library collections house a broad variety of materials on numerous different subjects and in many different formats. The challenge in making these things available for the use of library patrons is letting those patrons know what is in the library collection. This is the reason for having a library catalogue and for taking the time to correctly catalogue library materials.

The library catalogue might be compared to the index for a book. The index provides the reader with a way to find information in the book without having to read every page. The index tells the reader the page on which the information about a specific subject can be found. The library catalogue does the same thing. It tells the library user exactly where materials meeting their specific needs can be found, with the call number of the book corresponding to the page number in an index.

The information contained in the cataloguing record provides the many access points needed by the patron looking for information in the library. Traditionally, the library card catalogue provided access by the author's name, the title of an item, and the subject(s) covered in the item. Other points of access were additional authors, names of series, illustrators, and sometimes the titles of contents.

—Author

1

Library Catalogue

A library catalogue (or library catalogue) is a register of all bibliographic items found in a library or group of libraries, such as a network of libraries at several locations. A bibliographic item can be any information entity (*e.g.*, books, computer files, graphics, realia, cartographic materials, etc.) that is considered library material (*e.g.*, a single novel in an anthology), or a group of library materials (*e.g.*, a trilogy), or linked from the catalogue (*e.g.*, a webpage) as far as it is relevant to the catalogue and to the users (patrons) of the library.

The card catalogue was a familiar sight to library users for generations, but it has been effectively replaced by the online public access catalogue (OPAC). Some still refer to the online catalogue as a "card catalogue". Some libraries with OPAC access still have card catalogues on site, but these are now strictly a secondary resource and are seldom updated.

Many of the libraries that have retained their physical card catalogue post a sign advising the last year that the card catalogue was updated. Some libraries have eliminated their card catalogue in favour of the OPAC for the purpose of saving space for other use, such as additional shelving.

GOAL

Charles Ammi Cutter made the first explicit statement regarding the objectives of a bibliographic system in his *Rules for a Printed Dictionary Catalogue* in 1876.

Those objectives were:

* To enable a person to find a book of which either (Identifying objective)

  - The author
  - The title
  - The subject
  - The category
* To show what the library has (Collocating objective)
  - By a given author
  - On a given subject
  - In a given kind of literature
* To assist in the choice of a book (Evaluating objective)
  - As to its edition (bibliographically)
  - As to its character (literary or topical)

These objectives can still be recognized in more modern definitions formulated throughout the 20th century. 1960/61 Cutter's objectives were revised by Lubetzky and the Conference on Cataloguing Principles (CCP) in Paris. The latest attempt to describe a library catalogue's goals and functions was made in 1998 with Functional Requirements for Bibliographic Records (FRBR) which defines four user tasks: find, identify, select, and obtain.

TYPES

Traditionally, there are the following types of catalogue:

* *Author Catalogue:* A formal catalogue, sorted alphabetically according to the authors' or editors' names of the entries.
* *Title Catalogue:* A formal catalogue, sorted alphabetically according to the title of the entries.
* *Dictionary Catalogue*: A catalogue in which all entries (author, title, subject, series) are interfiled in a single alphabetical order. This was the primary form of card catalogue in North American libraries just prior to the introduction of the computer-based catalogue.
* *Keyword Catalogue:* A subject catalogue, sorted alphabetically according to some system of keywords.
* *Mixed Alphabetic Catalogue Forms:* Sometimes, one finds a mixed author/title, or an author/title/keyword catalogue.
* *Systematic Catalogue:* A subject catalogue, sorted according to some systematic subdivision of subjects. Also called a *Classified* catalogue.

* *Shelf List Catalogue:* A formal catalogue with entries sorted in the same order as bibliographic items are shelved. This catalogue may also serve as the primary inventory for the library.

HISTORY

Library catalogues originated as manuscript lists, arranged by format (folio, quarto, etc.) or in a rough alphabetical arrangement by author. Printed catalogues, sometimes called *dictionary catalogues*, began to be published in the early modern period and enabled scholars outside a library to gain an idea of its contents. Copies of these in the library itself would sometimes be interleaved with blank leaves on which additions could be recorded, or bound as *guardbooks* in which slips of paper were bound in for new entries.

Slips could also be kept loose in cardboard or tin boxes, stored on shelves. The first card catalogues appeared in the late 19th century after the standardization of the 5 in. x 3 in. card for personal filing systems, enabling much more flexibility, and towards the end of the 20th century the Online public access catalogue was developed.

These gradually became more common as some libraries progressively abandoned such other catalogue formats as paper slips (either loose or in sheaf catalogue form), and guardbooks. The beginning of the Library of Congress's catalogue card service in 1911 led to the use of these cards in the majority of American libraries. An equivalent scheme in the United Kingdom was operated by the British National Bibliography from 1956 and was subscribed to by many public and other libraries.

* *C. 245 BC:* Callimachus is considered the first bibliographer and is the one that organized the library by authors and subjects. The *Pinakes* was the first ever library catalogue. Variations on this system were used in libraries until the late 1800s when Melvil Dewey developed the Dewey Decimal Classification in 1876, which is still in use today.
* *C. 800:* Library catalogues are introduced in the House of Wisdom and other medieval Islamic libraries where

books are organized into specific genres and categories.

* *1595: Nomenclator* of Leiden University Library appears, the first printed catalogue of an institutional library.
* *1674:* Thomas Hyde's catalogue for the Bodleian Library.
* *1791:* The French Cataloguing Code of 1791

More about the early history of library catalogues has been collected in 1956 by Strout.

SORTING

In a title catalogue, one can distinguish two sort orders:

1. In the *grammatical* sort order (used mainly in older catalogues), the most important word of the title is the first sort term. The importance of a word is measured by grammatical rules. for example, the first noun may be defined to be the most important word.
2. In the *mechanical* sort order, the first word of the title is the first sort term. Most new catalogues use this scheme, but still include a trace of the grammatical sort order: they neglect an article (The, A, etc.) at the beginning of the title.

The grammatical sort order has the advantage that often, the most important word of the title is also a good keyword, and it is the word most users remember first when their memory is incomplete. However, it has the disadvantage that many elaborate grammatical rules are needed, so that only expert users may be able to search the catalogue without help from a librarian.

In some catalogues, person's names are standardized, i. e., the name of the person is always sorted in a standard form, even if it appears differently in the library material. This standardization is achieved by a process called authority control.

An advantage of the authority control is that it is easier to answer question (which works of some author does the library have?). On the other hand, it may be more difficult to answer question (does the library have some specific material?) if the material spells the author in a peculiar variant. For the cataloguer, it may incur (too) much work to check whether *Smith, J.* is *Smith, John* or *Smith, Jack.*

For some works, even the title can be standardized. The technical term for this is *uniform title.* For example, translations and re-editions are sometimes sorted under their original title. In many catalogues, parts of the Bible are sorted under the standard name of the book(s) they contain. The plays of William Shake-speare are another frequently cited example of the role played by a *uniform title* in the library catalogue. Many complications about alphabetic sorting of entries arise.

Some examples:

* Some languages know sorting conventions that differ from the language of the catalogue. For example, some Dutch catalogues sort *IJ* as *Y*. Should an English catalogue follow this suit? And should a Dutch catalogue sort non-Dutch words the same way?
* *Some Titles Contain Numbers, For Example 2001:* A Space Odyssey. Should they be sorted as numbers, or spelled out as *Two thousand and one*?
* *De Balzac, Honouré* or *Balzac, Honouré de*? *Ortega y Gasset, José* or *Gasset, José Ortega y*?

In a subject catalogue, one has to decide on which classification system to use. The cataloguer will select appropriate subject headings for the bibliographic item and a unique classification number (sometimes known as a "call number") which is used not only for identification but also for the purposes of shelving, placing items with similar subjects near one another, which aids in browsing by library users, who are thus often able to take advantage of serendipity in their search process.

ONLINE CATALOGUES

Online cataloguing has greatly enhanced the usability of catalogues, thanks to the rise of MAchine Readable Cataloguing = MARC standards in the 1960s. Rules governing the creation of catalogue MARC records include not only formal cataloguing rules like AACR2 but also special rules specific to MARC, available from the Library of Congress and also OCLC. MARC was originally used to automate the creation of physical catalogue cards. Now the MARC computer files are accessed directly in the search process.

OPACs have enhanced usability over traditional card formats because:

* The online catalogue does not need to be sorted statically. The user can choose author, title, keyword, or systematic order dynamically.
* Most online catalogues offer a search facility for any word of the title. The goal of the grammatic word order (provide an entry on the word that most users would look for) is reached even better.
* Many online catalogues allow links between several variants of an author name. So, authors can be found both under the original and the standardised name (if entered properly by the cataloguer).
* The elimination of paper cards has made the information more accessible to many people with disabilities, such as the visually impaired, wheelchair users, and those who suffer from mold allergies.

WHAT IS WRONG WITH THE LIBRARY CATALOGUE

Problems for the online library catalogue did not begin with the advent, quick development or broad adoption of the web. For more than 20 years, the library catalogue has been criticised for its difficult use and poor functionality. Despite a number of studies and papers suggesting ideas for improving library catalogues, changes have been slow and many of the ideas have not been implemented.

Most of the changes have been made on surface rather than in the core functionality, leaving library catalogues hard to use. Studies show that besides falling behind the trends on the web, the most problematic area is the catalogue's interface, lacking in functionality, intuitivity, and content.

Traditional library catalogues are poorly designed for the tasks of finding, discovering and selecting resources available in libraries. They are best at locating and obtaining known items, so the user must know precisely what he/she wants. But this emphasis on know-item searching does not follow the actual user behaviour and mental models in information retrieval.

Information retrieval process often begins with only a vague idea, which is then gradually formulated sufficiently to begin searching. Besides that, query formulation is difficult as the user needs to have the conceptual knowledge of how the terms can be combined and is required to use the terms that match those in the catalogue.

Boolean logic in query formulation is hard for the user to comprehend and research shows that there is in fact only minimal usage of Boolean operators. Due to the common use of the web, users are accustomed to naturallanguage searching and simply type multiple search terms (keywords) on a single line without connecting them with Boolean operators. They also build queries using only terms they have in mind, without consulting the controlled vocabulary the library uses, all leading to poor results.

That is why many think that a better alternative to query formulation would be searching by browsing, recognition and discovery. Browsing is recognized as a natural and effective way of searching that requires less effort and knowledge. It is also easier for the user to recognize than recall information.

As Bates points out "information seeking is, after all, about finding out things that one does not know before the search begins". These are all reasons for turning the traditional paradigm "query-first-then browse" upside down, making the exploration and discovery by browsing the primary search interface, supported by secondary query method.

The second problematic area in library catalogues is the results list and navigation between results. Queries often return hundreds or thousands of hits, but users are willing to look at only a very limited number. Web search engines have therefore developed very sophisticated systems for relevance ranking of results.

Accustomed to get the most relevant results first, users are confused when in library catalogues irrelevant records appear before items they were looking for. With a large number of search results it is also very time-consuming to look at every hit in order to decide whether it is relevant or not. To enable easier and faster selection, result clustering and faceted navigation should be applied to quickly narrow and filter the results to a manageable number.

One possibility for meaningful clustering of results is also the use of Functional Requirements for Bibliographic Records (FRBR). The third most frequent reproach against the library catalogue is the lack of information presented to the user. Most records in the library catalogue display only basic textual bibliographic data.

To improve the user experience, the library catalogue needs to be enriched with cover art images, tables of contents, summaries, reviews, excerpts, popularity ranks, recommendation lists and features such as "find similar" or "users who borrowed this book also borrowed...". These are all things already available on some other web destinations, especially online bookshops. They offer users all this additional information in order to promote their collection and to help users choose the items they need.

THE STATE OF CURRENT LIBRARY CATALOGUES

To estimate the state of current library catalogues an expert study was carried out in January 2008, based on the framework from a study performed in July 2007. Following the examined literature, six main areas of research were formed, within each a number of features were observed, analysing their presence and realization in the library catalogues.

For the purpose of the expert study, six library catalogues were chosen:

* *One Traditional:* The Slovene union catalogue COBISS and
* *Five More Modern and Innovative ones:*
  - Ann Arbor District Library catalogue,
  - Hennepin County Library catalogue,
  - Queens Library catalogue,
  - Phoenix Public Library catalogue, and
  - WorldCat.

Table 1.1 and Table 1.2 summarize the results of the expert study, showing which of the recommended features were found in the studied catalogues. In features most needed for easier and more intuitive searching there are only two catalogues showing good and promising results. Followed by WorldCat, these three catalogues have gone beyond traditional and offer users simple searching and quick results. The other catalogues are far behind in this area, still offering only complex searching that requires users to make many unnecessary steps.

Table1.1: Features in Six Current Library Catalogues—Part 1

	Library Catalogues					
	A	H	Q	P	W	C
Search						
Simple keyword search box on each page	+/–	+/–	++	++	++	–
Spell checking	++	++	++	++	–	–
Automatic spelling corrections	–	–	–	++	–	–
Begin search by browsing	+/–	+/–	+/–	++	–	–
Full text searching	–	–	–	–	–	–
Results page and navigation						
Relevance ranking	–	–	++	++	++	–
Clustering and/or faceted navigation	–	–	++	++	+	–
Breadcrumbs navigation	–	–	+	++	+	–
Enriched content and recommendation lists						
Cover art images	++	+	++	++	+	–
Reviews	++	++	–	++	–	–
Summaries/Annotations	++	++	++	++	+	+/–
Excerpts	–	++	++	++	–	–
Tables of content	++	++	++	++	–	+/–
New items, most popular, recently returned items and recommendations lists	+	++	++	++	–	–
"More like this"	+	–	–	++	–	–
Audio in video content	–	+	+/–	+/–	–	–

Key: A = Ann Arbor District Library.
H = Hennepin County Library.
Q = Queens Library.

P = Phoenix Public Library.
W = WorldCat.
C = COBISS
++ very good.
+ good, with some limitations.
+/– available, but very limited.
– not available

With the exception of WorldCat and COBISS, library catalogues have provided their users with additional information about the collection, offering enriched content such as cover art images, summaries, tables of content, and various recommendation lists. But there is still room for improvement, especially in the way this additional content is integrated in the catalogue. Libraries should also offer more multimedia content and recommendations on similar books. If features in table are focused on functionality, table is more about current trends library catalogues could adopt from the web. Taking a small lead in more social features are Ann Arbor and Hennepin library catalogues, followed by the Phoenix library catalogue.

The number of characteristics found in all six catalogues is smaller and more spread than in table, showing that each library chose a different set of trendy features. From reference point of view it is important to stress the potential of user participation and personalization. Personalization enables the system to adapt the interface to the end-user's wishes and recommend materials from the library collection according to the users' recent searches, favourite titles, or areas of interest. Another way to offer reading recommen-dations is also by using user participation features.

Tags and user created lists can be embedded in the library catalogue, pointing users to similar items chosen by other users. Ratings, reviews, comments, and forums bring to the library the wisdom of crowds that helps the user form an opinion on the material.

The expert study showed three different groups of library catalogues:

* Library catalogues that have not yet begun with this kind of modernization,
* Library catalogues that have focused more on improving functional features shown in table, and

* Library catalogues that devoted their attention to Web 2.0 trends.

Table 1.2: Features in Six Current library Catalogues—Part-2

	Library Catalogues					
	A	H	Q	P	W	C
User participation						
Ratings and reviews	++	+	–	+/–	++	–
Comments	++	++	–	–	–	–
Tags	++	–	–	–	–	–
Lists	–	+	–	++	+	–
Instant messaging (user-librarian)	–	+	+	–	–	+
Forum	–	–	–	–	–	–
User profile and personalization						
Automatic log-in	++	++	–	–	–	–
Saved searches	–	–	++	++	–	–
Recent activities	+/–	–	–	–	–	–
Overview and editing of created content	++	++	–	+	+	–
Saved items lists	+	++	–	++	++	+/–
Personalized web page	+	+	+	–	+/–	–
Personalized e-mail notices	–	++	+	+	–	+
Personalized recommendations	–	–	–	–	–	–
Other trends						
RSS feeds	+	++	++	++	–	–
Blogs	++	++	–	–	–	–
E-media for borrowing online	–	++	++	++	–	–

Notes:

Key:

A = Ann Arbor District Library.

H = Hennepin County Library.

Q = Queens Library.

P = Phoenix Public Library.

W = WorldCat.

C = COBISS

++ very good.

+ good, with some limitations.

+/– available, but very limited
.–not available

Interestingly, catalogues focused on functional improvements offer less user participation and personalization while catalogues with more enhanced 2.0 features have not modernized their search and navigation. Using and testing all catalogues in the expert study we found that the latter catalogues are much harder to use and are not user friendly despite offering users to participate.

The new features are shaded by poorly designed interfaces that can frustrate web-savvy users. On the other hand, catalogues that focused on modernizing functional aspects of catalogues are easy and fun to use, supporting discovery and serendipity. With many interesting features that encourage users to research the catalogue, the lack of direct user participation and personalization is not really problematic.

PURPOSE OF CATALOGUING LIBRARY MATERIALS

Library collections house a wide variety of materials on many different topics and in many different formats. The challenge in making these things available for the use of library patrons is letting those patrons know what is in the library collection. This is the reason for having a library catalogue, and for taking the time to correctly catalogue library materials.

The library catalogue might be compared to the index for a book. The index provides the reader with a way to find information in the book without having to read every page. The index tells the reader the page on which the information about a specific subject can be found.

The library catalogue does the same thing. It tells the library user exactly where materials meeting their specific needs can be found, with the call number of the book corresponding to the page number in an index. The information contained in the cataloguing record provides the many access points needed by the patron looking for information in the library. Traditionally, the library card catalogue provided access by the author's name, the title of an item, and the subject(s) covered in the item. Other points of access were additional authors, names of series, illustrators, and sometimes the titles of contents.

Computer catalogs can, in theory, provide access to any part of the information contained in the record for an item in the library. The development of MARC (Machine Readable Cataloguing) in the 1960's made it possible to encode all areas of a cataloguing record to be searchable. In MARC cataloguing, each piece of information in a catalogue record is given a numerical code, or field, and sometimes an alphabetical or numerical sub field. This coding makes it possible for a computer programme to be written that looks for particular numbered fields when a particular type of search, such as a subject or title, is requested.

Because all of the information in the cataloguing record is encoded, searches could optionally be done by ISBN number, by series, by publisher, by date or by any of the pieces of information stored in the cataloguing record. MARC has set the standard for all computer catalogs used in libraries today, and if the records contained in the catalogue comply with MARC requirements, the only controls on areas to be searched are the limits of the particular cataloguing programme.

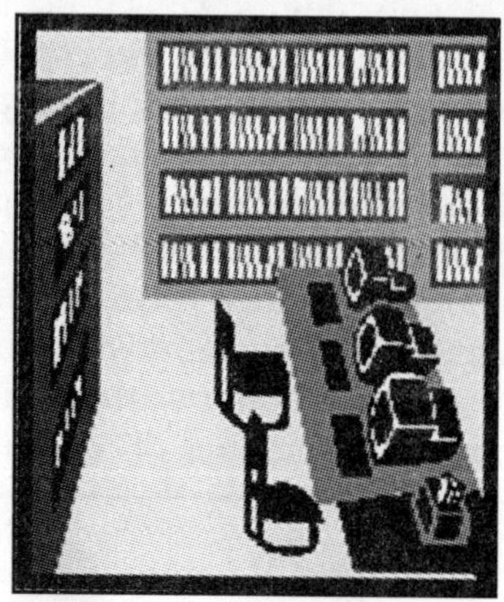

When library materials are catalogued in a careful and complete manner, access is provided for the library patrons and staff to all sources of information on a particular topic, by a particular author, or in a particular format, that the library possesses. The better the access, the more use the collection receives, and the more satisfied the patron is in his or her search for information in the library.

2

Catalogue

Cataloguing (or cataloging) is the process of listing or including something in a catalogue. In library science it is the producing of bibliographical descriptions of books or other kinds of documents. Today the study of cataloguing has broadened and merged with the study of metadata ("data about data contents") and is sometimes termed resource description and access.

CATALOGUING RULES

Cataloguing rules have been defined to allow for consistent cataloguing of various library materials across several persons of a cataloguing team and across time. Users can use them to clarify how to find an entry and how to interpret the data in an entry. Cataloguing rules prescribe which information about a bibliographic item is included in the entry and how this information is presented for the user. It may also aid to sort the entries in printing the catalogue.

The larger a collection, the more elaborate cataloguing rules are needed. Users cannot and do not want to examine hundreds of catalogue entries or even dozens of library items to find the one item they need. Currently, most cataloguing rules are similar to, or even based on, the International Standard Bibliographic Description (ISBD), a set of rules produced by the International Federation of Library Associations and Institutions (IFLA) to describe a wide range of library materials.

These rules organize the bibliographic description of an item in the following areas: title and statement of responsibility (author or editor), edition, material specific details (for example, the scale of a map), publication and distribution, physical description (for example, number of pages), series, notes, and standard number (ISBN). The most commonly used set of cataloguing rules in the English-speaking world are the Anglo-American Cataloguing Rules, 2nd Edition, or AACR2 for short.

AACR2 provides rules for *descriptive cataloguing* only and does not touch upon *subject cataloguing*. AACR2 has been translated into many languages, for use around the world. In the German-speaking world there is also the *Regeln für die alphabetische Katalogisierung* (RAK). Library items that are written in a foreign script are, in some cases, transliterated to the script of the catalogue.

STANDARDS

In libraries have versions of the AACR2 and MARC standards for a long time been internationally accepted standards. In subject databases such as Chemical Abstracts, MEDLINE and PsycINFO is no standards, but the "Common Communication Format" (CCF) is ment to serve such databases. In archives and museums are other principles followed. Resource Description and Access is a recent attempt to make a standard that crosses the domains. It should be considered that all these standards differ from the standards used by authors to refer to their sources. All these standards represent alternative way of bibliographical recording.

COMMON COMMUNICATION FORMAT

"The users of the CCF on the other hand, coming from many different backgrounds (some indeed national libraries), would never consider aiming at such a level of homogeneity between records originating in different systems. They have been able to accept that there will be different practices in record creation resulting in records which, when merged into a database, will show their different origins."

"Early in its deliberations the Group undertook a comparison of all of the data elements in:

* *The Reference Manual*: ASIDIC/EUSIDIC/ICSU-AB/NFAIS Interchange Specifications, and—the USSR-US Common Communication Format.

With these six standard formats as a guide, the Group identified a small number of data elements which were used by virtually all information-handling communities, including both libraries and abstracting and indexing organizations. These commonly used data elements formed the core of the CCF. A technique was developed to show relationships between bibliographic records, and between elements within biblio-graphic records. The concept of the record segment was developed and refined, and a method for designating relationships between records, segments, and fields was accepted by the group. The first edition of CCF: The Common Communication Format was published in 1984."

DESCRIPTIVE CATALOGUING

"Descriptive cataloguing" is a well-established concept in the tradition of library cataloguing in which a distinction is made between descriptive cataloguing and subject cataloguing, each applying a set of standards, different qualifications and often also different kinds of professionals. In the tradition of documentation and information science (*e.g.*, by commercial bibliographical databases) the concept document representation (also as verb: document representing) have mostly been used to cover both "descriptive" and "subject" representation.

Descriptive cataloguing has been defined as:

* "The part of cataloguing concerned with describing the physical details of a book, such as the form and choice of entries and the title page transcription."

SUBJECT CATALOGUING

This is mostly known as classification and (subject) indexing. Classification is the assignment of a given document to a class in a classification system. Indexing is the assignment of characterizing labels to the documents represented in a record. Classification is a kind of controlled vocabulary while indexing may use controlled vocabulary, free terms, or both.

CATALOGUING TERMS

* Main entry or access point – generally refers to the first author named on the item. Additional authors are

added as "added entries." In cases where no clear author is named, the title of the work is considered the main entry.

ONLINE PUBLIC ACCESS CATALOGUE (OPAC)

An Online Public Access Catalogue (often abbreviated as OPAC or simply Library Catalogue) is an online database of materials held by a library or group of libraries. Users search a library catalogue principally to locate books and other material physically located at a library.

HISTORY

Early Online Catalogs

Although a handful of experimental systems existed as early as the 1960s, the first large-scale online catalogs were developed at Ohio State University in 1975 and the Dallas Public Library in 1978. These and other early online catalogue systems tended to closely reflect the card catalogs that they were intended to replace. Using a dedicated terminal or telnet client, users could search a handful of pre-coordinate indexes and browse the resulting display in much the same way they had previously navigated the card catalogue. Throughout the 1980s, the number and sophistication of online catalogues grew. The first commercial systems appeared, and would by the end of the decade largely replace systems built by libraries themselves. Library catalogues began providing improved search mechanisms, including Boolean and keyword searching, as well as ancillary functions, such as the ability to place holds on items that had been checked-out.

At the same time, libraries began to develop applications to automate the purchase, cataloguing, and circulation of books and other library materials. These applications, collectively known as an integrated library system (ILS) or library management system, included an online catalogue as the public interface to the system's inventory. Most library catalogues are closely tied to their underlying ILS system.

Stagnation and Dissatisfaction

The 1990s saw a relative stagnation in the development of online catalogues. Although the earlier character-based interfaces were replaced with ones for the web, both the design and the underlying search technology of most systems did not advance much beyond that developed in the late 1980s.

At the same time, organizations outside of libraries began developing more sophisticated information retrieval systems. Web search engines like Google and popular e-commerce websites provided simpler to use (yet more powerful) systems that could provide relevancy ranked search results using probabilistic and vector-based queries. Prior to the widespread use of the Internet, the online catalogue was often the first information retrieval system library users ever encountered. Now accustomed to web search engines, newer generations of library users have grown increasingly dissatisfied with the complex (and often arcane) search mechanisms of older online catalogue systems. This has, in turn, led to vocal criticisms of these systems within the library community itself, and in recent years to the development of newer (often termed 'next-generation') catalogs.

Next-generation Catalogues

The newest generation of library catalogue systems are distinguished from earlier OPACs by their use of more sophisticated search technologies, including relevancy ranking and faceted search, as well as features aimed at greater user interaction and participation with the system, including tagging and reviews. These newer systems are almost always independent of the library's integrated library system (ILS), instead providing drivers that allow for the synchronization of data between the two systems.

While older online catalogue systems were almost exclusively built by ILS vendors, libraries are increasingly turning to next generation catalogue systems built by enterprise search companies and open source projects, often led by libraries themselves. The costs associated with these new systems, however, have slowed their adoption, particularly at smaller institutions.

UNION CATALOGUES

Although library catalogues typically reflect the holdings of a single library, they can also contain the holdings of a group or consortium of libraries. These systems, known as union catalogs, are usually designed to aid the borrowing of books and other materials among the member institutions via interlibrary loan. The largest such union catalogue is WorldCat, which includes the holdings of over 70,000 libraries worldwide.

RELATED SYSTEMS

There are a number of systems that share much in common with library catalogues, but have traditionally been distinguished from them. Libraries utilize these systems to search for items not traditionally covered by a library catalogue. These include bibliographic databases—such as Medline, ERIC, PsycINFO, and many others—which index journal articles and other research data.

There are also a number of applications aimed at managing documents, photographs, and other digitized or born-digital items such as Digital Commons and DSpace. Particularly in academic libraries, these systems (often known as digital library systems or institutional repository systems) assist with efforts to preserve documents created by faculty and students.

ANALYSIS OF COLLECTED DATA

Distribution of Questionnaires and the Responses Received

Table 2.1: Distribution of Questionnaires and Responses Received

Category of Users	No. of Questionnaires	No. of Questionnaires Distributed	% of Responses Received
	Total	Total	
UG students	1075	841	78.23
Faculty	430	364	84.65
Postgraduate students	155	104	67.10
Researcher	56	29	51.79
Total	1716	1338	77.97

The questionnaires were distributed to the respondents and the responses received from them are presented in Table 2.1.

From the Table 2.1, 1716 questionnaires were distributed to the different respondents of engineering colleges in Karnataka and the response rate was 77.97%. Among the total responses 841 respondents are UG students, 364 respondents are faculty. However 104 respon-dents are PG student community and only 29 respondents are researchers.

Age-wise Distribution of Respondents

Table 2.2 shows age group of the respondents. It has been observed that, 99 (7.40%) respondents belonged to the age group of less than 20 years. Among them most of the users were under-graduate students. Further 968 (72.35%) respondents belonged to the age of 20-25 years, followed by 174 (13.00%) of respondents belonged to the age group of 25-30 years. Eighty (5.98%) respondents were in the age group of 30-35 years, 12 (0.90%) respondents were in the age group of 35-40 years.

Table 2.2: Age-wise Distribution of Respondents

Sl. No.	Age in Years	Categories of Users				Total
		UGS	PGS	R	F	
1.	Less than 20 Years	99 (11.77)	0 (0.00)	0 (0.00)	0 (0.00)	99 (7.40)
2.	20-25 Years	721 (85.73)	70 (67.31)	14 (48.28)	163 (44.78)	968 (72.35)
3.	25-30 Years	21 (2.50)	31 (29.81)	13 (44.83)	109 (29.95)	174 (13.00)
4.	30-35 Years	0 (0.00)	3 (2.88)	2 (6.90)	75 (20.60)	80 (5.98)
5.	35-40 Years	0 (0.00)	0 (0.00)	0 (0.00)	12 (3.30)	12 (0.90)
6.	More than 40 Years	0 (0.00)	0 (0.00)	0 (0.00)	5 (1.37)	5 (0.37)
Total		841 (100.00)	104 (100.00)	29 (100.00)	364 (100.00)	1338 (100.00)

Note: Figures given in parentheses indicate percentages in respective category of users.

UGS = Undergraduate students, PGS = Postgraduate Graduate students, R = Researchers, F = Faculty.

Remaining five (0.37%) respondents were in the age group of more than 40 years. The chi-square calculated value = 544.842. P < 0.000 was found, significant. This study indicates that the major population surveyed belonged to the students group, followed by the faculty and then, researchers, etc. It is obvious that the students are more IT savy and feels comfortable in accessing computers.

Category-wise Distribution of Respondents

Table 2.3 exhibits that 841 (62.82%) respondents were undergraduates and 364 (27.20%) of the respondents formed the faculty. At the same time 104 (7.77%) users were postgraduates, followed by 29(2.17%) respondents, who were researchers.

Table 2.3: Category-wise Distribution of Respondents.

Sl. No.	Category of Users	No. of Respondents	Percentage
1	UG Students (UGs)	841	62.86
4	Faculty (F)	364	27.20
2	Postgraduate (PGs) Students	104	7.77
3	Researcher (R)	29	2.17
Total		1338	100.00

Gender-wise Distribution of Users

Table 2.4: Gender-wise Distribution of Respondents.

Sl. No.	Category of Users	Category of Users				Total
		UGS	PGS	R	F	
1	Male	489 (58.15)	80 (76.92)	24 (82.76)	192 (52.75)	785 (58.67)
2	Female	352 (41.85)	24 (23.08)	5 (17.24)	172 (47.25)	553 (41.33)
Total		841 (100.00)	104 (100.00)	29 (100.00)	364 (100.00)	1338 (100.00)

Note: Figures given in parentheses indicate percentages in respective category of users.

Table 2.4 exhibits that 785 (62.08%) users were males. Out of which 489 were undergraduate students, 192 were faculty, 80 were post-graduate students and the remaining 24 respondents were researchers, whereas, only 553 (41.33%) users were female, out of which 352 were undergraduate students, 172 faculty members, 24 were post-graduate students and remaining five respondents were researchers. The chi-square calculated value = 26.591. P < 0.000 was found to be significant.

Details about Library Software Used for Library Automation

Here the investigator has made an attempt to collect data relating to the library software packages used by the libraries of engineering college in Karnataka coming under this study. The data so collected are analysed and presented in Table 2.5. Table 2.5 shows that, out of 43 engineering college libraries. here 11 (25.58%) libraries are using Libsoft, while six (13.95%) libraries are using EasyLib. Whereas four (9.30%) libraries are using NetLib and four (9.30%) libraries are using Smart Campus.

Table 2.5: Details about Library Software for Qutomation.

Sl. No.	Name of the Software	No. of Libraries	Percentage
1	Libsoft	11	25.58
2	EasyLib	6	13.95
3	Netlib	4	9.30
4	Smart Campus	4	9.30
5	LiMS	3	6.98
6	ie-Lib	2	4.65
7	E-Granthalaya	2	4.65
8	SOUL	2	4.65
9	Libsuite	1	2.33
10	SLIM ++	1	2.33
11	Chancellor	1	2.33
12	Pal Pup	1	2.33

Table Contd...

13	NewGenLib	1	2.33
14	Libsys	1	2.33
15	YLAS	1	2.33
16	IOZEN	1	2.33
17	Lib-Manager	1	2.33
Total		43	100.00

Similarly, three (6.98%) libraries are using LiMs software followed by ie-Lib, E-Granthalaya, SOUL software packages are used by each two (4.65%) libraries. The software which is single installations are Libsuite, SLIM++, Chancellor, Pal Pup, NewGenLib, Libsys, YLAS, IOZEN and Lib-Manager and they are represented as 2.33% of the total respondents. It is observed from the study that, a large majority of respondents are using Libsoft for library automation.

Use of OPAC Services

Table 2.6 depicted the usage of OPAC at the libraries of engineering colleges in Karnataka. The study has identified that, 1092 (81.61%) of respondents were using OPAC. Among them 662 were under-graduates, 328 were faculty members and 81 were postgraduates, the remaining 21 respondents were researchers. Similarly 246 (18.39%) of respondents were not using this facility, among them 179 were undergraduates, 36 were faculty and 23 were post-graduates. Only eight respondents were researchers.

The students need more information for their academic pursuits. The colleges are nowadays, offering too many job oriented professional courses and it has become imperative, for the students to use modern technologies in fulfilling their academic requirements.

Frequency of OPAC Usage

It is necessary to find out how frequently, the staff and students make use of the OPAC facility, which is shown in Table 2.6.

A question was asked to find the frequency of OPAC usage. The results showed that 699 (64.01%) of the respondents were using it daily, 212 (19.41%) of the respondents used it, once in two days.

198 (18.13%) used it, once in a week and 152 (13.92%) used it, twice in a week. Similarly 40 (3.66%) of the respondents used it, once in two weeks. Only 37 (3.39%) of them used it, occasionally. Nearly 55% of the members used the OPAC at library, almost every day.

Table 2.6: Distribution of Frequency-wise and Category-wise Use of OPAC

Sl. No.	Frequency	Category of Users				
		UGS N=662	PGS N=81	R N=21	F N=328	Total N=1092
1	Daily	452 (68.28)	14 (17.28)	18 (85.71)	215 (65.55)	699 (64.01)
2	Once in two days	122 (18.43)	12 (14.81)	6 (28.57)	72 (21.95)	212 (19.41)
3	Once in a week	140 (21.15)	39 (48.15)	2 (9.52)	17 (5.18)	198 (18.13)
4	Twice in a week	107 (16.16)	14 (17.28)	3 (14.29)	28 (8.54)	152 (13.92)
5	Once in two weeks	15 (2.27)	14 (17.28)	0 (0.00)	11 (3.35)	40 (3.66)
6	Once in a month	5 (0.76)	11 (13.58)	0 (0.00)	21 (6.40)	37 (3.39)

Note: Figures given in parentheses indicate percentages in respective category of users. Total percentage will not be hundred because responses are more than one.

Locating Required Information in the Library and OPAC

Table 2.7: Locating Required Documents in the Library OPAC

Sl. No.	Locating Documents	Category of Users				
		UGS N=662	PGS N=81	R N=21	F N=328	Total N=1092
1.	Through OPAC	662 (100.00)	81 (100.00)	21 (100.00)	328 (100.00)	1092 (100.00)
2.	Browsing book(s) on shelves	239 (36.10)	67 (82.72)	19 (90.48)	122 (37.20)	447 (40.93)

3.	Consulting library staff	177 (26.74)	21 (25.93)	21 (100.00)	218 (66.46)	437 (40.02)
4.	From card catalogue	38 (5.74)	58 (71.60)	19 (90.48)	110 (33.54)	225 (20.60)
5.	Through help from friend(s)	187 (28.25)	44 (54.32)	19 (90m.48)	22 (6.71)	272 (24.91)

Note: Figures given in parentheses indicate percentages in respective category of users.

Table 2.7 showed how the users chose their books and other materials for their study. Analysis showed that 1092 (100.00%) of them chose the OPAC for finding information about books and other reading materials, 447 (40.93%) of them directly go to the shelves and browse books, without using OPAC. Nearly 437 (40.02%) of them got the required information with the help of library staff. Similarly 225 (20.60%) of them get their materials by consulting from the card catalogue, followed by 272 (24.91%) of the surveyed users, who got the information through peers. From the table, it is clear that OPAC has made a beginning with the users and will definitely dominate the scene in the years to come.

Table 2.8: Usage of Library OPAC

Sl. No.	Usage	Category of Users				Total
		UGS	PGS	R	F	
1.	Only library premises	314 (47.43)	54 (66.67)	11 (52.38)	198 (60.37)	577 (52.84)
2.	Stand alone system	187 (28.25)	9 (11.11)	4 (19.05)	99 (30.18)	299 (27.38)
3.	Wide Area Network (Internet)	99 (14.95)	6 (7.41)	1 (4.76)	8 (2.44)	114 (10.44)
4.	College campus network	62 (9.37)	12 (14.81)	5 (23.81)	23 (7.01)	102 (9.34)
Total		662 (100.00)	81 (100.00)	21 (100.00)	328 (100.00)	1092 (100.00)

Note: Figures given in parentheses indicate percentages in respective category of users. UGS=Under Graduate students, PGS=Postgraduate Graduate students, R=Researchers, F=Faculty

Usage of Library OPAC

Table 2.8 depicts the distribution of respondents on the basis of the usage of OPAC in their respective libraries. It showed that 577 (52.84%) of the respondents were using OPAC, in their library premises and 299 (27.38%) of the respondents were using the OPAC, through the stand alone system in their library. Nearly 114 (10.44%) of the respondents browsed OPAC through the Wide Area Network (Internet). Similarly 102 (9.34%) of the respondents got their access through the network at college campus. The chi-square calculated value = 63.207. P < 0.000 was found significant.

Table 2.9: Purpose of Using the Library OPAC

Sl. No.	Purpose	Category of Users				
		UGS N=662	PGS N=81	R N=21	F N=328	Total N=1092
1	To locate the book in the library	660 (99.70)	71 (87.65)	20 (95.24)	235 (71.65)	986 (90.29)
2	To find non-print materials	265 (40.03)	80 (98.77)	19 (90.48)	255 (77.74)	619 (56.68)
3	To cheek whether the required book is available in the library or not	470 (71.00)	70 (86.42)	18 (85.71)	246 (75.00)	804 (73.63)
4	To reserve the book which is borrowed by some one	305 (46.07)	67 (82.72)	17 (80.95)	278 (84.76)	667 (61.08)
5	To compile biblio graphy of books on a particular subject	275 (41.54)	66 (81.48)	18 (85.71)	195 (59.45)	554 (50.73)
6	To check the number of copies in library stock	225 (33.99)	61 (75.31)	20 (95.24)	295 (89.94)	601 (55.04)

Note: Figures given in parentheses indicate percentages in respective category of users. Total percentage will not be hundred because responses are more than one

Purpose of Using the Library OPAC

Table 2.9 depicted that a majority 986 (90.29%) of the respondents consult the OPAC to know the location of books in the library, followed by 619 (56.68%) and 804 (73.63%) to find the non-print materials or to check whether the required book was available in the library or not. Similarly 667 (61.08%) of the respondents consulting OPAC to compile bibliography of the books on a particular subject, 554 (50.73%) used OPAC to check the number of copies of the required books in the stock and 601 (55.04%) respondents did not respond to this query.

Users Information Search on OPAC

Whenever the users want to confirm the availability of a required document in the stock of the library, they can approach the OPAC with any of the search elements *viz.*, author, title, subject or call number, classification number, series and ISBN, shown in Table 2.10.

Table 2.10 shows that, 1056 (96.70%) of the respondents approached the OPAC by author, 1012 (92.67%) under the title, 330 (30.22%) approached the OPAC through the subject, similarly 204 (18.68%) and 211 (19.32%) of respondents approached through the accession number and classification number respectively. About 257 (23.53%) respondents did it, under the series search and 150 (13.74%) of respondents searched by ISBN. It is further observed that, when we compare all the approaches of the users, query approach through the author string is most popular followed by title, subject, series, classification number and call number.

Table 2.10: Users Information Search on OPAC

Sl. No.	Searching of Information	Category of Users				
		UGS N=662	PGS N=81	R N=21	F N=328	Total N=1092
1	By author	660 (99.70)	78 (96.30)	20 (95.24)	298 (90.85)	1056 (96.70)
2	By title	660 (99.70)	69 (85.19)	11 (52.38)	264 (80.49)	1012 (92.67)

Table Contd...

3	By subject	144 (21.75)	29 (35.80)	19 (90.48)	138 (42.07)	330 (30.22)
4	By call number	103 (15.56)	22 (27.16)	7 (33.33)	72 (21.95)	204 (18.68)
5	By classification number	125 (18.88)	22 (27.16)	9 (42.86)	55 (16.77)	211 (19.32)
6	By series	112 (16.92)	19 (23.46)	15 (71.43)	111 (33.84)	257 (23.53)
7	By ISBN	15 (2.27)	20 (24.69)	10 (47.62)	105 (32.01)	150 (13.74)

Note: Figures given in parentheses indicate percentages in respective category of users. Total percentage will not be hundred because responses are more than one

Reason for Not Using the Library OPAC

The study also investigated the reasons for not using the OPAC services by the respondents. From the analysis Table 2.11, it is evident that, the majority or 245 (99.59%) of the respondents have faced problems of password protection, 224 (91.06%) and 137 (55.69%) of respondents were not interested due to shortage of terminals and lack of awareness about the facilities respectively.

Table 2.11: Reason for not Using the library OPAC Services.

Sl. No.	Reason	Category of Users				
		UGS 3N=179	PGS N=23	R N=8	F N=36	Total N=246
1	OPAC access is password protected	179 (100.00)	22 (95.65)	8 (100.00)	36 (100.00)	245 (99.59)
2	Know the facility but Shortage of terminals not interested in using	178 (99.44)	11 (47.83)	6 (75.00)	29 (80.56)	224 (91.06)
3	Not aware of these facilities	81 (45.25)	15 (65.22)	5 (62.50)	36 (100.00)	137 (55.69)
4	OPAC module is not properly working	79 (44.13)	19 (82.61)	8 (100.00)	22 (61.11)	128 (52.03)

Table Contd...

5	No OPAC module is installed	17 (9.50)	20 (86.96)	3 (37.50)	19 (52.78)	59 (23.98)
6	System is not near to stack area	22 (12.29)	10 (43.48)	5 (62.50)	13 (36.11)	50 (20.33)
7	Lack of orientation from library staff	19 (10.61)	2 (8.70)	3 (37.50)	15 (41.67)	39 (15.85)
8	Did not get the book(s) required	15 (8.38)	5 (21.74)	2 (25.00)	5 (13.89)	27 (10.98)

Note: Figures given in parentheses indicate percentages in respective category of users. Total percentage will not be hundred because responses are more than one

Similarly 128 (52.03%) respondents faced problems, due to improper working of the OPAC module. Nearly 59 (23.98%) respondents said that the OPAC module was not installed, followed by 39 (15.85%) of respondents stated that lack of orientation from library staff. Only 27 (10.98%) of them expressed that they did not get book(s) required. It is further observed from this analysis that most of the respondents were facing the problem of shortage of terminals and lack of guidance or orientation.

Programmes for Promoting the Use of OPAC

The users were facing certain difficulties in making proper use of the OPAC facility. In view of this factor, a question was asked in the questionnaire, whether there is a need for conducting "User Education Programmes" like lectures/talks, seminars/conferences, orientations/training in using the OPAC module. The results are presented in Table 2.12.

Table 2.12: Programmes for Promoting the Use of OPAC

Sl. No.	Description	Category of Users				Total
		UGS	PGS	R	F	
1	Training	452 (68.28)	49 (60.49)	10 (47.62)	214 (65.24)	725 (66.39)
2	Seminars/Conferences	107 (16.16)	27 (33.33)	4 (19.05)	111 (33.84)	249 (22.80)

Table Contd...

3	Lectures/Talks	54 (8.16)	3 (3.70)	5 (23.81)	1 (0.30)	63 (5.77)
4	Stand on services	39 (5.89)	2 (2.47)	2 (9.52)	2 (0.61)	45 (4.12)
5	Any other programmes	10 (.51)	0 (0.00)	0 (0.00)	0 (0.00)	10 (0.92)
Total		662 (100.00)	81 (100.00)	21 (100.00)	328 (100.00)	1092 (100.00)

Note: Figures given in parentheses indicate percentages in respective category of users.

Table 2.12 shows that, the majority or 725 (66.39%) users responded for orientation or training programmes in using OPAC and 249 (22.80%) for seminars/conferences to be conducted, 63 (5.77%) were in favour of lectures/talks, Furthermore, 45 (4.12%) of the respondents expected, at least a staff to be posted, near the OPAC module, to provide assistance to the users. Only 10 (0.92%) of respondents wanted some other programmes to be conducted, apart from the following listed programmes. In fact, such programmes shóuld have been initiated by the library, for the better utilization of its electronic services. The chi-square calculated value = 95.686. P < 0.000 was found significant.

Assistance from the Library Staff for Using OPAC

In response to the opinion about the assistance from the library staff for using OPAC shows in fig. 2.1.

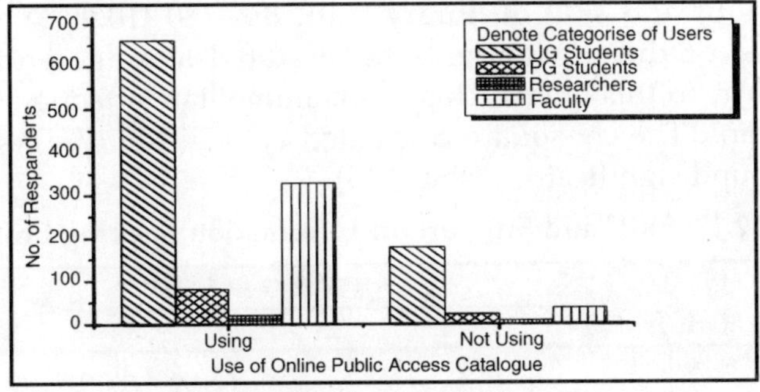

Fig. 2.1: Use of OPAC Services.

Majority (1000; 91.58%) of respondents has said 'Yes' and 92 (8.42%) of users are not interested in taking assistance.

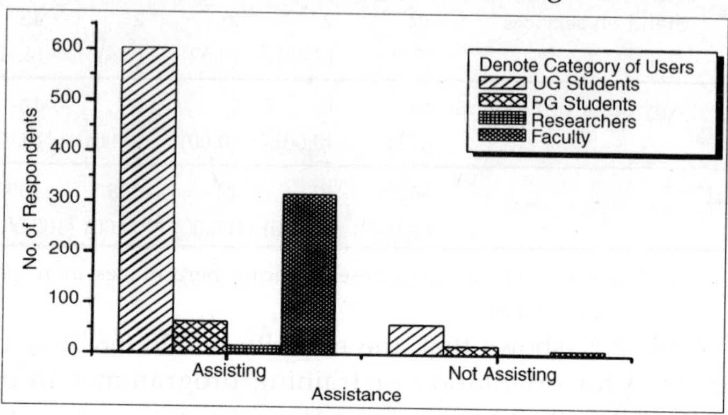

Fig.2.2: Assistance from the Library Staff for using OPAC

From this fig. 2.2, it is clear that maximum number of respondents needed assistance from the library staff for using OPAC, to help them in searching the required document(s). Such assistance is also necessary for fulfilling the Fourth Law of Library Science (Save the time of the reader)

Library Staff Skill and Support on Information Seeking Problems

The study found that, a high percentage of users, that is, 415 (38.00%) were happy with the excellent services provided by librarians. 288 (26.37%) and 175 (16.03%) respondents have expressed very good and good respectively, regarding the behaviour and skill of library staff. But 120 (10.99%) and 94 (8.61%) of the respondents have stated average and poor response, to this query. This needs immediate attention by the librarians. The chi-square calculated value = 105.173. $P < 0.000$ was found significant. (Table 2.13)

Table 2.13: Skill and Support on Information Seeking Problems

Sl. No.	Ratings	Category of Users				Total
		UGS	PGS	R	F	
1	Excellent	274 (41.39)	31 (38.27)	3 (14.29)	107 (32.62)	415 (38.00)

Table Contd...

2	Very Good	161 (24.32)	8 (9.88)	6 (28.57)	113 (34.45)	288 (26.37)
3	Good	96 (14.50)	15 (18.52)	5 (23.81)	59 (17.99)	175 (16.03)
4	Average	64 (9.67)	21 (25.93)	2 (9.52)	33 (10.06)	120 (10.99)
5	Poor	67 (10.12)	6 (7.41)	5 (23.81)	16 (4.88)	94 (8.61)
Total		662 (100.00)	81 (100.00)	21 (100.00)	328 (100.00)	1092 (100.00)

Note: Figures given in parentheses indicate percentages in respective category of users.

Opinions of Respondents

Some open questions were asked to students to know the opinion of the respondents and to obtain more information about OPAC for various purposes.

The respondents were making use of the OPAC for the following purposes:

* To find out particular book of the author or articles in journals.
* To know the arrival of new journals and other reading materials.
* To check the copies of available reading materials.
* To collect literature on seminars, thesis, dissertations, etc.
* For review of literature for the research work.

In this modern age, dominated by information and communication technologies, every human activity is being influenced by IT.

The libraries cannot function in isolation but have to embrace IT for providing new services for collecting, organizing, storing, retrieving and dissemination of varied forms of information with high speed and accuracy. Most of the activities in the libraries can be computerized, including the OPAC.

The opinions of the respondents can be summarized as below:

* It saves time and gives quick. accurate and efficient information.
* Retrieving of required information is at, a much faster rate.
* It is easy to search and to locate documents.
* Without wasting much time, one can find the required book or books.

The respondents have suggested the authorities to provide training in the use of OPAC.

3

Technical Processing Services

CATALOGUING

AACR2 defines a catalogue as:

* A list of library materials contained in a collection, a library, or group of libraries, organized according to some definite plan.

Obviously, cataloguing, or bibliographic control, is the process of preparing such a list. The catalogue consists of a description of each item, which is retrievable by several of its important characteristics used as headings, or access points: the author, title or subject matter. In a manual system, there are several copies of each description which are filed under the appropriate access points for the respective item. But in an automated system there is only one copy of the description which can be displayed using any access point for searching. The description is now called bibliographic record or just record.

Preparing and maintaining a catalogue require:

* Intellectual activity for the cataloguing process based on selected standards and rules, or for locating and using bibliographic records created externally.
* Choice of an overall organization of records within the catalogue and their specific filing sequence.
* Choice of the physical form(s) for the catalogue and the production of records in that form.
* Developing procedures for adding new records and modifying existing ones.

CATALOGUING PROCESS

Descriptive Cataloguing

This embraces the description of the bibliographic or physical significance of the item except its subject content. The cataloguer also decides here which bibliographic elements should be used as access points for the item in the catalogue and determines the appropriate form of access points used. The description normally has many different elements arranged in standard formats.

The rules that should be followed for descriptive cataloguing in a medical library are the Anglo-American Cataloguing Rules, second edition (AACR2) and its revisions. As these rules are more or less the most used rules internationally in both manual and automated systems, using them will enable the user to see the same descriptive record format in any library he may use, and enable the library to use records produced in other libraries.

Defining the Subject Content

This is normally done using two types of tools which produce a subject description in a coded form or in the language(s) used in the catalogue, which is the only difference between using them, otherwise the processes are identical. The two processes are:

* *Classification*: Classification, through the notation of the classification scheme used, decides the general area in the collection where the item will be shelved. Most classification schemes lead to an arrangement of items based on their subject content. This allows the user to browse the shelves. Normally, a more specific shelving number or symbol must be added after the class number to give the item a unique place among other items in the same class. The resulting number is called " call number ".

* Standardization in classification, contrary to descriptive cataloguing, has not yet been achieved internationally. The library may choose a generalized scheme or a specialized one.

The general schemes most widely used in medical libraries are:

* Dewey Decimal Classification (DDC), which is now in its 21st edition and the second on CD-ROM.
* Library of Congress Classification (LCC), which is continuously subjected to revision.
* Universal Decimal Classification (UDC), which is widely used in Europe.
* Among the specialized schemes the most widely used one in medical libraries is NLM Classification.
* *Subject Cataloguing or Indexing*. The problem of this process is that it is language dependent and thus no standardization can possibly be achieved.

The process depends on two types of tools:

* *Lists of subject headings:* These may be general or specialized. Among the general ones, the most widely used list is Library of Congress List of Subject Headings (LCSH), while Medical Subject Headings (MeSH) is the most widely used list by medical libraries. It is now available in many languages.
* *Thesauri:* These are more recent than lists of subject headings and are more associated with automation in libraries. Most thesauri are specialized in their nature.

The choice between lists and subject headings and thesauri is mostly dictated by the indexing method, whether it is pre-coordinated or post-coordinated, as the former favours the lists while the latter adopts thesauri. Automation has introduced yet another way of indexing using free text search or selecting keywords as access points. Cataloguing may involve original cataloguing, that is the creation of cataloguing records in the library from scratch, or using existing records elsewhere which is known as copy cataloguing.

This may be carried out manually or automated. The sources for copy cataloguing may be:

* *Cataloguing-In-Publication (CIP)*: The data in CIP is created on the basis of prepublication galley proofs or preproduction information for the item. This data is usually given on the verso of the title page. CIP data has to be handled with care and should be compared

carefully with the item itself when it is used as the basis for a cataloguing record, as it may have erroneous elements or is not in conformance with standards and rules adopted by the library.

* *Published Bibliographies*: Whether these bibliographies are catalogues of library holdings or published bibliographies, such as national bibliographies, they may be used for creating cataloguing records.
* *Machine-readable Records on Tape*: Some major libraries, such as NLM, may distribute their records on tapes in MARC format. The subscribing library may get such tapes, then use local computer system to select the records needed for the local catalogue. This approach requires significant local hardware and software. Recent development for this is the use of CD-ROM instead of tapes which is cost-effective.
* *Online Services*: Some files simply offer copies of cataloguing records, other online services allow user libraries to modify or create cataloguing records in a variety of formats for incorporation into their local catalogues. Among these are OCLC, RLIN, WLN, UTLAS, and BCMP. NLM has three online files with cataloguing data: CATLINE (Catalogue-on-line) for printed materials, AVLINE (Audiovisualson-line) for audiovisuals since 1975, and NAF (Name Authority File) for name and series authority records.
* *Service Bureaus*: Several agencies and companies in some countries produce catalogue cards or other catalogue formats on demand. The cataloguing copy is provided in a form that is immediately usable in a local catalogue.
* *Book Suppliers*: Some book suppliers provide catalogue records (cards or otherwise) with the books they ship to their library customers.

Regardless of the source of the cataloguing copy, individual libraries may modify or augment cataloguing records they find in order to make them more useful in local catalogues.

Among such amendments the following are necessary:

* If the copy has subject headings and/or classification which the library does not use.
* If the edition of cataloguing rules used for the copy is different from the one applied by the library.
* If the library may wish to add further access points and explanatory notes to records to emphasize some local interest.

But if the cataloguer comes across an error in an access point or in another part of a cataloguing record, he should write to the appropriate institution and ask for clarification.

Other kinds of modifications are probably unnecessary, such as:

* Eliminating data to simplify records.
* Deleting data that the library feels does not assist users very much, such as ISBN or ISSN.

ORGANIZATION OF THE CATALOGUE

In a manual system, most library catalogues are divided into at least two parts:

Shelflist

The shelflist contains one record for each item in the collection. It is usually arranged by call number in exactly the same order of items on the shelf. It is useful for assigning individual shelving numbers, in making an inventory of the collection, provided it is annotated when the library has multiple copies in the same order. This shelflist may not be available for serials when they are not classified. A list of serials may replace it.

Main Catalogue

The main catalogue contains several copies of the record for each item in the collection. A copy of each record is entered: under the author's name, the names of any of the other persons or corporate bodies associated with the work described, its title, its series title, and various subject headings. It also includes cross-references, guiding users from unused forms of names and subject headings to those that have been used.

Many catalogues may also include guide or special heading to enable a user to determine quickly where in the overall sequence of records a particular catalogue file drawer, page of book catalogue, or part of a microform catalogue is located.

DICTIONARY VERSUS DIVIDED CATALOGUE

There are three major arrangements for manual main catalogues:

* *Dictionary catalogue,* in which author, title and subject access points are interfiled.
* *Divided catalogue,* in which subject access points are arranged in a separate sequence from author and title sequence. Some libraries divide even author and title access points as well.
* *Classified catalogue,* in which the call numbers serve as subject access points and are in a separate sequence from author and title access points. This arrangement usually requires a language subject index to class numbers used in the catalogue, although some libraries may be satisfied with the published index of the classification scheme used.

In an online catalogue there will be no need for such arrangements although the automated systems produce any arrangement as a by-product.

AUTHORITY FILES

The authority file is the file that contains the forms of names (of persons, corporate bodies or places), title, series, or subject headings and descriptors used in the bibliographic record, as well the required cross-references to and from these forms, and their relationship with other used forms.

Authority records may be interfiled in the main catalogue, or may be kept in separate authority files, in a manual system. They must be accessible to cataloguing staff. In automated system, they are usually separate from the bibliographic records database but transparently interlinked with the number or symbol of the authority record.

The following is a brief description of the types of authority files:

* Name Authorities: A name authority record consists of:
  - The authoritative name form chosen for use in the catalogue.
  - Alternate forms of the name, and an indication as to whether cross-references from these forms are maintained in the catalogue.
  - Any related names such as previous names of an institution.
  - Source of the authoritative name.
  - Any historical or biographical information about the name necessary to distinguish it from another name.
  - An indication as to which set of cataloguing rules was used to establish the authoritative form.

Name authorities may be imported from cooperative ventures or from major libraries that have such files, such as NLM. They may be initiated also on cooperative basis particularly among libraries with a common language such as Arabic, because the forms of names may differ among the speakers of that language, and the library in the respective country is the best to verify them. With automated systems, it may be easier to use as a search tool as well if the file is constructed in a thesaurus form. These systems and the thesaurus structure will enable making the file multilingual.

* *Title Authorities*: These files will be particularly useful if the library uses uniform titles in its catalogue, or when variant titles exist among various editions of the same work.
* *Series Authorities*: A series authority record is required only for a monographic series, where individual works bear individual title and authorship information, in addition to an overall series title. This file should record the decision on how to handle series.
* *Subject Authorities*: The library may consider the list of subject headings or the thesaurus it applies as a subject authority, or restrict the file to the subject

headings or descriptors it actually uses. This latter type has been eliminated when an automated system is used as it is going to do both purposes.

Catalogues of Special Collections

Some libraries maintain separate catalogue for special types of materials, such as audiovisuals, in addition to their inclusion in the main catalogue. In automated systems, such catalogues may be produced as by-product from the bibliographic database.

Filing Rules

Records in main catalogue in a manual system must be filed alphabetically according to standard filing rules, while those in the shelflist according to the filing order of the classification scheme in use. In an automated system, the system itself contains filing values for the elements of description that are considered in filing. These values are in fact interpretation of the filing rules adopted. As filing is always language dependent, the rules must cope with all languages represented in the catalogue, whether the characters are in roman or non-roman alphabets.

The major existing filing rules are:

* ALA filing rules/Filing committee, Resources and Technical Services Division, American Library Association. Chicago: ALA, 1980.
* Blaise filing rules/British Library Filing Rules Committee. London: British Library, 1980.
* BS 1749: 1985-British standard recommendations for alphabetical arrangement and filing order of numbers and symbols. London: BSI, 1985.
* ISO 7154-ISO bibliographic filing rules. Geneva: ISO, 1985. and ISO/TR 8393-1985, Exemplification of bibliographic filing principles in a model set of rules. Geneva: ISO, 1985.
* Library of Congress filing rules/prepared by John C. Rather and Susan C. Biebel. Washington, DC: Library of Congress, 1980.

The set of filing rules for Arab libraries discusses the agreement and disagreement of these filing rules and those used in some major libraries in the Arab region as well as standard rules for the region:

* ARIS-Net filing rules for catalogues, bibliographies and directories. Tunis: ALDOC, 1989.

The basic principles behind all these rules are:

* Filing is word by word rather than letter by letter.
* Filing must be strictly as is rather than as if which means that the word is filed as written not as it sounds or means, whether written in full or abbreviated form.
* A numeral files before the alphabet.
* Order of characters must be strictly adhered to.

This order is as follows:

- Space, dash, hyphen and diagonal slash are given equal filing character and come first
- Ampersand
- Arabic numerals
- Alphabet letters

* Different forms of the same letter have equal value and must be interfiled.
* All records in the same catalogue must be filed according to the same principles-the same rules.

PHYSICAL FORMS OF CATALOGUES

Card Catalogues

This form is still prevalent in medical libraries. It can include all records regardless of their source. Records are on cards which file into drawers housed in cabinets. Standards are 12.5 x 7.5 cm. Rods may be inserted through holes in the bottom of the cards to help retain them in drawers.

Sheaf Catalogues

A loose-leaf binder format providing some of the convenience of the book. Usually each record is on a separate slip of paper. There may be a number of records on each slip.

Visible Index

This form consists of strips mounted in a frame, or cards held flat, hinged, and with the edge of each card protruding to make the heading visible. This form is used for displaying the list of serials holdings of a library.

Microform Catalogues

This is a form in which records are greatly reduced and "printed" upon a film. So a suitable reader which magnifies the film and project it on to a screen is required. It may be a microfilm or a microfiche.

Machine-readable Catalogues

This is a form which permits input and storage for manipulation in a computer. Access may be online or offline. Data are displayed on a screen or visual display, and may also be output to magnetic tape, disk or printed in hard copy. An offshot of the machine-readable form is the CD-ROM. Another is the computer output microform (COM). But the form which facilitates continuous updating, with amended records being available to the user as soon as they are input, is the online public access catalogue (OPAC). It can be accessed from outside the library through remote terminals.

Finally, the form the library decides to choose should possess as many as possible of the following:

* It must be easy to use.
* It must be easy to keep uptodate.
* It must be easy to scan.
* It must be easy to produce multiple copies.
* It must take up as little space as possible.
* It must be easy to guide.

DESCRIPTIVE CATALOGUING

International Efforts

The major contribution in cataloguing at the international level is that of IFLA. This is in the form of international standard bibliographic descriptions (ISBDs) which have influenced almost all existing cataloguing rules.

IFLA has so far issued the following ISBDs and is continuously subjecting them to revision:

* ISBD (G)-General

* ISBD (M)-Monographs
* ISBD (NBM)-Non-book Materials
* ISBD (CM)-Cartographic Materials
* ISBD (A)-Antiquarian Books
* ISBD (PM)-Printed Music
* ISBD (S)-Serials
* ISBD (CF)-Computer file, Machine-Readable files (MRF)
* ISBD (CP)-Component parts
* ISBD (ER)-Electronic Resources (replaced ISBD (CF)

Other international efforts include those of Unesco particularly the creation of the International Serials Data System (ISDS). ISDS seeks to develop a registry of world serials publications. containing sufficient bibliographic information for their identification and bibliographic control.

The cornerstones of ISDS are the ISSN and a corresponding "key title", to which geographic qualifiers may be included in parentheses at the end of the title when necessary to make the key title unique.

Another international organization is the International Standardization Organization (ISO) which is responsible for many relevant international standards, in addition to those previously cited on filing rules:

* ISO 690, Bibliographic references: contents, form and structure.
* ISO 9115, Bibliographic identification (biblid) of contributions in serials and books.
* ISO 2108, International standard book numbering (ISBN).
* ISO 3297, International standard serial numbering (ISSN).
* ISO 3901, International standard recording code (ISRC).
* ISO 2709, Format for bibliographic information interchange on magnetic tape.
* ISO 10444, International standard technical report number (ISRN).

AACR2

AACR2 incorporates the ISBD system aiming at eliminating inconsistency in the descriptive treatment of various types of materials. It allows local cataloguers to choose among three levels or degrees of detail in constructing descriptive cataloguing data and also includes some optional rules. This flexibility improves the utility of the rules by a wide range of sizes and types of libraries.

Levels of Description

Rule 1.OD of AACR2 specifies these levels as follows:

* *First level:* Title proper/first statement of responsibility if different from main entry in form or number or if there is no main heading.—Edition statement.—Material (or type of publication) specific details.—First publisher, etc., date of publication, etc.—Extent of item.—Note(s).—Standard number.
* *Second Level:* Title proper [general material designation] = Parallel title: other title information/first statement of responsibility.—Edition statement/first statement of re-sponsibility relating to the edition.—Material (or type of publication) specific details.—First place of publication, etc: first publisher, etc, date of publication, etc.—Extent of item: other physical details. dimensions.—(Title pro-per of series/statement of responsibility relating to series, ISSN of series. numbering within the series. Title of subseries. ISSN of subseries. numbering within subseries).—Note(s).—Standard number.
* *Third Level*: All the elements set out in the rules that are applicable to the item being described.

The information stated here is considered the minimum to be given by the cataloguer, as he may add additional elements in the first two levels. Moreover, the cataloguer may use different levels for different materials. if he does he must be consistent. It is noted that a punctuation pattern is used, which is very important element in bibliographic standardization. This pattern is defined for every element of description.

Areas of Description

The description is divided in both AACR2 and ISBDs into eight areas or fields.

They are as follows:

* *Area 1:* Title and Statement of Responsibility Area
  - 1.1 Title proper
  - 1.2 General material designation
  - 1.3 Parallel title(s)
  - 1.4 Other title information
  - 1.5 Statement(s) of responsibility
* *Area 2:* Edition Area
  - 2.1 Edition statement
  - 2.2 Parallel edition statement(s)
  - 2.3 Statement(s) of responsibility relating to the edition
  - 2.4 Statement relating to a named revision of an edition
  - 2.5 Statement(s) of responsibility relating to a named revision of an edition
* *Area 3:* Material (or Type of publication) Specific Details area (Used only for cartographic materials, printed music, computer files, and serials).
* *Area 4:* Publication, production, Distribution, etc, Area.
  - 4.1 Place(s) of publication, distribution, etc.
  - 4.2 Name(s) of publisher, distributor, etc.
  - 4.3 Date of publication, distribution, etc.
  - 4.4 Place of manufacture
  - 4.5 Name of manufacturer
  - 4.6 Date of manufacture
* *Area 5:* Physical Description Area
  - 5.1 Specific material designation and extent of item
  - 5.2 Other physical details
  - 5.3 Dimensions
  - 5.4 Identification of accompanying material
* *Area 6:* Series Area
  - 6.1 Title proper of the series
  - 6.2 Parallel title(s) of the series
  - 6.3 Other title information of the series

- 6.4 Statement(s) of responsibility relating to the series
- 6.5 International Standard Serial Number (ISSN) of the series
- 6.6 Numbering within the series
- 6.7 Enumeration and/or title of subseries
- 6.8-The same as for 6.2 through 6.6 for subseries
- 6.12

* *Area 7:* Note(s) Area (repeatable, each note being a separate area)
* *Area 8:* Standard Number, etc Area (a repeatable area)
  - 8.1 Standard number: ISBN, ISSN, ISRC etc.
  - 8.2 Key-title (associated only with an ISSN)
  - 8.3 Terms of availability and/or price
  - 8.4 Qualification(s) following 8.1 and/or 8.3

Access Points (Headings) and References

AACR2 is of two parts: The first covers descriptions as stated before and consists of (13) chapters where the first covers all types of materials, and chapters 2-12 cover a certain type each, while chapter 13 concerns analytical cataloguing. The second part starts with chapter 20 which is an explanation of the rules of this part, while no chapters 14-19 exist.

Chapter 21 covers the choice of access points, chapter 22 deals with headings for persons, chapter 23 deals with headings for geographic names, chapter 24 deals with headings for corporate bodies, chapter 25 deals with uniform titles, while chapter 26 collects together the various rules for references.

The rules are completed by four appendices:

1. *A:* Capitalization
2. *B:* Abbreviations
3. *C:* Numerals
4. *D:* Glossary

Numerous handbooks and illustrations have been published in different languages, as well as in the local formats adopted such as CEHANET procedures manual.

SUBJECT ANALYSIS

CLASSIFICATION

Classification is basically grouping similar objects or ideas together. This grouping is done through the notations assigned as class numbers from the classification scheme adopted. There are three major general classification schemes that may be encountered in some medical libraries.

Library of Congress Classification (LCC)

This is a general enumerative scheme consisting of 21 classes in individual schemes, although they are now available on CD-ROM as well. The main classes and subclasses are designated by capital letters. Further subdivision is by integral numbers ranging from 1 to 9999, which may be extended decimally.

The classes of this classification that concern medical libraries are:

* *GN:* Anthropology
* *HN:* Social History and Reform
* *QR*: Bacteriology
* *TC:* Hydrology
* *TD:* Sanitary and Municipal Engineering
* *TH*: Building construction
* *TX:* Domestic Sciences

Note here that medicine is assigned class R which is not recommended for medical libraries.

This class is subdivided as follows:

* *R:* Medicine in General
* *RA:* Government Medicine and Public Health
* *RB:* Pathology
* *RC:* Practice of Medicine
* *RD:* Surgery
* *RE:* Ophthalmology
* *RF:* Otorhinolaryngology
* *RG:* Gynecology and Obstetrics
* *RJ:* Paediatrics
* *RK:* Dentistry

* *RL:* Dermatology
* *RM:* Therapeutics
* *RS:* Pharmacy
* *RT:* Nursing
* *RV:* Herbalism
* *RX:* Homeotherapy
* *RZ:* Various Schools and Arts

The LCC uses auxiliary tables for individual classes, but not for the scheme as a whole. There are five types of these tables: form, geographic, historical, topical and mixed.

Dewey Decimal Classification (DCC)

Knowledge in this scheme is divided into ten major classes using arabic numerals 0-9 provided that the number is of three digits. After this base number numbers may be expanded decimally.

Medical sciences are placed in the main class 600-Technology as follows:

* *610:* Medical Sciences Medicine
* *611:* Human Anatomy, Cytology, Histology
* *612:* Human Physiology
* *613:* Hygiene
* *614:* Forensic Medicine, Disease Incidence, General Preventive Medicine
* *615:* Pharmacology
* *616:* Diseases
* *617:* Various Medicine Branches. Surgery
* *618:* Other Medicine Branches. Gynecology and Obstetrics
* *619:* Experimental Medicine

In addition, there is a large number of class numbers relevant to health sciences, among which are:

* *334:* Social Law, Social welfare, Labour, Health, Safety, Education and Culture Law
* *363:* Social Issues and Services
* *574:* Biology
* *628:* Sanitary and Municipal Engineering, Environmental Protection Engineering

* *632:* Plant Injuries, Diseases, Pests
* *636:* Veterinary Medicine

The scheme has seven auxiliary tables for using with the various class numbers as instructed in the schedules. The scheme is now in its twenty-first edition in four volumes, of which the fourth volume is an alphabetical relative index and a manual. It is also on CD-ROM.

Universal Decimal Classification

This scheme is originally based on DDC but deviated from it in many aspects particularly the obligation of using the three digits base numbers. But the major classes are nearly the same except for cancelling class 4 to be combined with class 8.

Medical sciences have 61 and its subdivisions are as follows:

* *61:* Medical Sciences (Medicine)
* *611:* Anatomy. Human and Comparative Anatomy
* *612:* Physiology. Human and Comparative Physiology
* *613:* Hygiene in General. Personal Health and Hygiene
* *614:* Public Health and Hygiene. Accident Prevention
* *615:* Pharmacology. Therapeutics. Toxicology
* *616:* Pathology. Clinical Medicine
* *617:* Surgery. Orthopaedics. Ophthalmology
* *618:* Gynecology. Obstetrics
* *619:* Domesticated Animal Diseases. Veterinary Medicine

Class numbers related to health sciences are also scattered in nearly the same way as DDC. The scheme also uses ten auxiliary tables. The latest medium English edition was published in 1993, and its amendments in 1996. It is also on CD-ROM.

NLM Classification

This scheme covers medicine and other related sciences using the classes QS-QZ and W-WZ permanently excluded in LCC. So, LCC may be considered supplementary to this scheme for classifying other disciplines, except QM (human anatomy),

QR (microbiology) and R (medicine) in LCC which cannot be used in this scheme.

The classes are subdivided as follows:

* QS-QZ Preclinical Sciences
  - QS Human Anatomy
  - QT Physiology
  - QU Biochemistry
  - QV Pharmacology
  - QW Microbiology and Immunology
  - QX Parasitology
  - QY Clinical Pathology
  - QZ Pathology
* W-WZ Medicine and Related Subjects
  - W Health Professions
  - WA Public Health
  - WB Practice of Medicine
  - WC Communicable Diseases
  - WD100 Nutrition Disorders
  - WD200 Metabolic Diseases
  - WD300 Immunologic and Collagen Diseases. Hypersensitivity
  - WD400 Animal Poisons
  - WD500 Plant Poisons
  - WD600 Diseases and Injuries caused by Physical Agents
  - WD700 Aviation and Space Medicine
  - WE Musculoskeletal System
  - WF Rispiratory System
  - WG Cardiovascular System
  - WH Hemic and Lymphatic System
  - WI Digestive System
  - WJ Urogenital System
  - WK Endocrine System
  - WL Nervous System
  - WM Psychiatry
  - WN Radiology. Diagnostic Imaging
  - WO Surgery
  - WP Gynecology

- WQ Obstetrics
- WR Dermatology
- WS Paediatrics
- WT Geriatrics. Chronic Disease
- WU Dentistry. Oral Surgery
- WV Otorhinolaryngology
- WW Ophthalmology
- WX Hospitals and Other Health Facilities
- WY Nursing
- WZ History of Medicine

In addition the scheme has two types of auxiliary tables, the first covers form subdivisions which are listed under main class numbers, and the other is list (G) which is common to all schedules and covers the geographic subdivision. This list divides the world into nine geographic regions, and one notation for international organizations that publish materials related to medicine.

It has an alphabetical relative index, which uses terms derived from Medical Subject Headings (MeSH), and includes subjects outside the scope of the scheme and have LCC numbers. The scheme is now in its fifth edition.

CONTROLLED VOCABULARY

There are two types of tools for controlling vocabulary to be used in subject cataloguing and indexing:

* Lists of Subject Headings; and
* Library of Congress Subject Headings (LCSH)

This is the largest list of subject headings in English. It is a general list originally constructed for the use of the Library of Congress. Now it is published annually, as well as quarterly on CD-ROM under the title: CDMARC subjects.

Recent development include:

* The use of accepted abbreviations such as BT and NT, generally used in thesauri.
* Eliminating inverted forms of subject headings gradually.

Gradual elimination of subject headings that have the conjunction " and " or qualifiers.

The list has four types of subdivision:

* Topical subdivision
* Form subdivision
* Geographic subdivision
* Chronological subdivision

The list is not recommended for medical libraries as it is too general and lacks the subject headings required in health sciences.

Medical Subject Headings (MeSH)

This is the largest list of medical subject headings in English and in other languages to which it has been translated. It is published annually by the NLM, and is used in Medline and in most large medical libraries in the world. It is unique in having the following features that are absent in traditional lists of subject headings:

* Subject headings have classification numbers based on the tree structure of the list. Some headings bear more than ten different numbers each.

The major categories of the tree structure are:

- A Anatomy
- B Organisms
- C Diseases
- D Chemicals and Drugs
- E Analytical, Diagnostic and Therapeutic Techniques and Equipment
- F Psychiatry and Psychology
- G Biological Sciences
- H Physical Sciences
- I Anthropology, Education, Sociology and Social Phenomena
- J Technology, Industry, Agriculture
- K Humanities
- L Information Science
- M Named Groups
- N Health Care
- Z Geographic Locations

Each main category is further subdivided once or more as required using arabic numerals and decimal points:

* The list has an index to the tree structure which is published as a separate volume.

* The list has a KWOC index for the terms used. This feature is used in thersauri.
* The topical, geographical, chronological and form subdivisions are not repeated in the list under the related headings but the notes give instruction on their use.
* *The print edition has the following lists as appendices:*
  - Types of publications. The types are also listed in the main list.
  - Topical subdivisions which are only used with main headings. They are also given in the main list.
  - Form subdivisions for cataloguers with annotations. They are also given in the main list.
  - Geographical locations for cataloguers. They are not given in the main list.
  - Language subdivisions. These are not given in the main list.

Entries of MeSH are of three types:

* Entry of the main heading which typically includes the following information as required:
  - The Heading
  - Consider also cross-reference to other terms
  - Tree number(s)
  - Indexing annotation
  - Cataloguing annotation
  - History note
  - Online note
  - See related
  - X See cross-reference, for entry vocabulary
  - XR See related from other headings
* *Subheading:* This is printed in lower case and preceded by a slash. The entry includes the following information:
  - Subheading
  - Indexing annotation
  - History note
  - Online note
* *Vocabulary Terms:* These include synonyms, near-synonyms, abbreviations, alternative spelling and

alternate forms that may be more familiar or easier to type. The entry includes the following information:

- The vocabulary term
- The word "see"
- The main heading preferred
- The tree number(s) of the main heading

Thesauri

A thesaurus is the vocabulary of a controlled indexing language, formally organized so that the relationships between concepts are made explicit.

Fortunately the establishment and development of thesauri have been handled by ISO:

* ISO 2708, Documentation-Guidelines for the establishment and development of monolingual thesauri.
* ISO 5964, Documentation-Guidelines for the establishment and development of multilingual thesauri.
* ISO 5963, Documentation-Methods for examining documents, determining their subject and selecting indexing terms.

These standards, the relationship or function of term or note which follows is expressed by the following abbreviations and symbols:

* *SN:* (Scope note). A note attached to a term to indicate its meaning within an indexing language.
* *USE:* The term that follows the symbol is the preferred term, when a choice between synonyms or quasi-synonyms exists.
* *UF:* (Use for). The term that follows the symbol is a non-preferred synonym or quasi-synonym.
* *TT:* (Top term). The term that follows the symbol is the name of the broadest class to which the specific concept belongs. It is sometimes used in the alphabetical part of a thesaurus.
* *BT:* (Broader term). The term that follows the symbol represents a concept having a wider meaning.
* *NT:* (Narrower term). The term that follows the symbol refers to a concept with a more specific meaning.

* *RT:* (Related term). the term that follows the symbol is associated, but is not a synonym, a quasi-synonym, a broader term or a narrower term.

Although these abbreviations have acquired status as generally recognized conventions, some agencies have developed different symbols such as using ® instead of USE, = instead of UF, < for BT, > for NT and—for RT.

The concepts that are represented by indexing terms may be:

* *Concrete entities:*
  - Things and their physical parts
    a. Limbs
    b. Microforms
  - Materials
    a. Adhesives
    b. Drugs
* *Abstract entities:*
  - Actions and events
    a. Treatment
    b. Marketing
  - Abstract entities, and properties of thing, materials or actions
    a. Elasticity
    b. Speed
  - Disciplines or sciences
    a. Chemistry
    b. Microbiology
  - Units of measurement
    a. Hertz
    b. Kilometers
* Individual entities', or classes-of-one, expressed as proper nouns
  - World Health Organization

The indexing term should preferably consist of a noun or a noun phrase.

The latter occurs in two forms:

* *Adjective phrase:* Handicapped children
* *Prepositional phrase:* Hospitals for children

UNCONTROLLED VOCABULARY

Uncontrolled, or natural language, words and terms can be of considerable value as subject access points when they come from such sources as the title of a document, cataloguer's note on its bibliographic record, abstract or full text. Such words are often called keywords. Use of these keywords was made for creating KWIC (Keyword-incontext) and KWOC (keyword-out-of-context) indexes particularly by using the computer. In addition they are used for searching databases particularly those without controlled vocabulary. This requires compiling stop-list to identify those words of natural-language text which the computer programme is not to make accessible in an index, thus marking accessible only those words which are highly significant for retrieval purposes.

But natural language indexing compared to that of controlled vocabulary has some stronger and weaker characteristics:

* *Synonym Control:* Suppose that we consider "renal stone" as the keywords to be searched. We must look into several places if our search is to be fairly comprehensive. We have look under renal calculi, kidney calculi, and kidney stones, as well as their singulars. If the system develops some sort of synonym control then searching will be efficient.
* *Singular and Plural:* The same problem occurs here as in synonym control. This has to be solved through truncation and other devices that enable the retrieval of singulars and plurals.
* *Different Spelling:* An important example is the different spelling in British and American English.
* *Hierarchical Relationships:* Prevalent in controlled vocabulary.
* *Specificity:* This is represented better in natural language indexing than in controlled vocabulary.
* Uptodate Vocabulary. Natural language indexing is always uptodate.
* *Ease:* Natural language is easier to use than controlled vocabulary, if the need is for few articles, but is very hard if the need is for comprehensiveness.

* *Lower Cost:* Natural language is quicker and cheaper for the index producer to develop. There is no need for well-trained indexers.
* *Compound Terms:* The controlled vocabulary takes care of this problem fairly easy. Natural language should have the required capability in the system.
* *Inconsistency of the Indexer:* This is not existing in natural language indexing.

4

Cataloguing Principles in an Online Environment

INTRODUCTION

It is often claimed that current cataloguing codes (cataloging codes)are based on concepts and principles from the pre-machine period and that they do not serve us well in giving guidance in the construction of electronic catalogues. Thus, in organising bibliographic information for an electronic environment, it is essential to examine the validity and adequacy of the principles on which current cataloguing codes are based. By assessing the extent to which cataloguing principles accord with the capabilities of the online environment, this chapter will answer some of the questions that have been highlighted in the literature of the last two decades on the relevance of current cataloguing principles to the online environment. To many writers, for example, Martin the online catalogue has meant a re-examination of the principles and practice of cataloguing.

Carpenter and Svenonius raise the issue that:

"At the time the Paris Principles were composed, there was some awareness that computers might change cataloguing. the direction of this change could not then be imagined. It remains to be seen whether this change will require the composition of a new set of principles, this time without ambiguity or compromise".

Another aim of this chapter is to establish whether cataloguing principles for the online environment should encompass a broader range of information sources, *i.e.*, different bibliographic databases such as library catalogues, databases constructed by publishers, booksellers, library suppliers and A&I services.

Boll Asks:

> "Whether there is now a need to include rules for A&I services, which constitute a major component of the online environment".

In general, the aim is to investigate whether the conceptual foundations developed over the last two centuries for the creation of bibliographic records and the construction of catalogues are still valid in the new environment. A similar question is posed by Svenonius who questions whether changes in technology call for changes in the conceptual foundations of cataloguing.

This chapter is in two parts. In Part one some of the basic cataloguing principles, which have been highlighted in the literature as those most likely to be influenced by the new technology, will be re-examined in the light of both the present and the potential characteristics and capabilities of the online environment. Part two will deal with a comparison of A&I conventions with library cataloguing principles and identify in what areas the same principles can be applied by both communities.

What are 'Cataloguing Principles'

In terms of descriptive cataloguing, 'principles' are regarded as underlying concepts for the design and development of cataloguing rules and the construction of library catalogues. Principles can also be Cataloguing principles do not necessarily mean that we must have a single standard for descriptive cataloguing, or that all cataloguing codes must be the same.

Cataloguing principles mean that we can have different, but compatible standards within the same framework. The Paris Conference was an international attempt to make national codes compatible. The Paris Principles are, in fact, an expansion of a few basic concepts developed over the last two centuries.

These concepts, which are repeated in various parts of the Statement of Principles are:

* The functions of the catalogue,
* The concept of multiple entries,
* The concept of uniformity in the choice and form of headings and entry words,
* The concept of functionality of entries and catalogues, and
* The concept of authorship, personal and corporate.

However, this chapter deals only with some of the principles that might be influenced by the new environment and that have been the subject of arguments among cataloguers for a long time, namely:

* The objectives and functions of the catalogue which influence all other principles,
* The structure of the catalogue and the kinds of entries and indexes, *i.e.*, main entries, added entries and references,
* Uniform headings for works and uniform headings for authors, and
* The form of personal headings and corporate headings.

The concept of main entry will be dealt with in detail, because it has been considered important in the literature on the impact of computerised catalogues on cataloguing principles.

There are other pre-existing principles, unstated or overlooked, in the Paris Principles, such as the general assumption that catalogued items are almost always stand-alone publications rather than 'dependent works'. This issue, and other related questions, such as the 'basic unit of description' and the 'edition' issue, will be discussed in the next chapter in relation to their treatment in the online environment, particularly in shared cataloguing systems.

In the extrapolation of cataloguing principles, it is necessary to be aware of the context within which they were originally meant to operate. The Paris Principles have been indirectly influenced by both the characteristics and the limitations of the manual catalogue. They were principles for a catalogue which had limited capabilities in providing access to bibliographic information. Those who contributed to the formulation and compilation of earlier cataloguing principles implicitly assumed that the physical form of the catalogue would be the card or printed book catalogue, either as individual catalogues or national bibliographies. On the whole, the Paris Principles were formulated at a time when there was little perception of approaches other than the traditional ones of author, title and subject.

Major Developments and Changes in Descriptive Cataloguing Since the Paris Conference

Nearly 35 years have passed since the Paris Conference and cataloguers have witnessed profound changes in many aspects of bibliographic control in general, and in descriptive cataloguing in particular, during this period of time. There has also been a considerable increase in unconventional forms of publications as well as various types of information sources and a considerable growth in different presentations of documents which demand increasing detail to retain precision in identification. Martin reviews some of the major issues which influence bibliographic control and access in the new environment.

The cataloguing world has also faced major challenges such as the increasing costs of cataloguing and the need for simplified cataloguing or *minimal level cataloguing* (MLC), the question of duplicate records in cooperative cataloguing systems and the potential danger that cataloguing principles and concepts might be de-emphasised by those coming from the new technology environment. The cataloguing community is now working in an environment totally different from that of the early 1960s. Given the influence of all these changes and developments in the world of cataloguing, a fundamental re-examination of cataloguing principles seems very necessary.

A Re-examination of Cataloguing Principles in an Online Environment

While current cataloguing principles deal with basic questions concerning the organisation of author/title catalogues, online catalogues have revolutionised access to bibliographic information beyond that approach. An important change in relation to providing access to bibliographic information in the online environment is that access is no longer controlled by cataloguing principles and rules to the same extent as previously but, to some extent, is now governed by various search/retrieval capabilities that were not available in the manual catalogue.

For example, access through keyword searching, truncation, Boolean searching, hypertext searching and, most importantly, access to the full text of items, lie outside of cataloguing rules. This is one of the most fundamental differences between an online system and a manual system that should be taken into consideration when re-examining cataloguing principles. Furthermore, while the boundary between description and access has faded in the online environment, cataloguing principles have traditionally placed little emphasis on description.

In the following parts some of the principles will be analysed with regard to the present and potential influences which the various capabilities of the new technologies might have upon them.

Objectives and Functions of the Catalogue in An Online Environment

In our re-examination of cataloguing principles, major consideration should be given to the objectives and functions of the catalogue. Most cataloguing principles, such as the basis for description, the structure of the catalogue and the choice and form of access points are, to a great extent, influenced by the objectives and functions of the catalogue.

The present cataloguing objectives, which were proposed by Lubetzky to the Paris Conference, have their origin in the work of Panizzi and Cutter dating from the nineteenth century. The traditional approach in the Paris Principles towards the functions of the catalogue has not been able to solve the controversies between the 'finding function' and the 'collocating function' of the catalogue. It is often stated that the first and second objectives are inherently in conflict, and to consider one as primary means to sacrifice the other. While the first function puts emphasis on the finding of specific items within a library collection, the second function focuses on collocation of the works of a particular author and the editions and manifestations of a particular work. These two different approaches influence the choice and form of main and added entries, references and the linking devices to connect related entities.

For example, in the finding function approach the focus of description and the basis for cataloguing data is the physical item in hand. Thus the main entry and added entries are provided according to the information on the title page because it is more familiar to readers. In this context, the relationship of the item to other works and its place in the bibliographic hierarchy is not identified and recorded. Wilson presents a well account of the conflict between the two objectives and their implications for the functions of the catalogue.

It is further stated that these objectives are not fully achieved in the manual environment because of its limitations in finding the actual location of items and the huge cost of making analytics and assembling all the works of a given author, *i.e.*, the collocating function.

A general question raised in the literature is whether the objectives and functions of the catalogue as set forth in the Paris Principles are still valid in the online environment. Another question which has to be addressed in this regard is: whether the catalogue in the online network environment should still maintain the same functions formulated for a pre-machine environment or should widen its scope to include new functions? While it is claimed by some writers that the current objectives and functions of the catalogue continue to be valid in the new environment and even that the new technology may help fulfil them more comprehensively and accurately others have challenged the validity and adequacy of the traditional objectives of the catalogue in the new environment.

Ayres states that the scope of the objectives must be expanded to include the impact that online catalogues have on the content of the catalogue. Buckland discusses the need to change our basic assumptions about the catalogue's purpose in order to design the catalogue of the future. He claims that we should pay more attention to bibliographic access and selection and should design the catalogue as a selecting aid. Heaney notes that library catalogues function not solely as descriptive lists of books but as elements of library management systems and as sophisticated information tools.

In addition to the finding and collocating functions, which are valid in any environment, the online catalogue helps to better identify and characterise entities in terms of their nature, scope and orientation through different data fields such as intellectual level, document type, genre, language code, geographic area code and additional notes. Similarly, a fuller description of the item helps the online catalogue to be used as a means for different users to choose one item over similar items. The locating of items is another function of the catalogue and, in this respect, online catalogues are far more capable of showing the location and status of the item(s) being sought.

In the following part, the functions of the catalogue will be analysed with regard to the impact of some of the major characteristics of the online environment.

These are:

* The integration of library operations,
* Developments in networking and in global access to catalogues,
* Access to other types of bibliographic databases, and
* Online search/retrieval/display capabilities.

Integration of Different Library Operations

The integrated online library system has made it possible for different library modules to use the same bibliographic records within the same database management system. Acquisitions librarians, cataloguers, circulation librarians, serial librarians and reference librarians all have access to the same database and use it for different purposes. In an integrated system, the end user may have access to parts of acquisition status, circulations and holdings information. It is therefore necessary for the online catalogue to fulfil the various bibliographic needs of different operations, from housekeeping functions to reference services. In this context, not only should the catalogue function as a finding tool as well as a collocating tool but it should also help in the choice between one work and others.

The combination of approaches to an integrated catalogue not only makes it necessary to expand the current objectives but also to put more emphasis on principles for the choice and form of access points as well as for description, *i.e.*, data elements beyond author/title information. For example, a reference librarian may need to find a specific item and at the same time identify different editions and manifestations related to that item to provide more help to the user.

Networking and Global Access to Catalogues

The fact that the resources and bibliographic information of hundreds of libraries participating in national and international networks are now accessible to any remote user calls for a reconsideration of the functions and objectives of the catalogue. The concept of 'catalogues on demand' extends the functions of the catalogue beyond providing access to a library's own collections.

With international access to individual catalogues, the question arises as to whether a catalogue should serve in the first place its local users, that is, to identify the holdings of a particular library, or to enable any user to access the collections of other libraries available through the network. Buckland asks: "What difference does it make that the catalogue now is concerned with the collectivity of collections rather than the local holdings of the individual library?" While catalogues should serve their local patrons well, they should also be useful to remote users. In such an environment, consideration should always be given to the fact that the item in hand for cataloguing may be a manifestation of another work known under a different title being held in another collection.

With respect to the network environment, there is some support for the precedence of the collocating function of the catalogue over its finding function. In a conceptual approach to a catalogue's functions as presented by Lubetzky to the Paris Principles, Wilson proposes that, with regard to the availability of different catalogues in an online network and with respect to the significance of 'work' over 'publication', priority should be given to the collocating objective. He proposes a redefinition of 'work' to be taken as the basic unit of cataloguing.

Dempsey points out that a lack of sufficient attention to the collocating objective of the catalogue has resulted in two problems in large shared databases: difficulty in authority control and an increase in duplicate records. Ayres supports a similar concept. In general, in a network, online environment and with regard to the needs of different users, we cannot give precedence to any function. Rather, all functions of the catalogue should equally be taken into consideration.

On the other hand, while in a large shared database the potential number of editions and manifestations of a work increases, it is more likely that access to a very specific bibliographic manifestation of a work, for example, a particular version, would be a common need for some users. The result of a study of MELVYL at the University of California using transaction logs of remote users showed that known item searches constituted 40% of searches. It is evident that in a shared system or network of catalogues there will be a good chance for the user to select those that suit his/her needs best among different representations of a work. Copy cataloguing through bibliographic utilities, which is usually a known-item search, is another example of such a user approach.

With the availability of catalogues to different remote users, it is hard to give absolute priority to either of the two traditional functions of the catalogue. A catalogue accessible to all types of users through a network will be expected to satisfy, as far as possible, different needs.

Availability of Different Types of Bibliographic Database

With respect to the accessibility of different types of online and/or on-disk bibliographic databases to various users, a combination of approaches in terms of the functions of the catalogue should be considered.

With access to book trade databases, the catalogue goes beyond providing holdings information and becomes a gateway to explore what is newly published, what is to be published and what is in print. In such an environment, emphasis is also put on other functions such as the crucial choice of one item over another. From a different point of view, the functions of the bibliographic database in the library world and book trade world are similar in many respects, such as the finding function, the selecting function and housekeeping function. Even the bringing together of works by a particular author and also collocation of series, are functions wanted by the two communities. A major difference is in the collocation of different editions and manifestations of a work, which libraries appear to consider important enough to control by rules of entry.

Online Search/Retrieval/Display and Functions of the Catalogue

All a catalogue's functions can be achieved more comprehensively through the search/retrieval/display capabilities of the online catalogue. An interesting aspect of the online catalogue which is duplicated from A&I services is the ability of the searcher to choose and/or combine a number of different searching options. For example, keyword searching on place of publication, name of the publisher, date of publication, series information and ISBN or ISSN not only facilitates the finding function but it can also help in the choice of one item over another. Boolean searching can facilitate both the finding function and the collocating function. Hypertext searching on any term or a combination of terms can extend a known-item search to other items which may be unknown to the searcher but may have some kind of relationship with the item first found.

There is an important difference between the manual environment and the online environment in terms of search/ retrieval/display capabilities of the catalogue and their influence on the two objectives. Whilst collocation in the manual catalogue is achieved through the physical pre-arrangement of records of related editions and manifestations of a work, in the online environment it can be achieved through the pre-coding and display of search results.

With many more data elements in MARC records, additional indexes and extensive search and retrieval capabilities, the online catalogue can be used as a selecting aid to choose specific items. This function, *i.e.*, the choosing function, which is of interest to different users such as acquisitions and reference librarians as well as the book trade, can be carried out more effectively. For example, combining key data elements, such as author or title with date of publication, country of publication, name of publisher and language of the item is a useful way to choose appropriate items.

Conclusion

The catalogue in the global online environment is supposed to satisfy all possible approaches. From the preceding paragraphs, it can be concluded that the functions of the online catalogue go beyond those laid down in the Paris Principles. The online catalogue with its extensive capabilities can widen the scope and content of the functions and fulfil new functions. It is therefore necessary that cataloguing principles for the online environment should cover all these different functions equally and should also take into consideration the influence of each function on other principles.

Structure of the catalogue and the concept of multiple entries

The structure of the catalogue has an important role in the fulfilment of its functions. Sections 3 (Structure of the Catalogue), 4 (Kinds of Entry), 5 (Use of Multiple Entries), 6 (Function of Different Kinds of Entry) and sub-sections 8.1, 9.1, 9.2, 9.5, 9.6 and also sections 10 and 11 of the Statement of Principles relate to the structure of the catalogue. The principles underlying the structure of the catalogue and choice of entries in the Paris Principles include statements concerning the determination and construction of necessary entries for a linear, alphabetical catalogue. Such a linear catalogue consists of main entries, added entries and references.

Online catalogues, on the other hand, go far beyond the linear author/title catalogue. they permit dynamic linking, merging and rearrangement of files. The structure of an online catalogue usually consists of bibliographic, authority and holdings records linked to one another, each of which is arranged in a given order. Multiple access points and related index files in an online system are not limited to traditional author/title headings. Since it is possible to specify more data elements in a record as access points, the structure of online catalogues may include other index files such as keywords, author/any keyword from title, standard numbers, language of the item, country of publication, date of publication, type of material, genre and readership level.

Cataloguing principles should take into consideration the complex structure of the online catalogue and provide principles for the construction of different files and also for the indexing of different fields and sub-fields concerning access to required elements in the record. They should also suit the structure of the catalogue including different indexes for searching and browsing. A possible approach would be to provide principles for the construction of browsable indexes which can help the searcher to get a clear idea of what sort of indexes are available for searching and retrieval. It is also useful to provide name authority files for browsing, like those offered by SIRSI and PALS systems and a uniform-title authority file for making the catalogue more effective in its collocating function. A possible development in the structure of the catalogue is through the concept of 'super records'.

The Concept of Main Entry

As a typical example of the impact of the online environment on cataloguing principles, it has been claimed that the concept of main entry has lost its value. It was indicated that with the advent of computerised catalogues the value of the main entry concept, which developed in the context of book and card catalogues, has been questioned, but no satisfactory and practical solution has emerged as to how its functions can be otherwise fulfilled.

Svenonius asks:

> "If the main entry were to be abandoned, what would replace its role in the construction of uniform

headings? what would take its place in the structuring displays in online catalogs? how would abandoning the main entry affect single-entry and minimal-level catalogs"?

A review of the related literature of the last two decades shows a developing discussion in favour of abandoning the main entry concept in the online environment. Although before the advent of automated catalogues there were some proposals for the no-main-entry concept such as '*Description Independent System* (DIS)', 'alternative entry', and 'title main entry', developments in online catalogues of access to bibliographic information have given the issue a new dimension and the number of those who advocate the abandonment of the main entry concept has increased.

To many writers, the concept arose out of pre-machine systems and is said to be irrelevant in a developed online catalogue where the technology permits many more access points of equal value in the retrieving of bibliographic information. It is often also claimed that the process of determining main entries is one of the most complex, costly and time consuming processes in descriptive cataloguing.

In contrast to those supporting the simple abandonment of the main entry principle, others argue for its continued use in computerised catalogues. In a survey of the attitudes of cataloguers and cataloguing educators, Musavi found that more than half of the respondents disagreed with the abandonment of the main entry concept even in the online catalogue. The majority of respondents believed that online catalogues will not devalue the concept of main entry. Baughman and Svenonius assessed the implication of the possible abandonment of main entry in AACR2 and found that a number of problematic rules would result. Exploring the definitions and functions of main entry, Carpenter stated that some of the functions of main entry, particularly its collocating function, are still valid in the online environment.

The following part is an analysis of the main entry concept in terms of its functions in an online environment. The focus of this part is only on main entries for personal names.

Functions of Main Entry

Discussions of the main entry concept have been mostly concerned with the objectives and functions of the catalogue rather than merely its definitions.' Verona any consideration about the functions of the main entry has to be based on an evaluation of the general objectives and functions of the alphabetical catalogue. A similar idea comes from Carpenter who points out that: "If main entry is to have any function, it must be in the context of fulfilling an objective of a catalogue."

A major justification for the concept often lies in its collocating function, in bringing together both different editions of a work and the works of an author.

Carpenter states that other functions, i.e.:

* Naming a work,
* Providing credit to the principal author,
* Providing the only full entry, and
* Being the entry to which all others refer, are of historical interest.

Looking from a database perspective, Brooks and Bierbaum consider the uniform main entry as an essential device to link all the occurrences of a bibliographic mutation. Tillett emphasises the role of main entry in specifying the nature of the relationship between a work and the person associated with it. Heaney notes that the issue of the main entry is more complicated than its being only considered as a primary heading. it involves not the idea of "main" entry but also the adequate identification, within the record, of related works. As a collocating device, the concept of main entry has been retained not only in multiple-entry card catalogues but also with the same justification in automated catalogues.

In terms of collocation, main entry has two specific functions:

* Assembling and displaying works by an author, and
* Assembling and displaying different editions of a work.

Assembling and Displaying Works by an Author

Assembling of the works of an author can be achieved through a uniform heading for the author, whether recorded as the main entry heading or as an added entry. This function is thus not exclusively achieved by the main entry heading. Furthermore, the main entry heading alone cannot assemble all the works by an author. In many cases where an author is a joint author, editor, compiler or author of one part, his/her name may be presented as an added entry heading.

Assembling and Displaying Different Editions of a Work

While the most important justification for the main entry is in its role of assembling and displaying, in a meaningful and logical order, the various editions of a work, it has been a complex and debatable concept in the history of descriptive cataloguing. Although this function is attributed to main entry, it cannot be fully achieved through the main entry heading alone. In assembling the different editions of a work, the main entry heading is dependent upon a second collocating device: the uniform title.

Without the inclusion of a uniform title following the main entry heading in the record, the assembling function of the main entry is only partially achieved: it would be limited only to those works whose editions and manifestations have identical titles proper. Thus, neither of the two functions perceived for main entry in the Paris Principles can be fully achieved through the main entry heading alone. As will be discussed further in this part, a combination of the author's uniform heading and the uniform title that is considered as a 'unifying mode of identifying' different editions of a work will fulfil the collocating function in a more comprehensive way.

Online Search/Retrieval/Display and the Concept of Main Entry

Keyword Searching

In an online database with keyword access, it is possible to retrieve a record through keywords, whether in main entries, added entries or any other significant word indexed from the text of the record. A major characteristic of keywords is that they are not controlled by cataloguing rules and they are not subject to authority control. Therefore, keyword searching on names will retrieve only those records that match the term(s) keyed in by the searcher. Keyword searching capability cannot replace the main entry in terms of its collocating function. It can, however, facilitate the collocating function: once access to one or more specific items has been provided through keywords, the searcher can extend the search by keying the exact form of the author heading or the uniform title found on the retrieved record(s) to search for related editions with the same terms only.

Boolean Searching

Boolean search is another capability for bringing together different editions of a work. This can be done by keying in two or more data elements such as the author heading and the title proper or the uniform title, by using the 'AND' operator. Since the title proper of different editions of a work may vary, titles proper in conjunction with author heading cannot be a useful element for the collocating function. The 'author/title' search key, which many systems provide, is an implicit Boolean search which has the same limitation. Instead, a Boolean search on the author uniform heading and the uniform title, including relevant qualifiers, can achieve the collocating function more effectively. This approach is another justification for the main entry concept.

Index Browsing

The browsing capability removes the burden of entering the exact search terms and enables the searcher to gain an overview of an index containing an alphabetical list of all headings. Browsing, for example, the author index will display together all the works by an author irrespective of his/her type of contribution. Nevertheless, for the uniform citation and display of entries in the browsable author index we need to identify the primary author. To link works, however, the primary author's name should be in a uniform heading. This is again another justification for the concept of main entry in an online environment.

It can be seen that, even with browsing capability, a useful collocation of different editions of a work is not possible with the present structure of entries. Browsable indexes could help solve the collocation problem if the author and the title indexes are pre-coordinated for meaningful arrangement and display of related entities.

Online Display and the Concept of Main Entry

Since the display format in online catalogues is independent of the storage format, when a number of records are displayed in response to a query, the retrieved titles need to be displayed in conjunction with a second primary identifier such as the author heading.

Otherwise, not only is the identification of the retrieved items not complete, but different works by an author are also not distinguished and assembled. This primary element is necessary in online displays of related works. Carpenter states that the primary key provides a unique identification of the record. He also points out that: "Discussions about main entry have changed focus from records to useful displays". Online displays, for instance, default listings in brief displays, require that, in addition to titles proper, another principal element must be displayed.

The following example may help to make this idea clearer:

* As the convention now exists in many OPACs, when there is an editor or a compiler for a work and the work goes under title main entry or a corporate heading and the editor or the compiler is given an added entry as opposed to main entry, his/her/its name would still need to be displayed in conjunction with the title proper in the brief display to uniquely identify the work and to differentiate between works with identical titles. From another perspective, that of the catalogue user who does not understand what main entry is, an editor or a compiler may seem to be the primary identifier or access point which should be displayed in conjunction with the title in brief displays and in single entry listings.

Conclusion

As a concept, the main entry relates rather to the nature of relationships between entities than to the physical medium through which those entities are to be described. Many works, particularly in the fields of literature, law and music, require such a uniform construct for identification and collocation. Even if technology provides catalogues with sophisticated devices to link two or more related entities to one another, it would not help the user if catalogues do not show him/her the nature of these relationships. Without such a concept the catalogue, whether manual or computerised, would lose its integrity and usefulness.

From the preceding discussions concerning the possible influence of different online search/retrieval/display capabilities, it can be concluded that online catalogues still need a construct to carry out some specific functions which cannot be fulfilled thoroughly through other devices. Of great concern is the fact that the main entry concept is not meant to be a single function element but rather a concept that is essential to fulfil some basic functions. Thus it is in need of a re-definition that will focus on its multiple functions.

Main entry is a uniform construct for the naming and identifying of works and also for the useful collocation and arrangement/display of the different editions and manifestations of a work. In addition to the identification of the primary author, the concept of uniform citation is dependent on two key identifying elements: uniform titles for works and uniform headings for authors.

Uniform Headings for Titles

A work can potentially be produced in different editions, different versions, in various languages and/or in a variety of physical formats. This concept is intrinsic to the bibliographic universe and its control is an essential principle for catalogues. In this context, the name of the work, *i.e.*, the 'uniform title', has been devised in descriptive cataloguing to control the conditions of a work.

For this reason, the use of uniform titles has greatly increased and their application has gone beyond anonymous classics, sacred scriptures and works of music. However, the Paris Principles are less concerned with the concept of uniform titles: principles 7.1, 11.3 and 11.4 only deal vaguely with the choice and form of uniform titles. In the following parts, the rationale and the functions of uniform titles will be examined in the context of the online environment.

Functions of the Uniform Title

The functions of uniform titles are:

* To standardise the original title of a work,
* To standardise the form of the main entry heading for anonymous works,
* To group together all editions and manifestations of a work under one particular title, and
* To identify the relationships between an edition and a work.

The rationale for the principle of uniform titles, however, rests mainly with two functions:

* The uniform identification of a work; and
* The assembling of entities derived from or related to the same work.

Uniform titles support at least four types of bibliographic relationship: equivalence, derivative, whole-part, and sequential relationships.

Online Search/Retrieval/Display and the Concept of Uniform Titles

No research has yet attempted to study the influence of different search/retrieval/display capabilities of online catalogues on the principle of uniform title. Tillett states that some Western cataloguing practices that arise from the physical limitations of manual catalogues do not make sense in the online environment and should be rethought. Of such practices, the uniform title is one of the most important. Tillett states that we should simplify the entire issue of uniform titles to make it relevant to the online catalogue in a network environment. Vellucci emphasises the need to explore more fully the potential of uniform titles as linking devices and as foundation points for online catalogues.

She states:

> "As we move into the online environment, the uniform title will continue to evolve. The terminology might

change again, and new functions might be identified. But the important role of the uniform title in identifying works and serving as a linking device for bibliographic relationships will no doubt be a primary focus for uniform titles of the future".

Boll points out that, in an online catalogue, both the primary heading and the uniform title "are needed to recall, as a group, manifestations of the same work that have different titles proper". As in the case of the main entry concept, the examination of individual search/retrieval/display capabilities in online catalogues reveals that not only do those capabilities not diminish the need for the concept of uniform titles but they also emphasise their role in the effective collocation and display of related works and items.

Without the uniform title associated with the main entry heading, one can see that different editions of the same work are scattered among the retrieved records for other works by the same author. For example, translations or selections of a work, while being scattered among different works by the same author, are treated as if they are new works by the same author. This problem is highlighted in online catalogues: they may need a number of screens to list all retrieved items and the searcher may have to spend considerable time to find his/her needed item.

With regard to the catalogue's collocating function, uniform titles will play a more important role in the online catalogue. In an online environment, the linking of different editions and manifestations of a work is essential for increasing recall in response to user queries and could be a critical part of the file structure for new system designs. While uniform titles alone increase the search results, the addition of other data elements, such as version, language, date and part of the work, to the uniform title will narrow down the search results and will increase precision.

In their present state, formal or conventional titles, such as "Laws, etc." and "works", may not be useful in online retrieval unless in conjunction with, for example, a name or date. The search expression "Laws, etc. AND New South Wales" is useful in an online catalogue. In such systems some of the qualifiers can be specified by Boolean means or can be simplified into natural language terms.

While the occurrence of editions of the same work with different titles and different works with similar titles increases in large catalogues and union databases, the concept of uniform titles can help control this problem. In the context of searching a large bibliographic database, there should be a means for the user to realise that what has been retrieved in response to his/her query may be different editions of the same work.

Uniform headings for persons

Another principle that is essential to the fulfilment of the main entry's functions is a uniform heading for persons. A rigid ideal in modern cataloguing codes and one of the first principles in the Anglo-American cataloguing tradition has been to list all works by or about a given person under a uniform heading. In this context, uniform headings have been regarded as a necessary device for the integrity of the catalogue.

While the need for uniformity of headings in an online environment and for links among variant forms of a name has been reaffirmed by a number of writers, the necessity to enter an author's works under one uniform heading and the provision of references for other forms of a name for the same author has come into question in online catalogues.

In terms of the implication of adhering to the principle of uniform headings in an online environment Chan asks:

> ". . . does the principle of uniform heading have the same meaning or import in the automated catalogue as in the card catalogue?... What are the implications of the principle of uniform heading in the maintenance of the name authority file? To what extent does the designation of a focal point facilitate and economize such operations?"

However, as discussed in relation to the collocating function of the catalogue, the bringing together and display of an author's works require that all records be presented under a uniform heading for the author. Divergence in the form of headings is not consistent with the requirements of the online environment.

Normalisation of names is a principle which is also essential to database management systems.

However, a major problem in the online environment is that there are different bibliographic databases and a wide variety of users. A difficulty in searching different databases is that, while there is a uniform approach in library cataloguing in relation to uniform headings, other communities such as the book trade and A&I services are less concerned with this principle. In many bibliographic databases it is often the case that the same person has been entered under a variety of unlinked names leading to irretrievability of all the works by a particular author.

Online Search/Retrieval/Display and the Principle of Uniform Headings

Keyword searching

Keyword searching facilitates the finding function of the catalogue through the form of an author's name that appears on the title page or in information sources, *i.e.*, the form which is usually familiar to both the book world and the searcher. However, with keyword searching it is possible only to search names under the form in which they have been recorded in the bibliographic record. Keywords are not subject to authority control and therefore cannot always collocate all the works by or about an author in a catalogue, especially if the form of name differs. However, keyword searching facilitates the collocation of an author's works: once access is made to a record through any form of the name, it is possible to assemble works by or about a particular author through a further search on the uniform author heading.

Truncation

With right-hand truncation, the online catalogue is able to retrieve those names which begin with the characters defined by the searcher. In other words, names must be uniform, at least for the few beginning characters, to retrieve all the works by a given author. For example, truncation on a surname will retrieve works by those authors whose forenames or initials may differ from one another.

Truncation, particularly automatic right-hand truncation, influences uniform headings in two ways:

* It retrieves all the works by an author when only the surname is known to the searcher,
* It increases the number of retrieved records, some of which may not be relevant to the needs of the searcher.

In effect, not only does truncation not devalue the principle of uniform headings, but it also emphasises it, in that the more complete the uniform heading is, the more chance there will be for retrieval precision.

Index Browsing

In systems allowing the browsing of name indexes, it is necessary, in general, that works by an author be assembled under a single form of name. The browsing capability thus reinforces the need for the principle of uniform headings. The value of uniform headings can also be seen in single-entry printouts and lists both in library cataloguing and in publishers' activities. The 'author index' volume in the *Books In Print* is a good example of a name browsable index.

Authority Control Systems

In an online catalogue utilising name authority files, access to the works of a given author by any variant forms of the name would be as effective as access by the uniform heading. The distinction between the established form of a name and any cross reference to it is invisible to the user. It has been said that in future catalogues a complete listing of an author's works under any form of the author's name is quite feasible.

Even in authority control systems there is still a need to establish one form of a person's name as the uniform heading and others as references. In fact, uniform headings are still considered to be an important principle in authority work.

While name authority systems make it possible to achieve the finding function in a one-step search for any work by a given author, adherence to the principle of uniform heading is a means to maintain the one-to-many relationship in bibliographic databases and, thus, to achieve the collocation of all works available by a given author in the catalogue.

Online Displays and the Principle of Uniform Headings

With regard to differences in the physical forms of the manual catalogue and the online catalogue, the very rigid ideal in the card catalogue of assembling *in one place* all the works a library has by a given author has shifted, in the online catalogue, to the ideal of the system's ability to retrieve all the works of an author through any searched form of his/her name and to display them together under one uniform heading for the author. Under whatever form of name the works by a given author have been searched, the default listing of those works requires that the name of the author needs to be displayed in a uniform manner.

Networks and the Concept of Uniform Headings

Uniform headings are an essential principle in bibliographic control, especially in shared cataloguing environments and union catalogues, facilitating bibliographic cooperation between libraries.

The communication of bibliographic records for cataloguing purposes, reference services and inter-library loan depends to a large extent on the uniformity of headings. In searching the different catalogues accessible in a network, the patron, the technical services librarian and the reference librarian usually look for the works of a given author under the same heading.

The ability to look for particular bibliographic information in different catalogues irrespective of their size, type and location requires an ever-increasing need for standard bibliographic records.

Except for differences in user interfaces, a first requirement is to conform to the concept of uniform headings at the national level. National name authority files would be the most desirable answer to complications in the forms of authors' names and can provide consistent access to catalogues and other bibliographic lists. It is then possible to share bibliographic and authority records on the international level.

Criticising the way that cataloguers prepare headings as if they are cataloguing for a single library, Wajenberg states that:

"The cataloguing code for the third millennium should rise the parochial emphasis on the local catalogue. It should provide instructions for preparing headings for a national online authority file, and eventually for an international equivalent".

Form of Headings in an Online Environment

In addition to the principle of uniform headings, which is essential to the integrity and the collocating function of the catalogue, the form of names in headings, as emphasised by IFLA/Unesco in 1961 should be agreed upon both nationally and internationally. This principle needs to be examined with respect to searchers' expectations and also to the searching/retrieval/ display capabilities of the online catalogue. The form of personal and corporate names will be discussed with respect to the possible influence of the online environment.

Form of Personal Name Headings

The form of a name is an important factor in searching and retrieval, particularly in online systems in which the searcher has to key in the name as the search string. In online catalogues with many search/retrieval capabilities it is important to see whether this principle needs a rather different approach. In a manual environment, a problem with the form of heading is that searches for works of authors must be in the exact form and order of their name headings. This requirement is no longer totally necessary since cross references in authority records and keyword searching allow for the searching of names in different ways. If the searcher is not sure as to which part of the name forms the surname for efficient searching, for example, Jean De La Fountaine, Walter De La Mare, Dante Alighieri, cross references or keyword access offers the possibility to search names in any order. Keyword searching capability also reduces the need for complete "surname+initials+(full forenames)+dates" headings as in AACR2R.

Truncation of headings, especially automatic right-hand truncation, can help retrieve works by authors whose complete heading is not known to the searcher. Variations in the fullness of forenames seem unimportant in systems with a truncation capability. Using 'Price, H H' and 'Grossman, Allen R.' as examples, Arlene Taylor proposes that an online catalogue with keyword searching of headings and automatic right-hand truncation needs rather different rules for the formulation of headings and references.

Wajenberg claims that, with keyword searching, the inversion of surnames and rules for the choice of entry-element in compound surnames and names with prefixes become unnecessary. Using the heading 'Mozart, Wolfgang Amadeus' as an example, he points out that the most useful form of name is the fullest form. Kilgour on the other hand, proposes that for a single-screen miniature catalogue author entries can be reduced to surnames alone. His survey of two online catalogues in the North Carolina State University, containing approximately 3.4 million entries, showed that surname searches produced mini catalogues of one screen 12.6% of the time, two screens 22.5%, and three screens 30.1%. He claims that his finding, that nearly two-fifths of the cataloguing of books in a large university library produces entries that will be displayed in mini catalogues of one screen, demands revision and simplification of cataloguing practices in large research libraries For example, he proposes that with keyword search function no added author fields will be necessary for multiple surnames.

There are other factors, such as the need for default listings of the works of an author and the needs of the book world, citation traditions and international exchange of bibliographic data, which require the standard order of 'surname, forename' in full form for personal headings. There is at present no consensus on the form of headings among the different creators of bibliographic records. There are, however, to some extent similarities between library cataloguing and the book world: both tend to use the best known form of name with library cataloguing more inclined to use the complete form.

Form of Corporate Headings

The issue of corporate headings was one of the problems on which there was no international consensus at the Paris

Conference. Even today different national codes have different approaches towards the form of headings.

Searching, retrieval and display of corporate names in online systems are often frustrating to the user. Many of the problems concerning the searching of corporate bodies' publications relate to the form of headings for these bodies. Little has been written on the form of corporate headings in an online environment. Some of the implications of searching corporate names in online systems have been briefly addressed by Arlene Taylor, Brunt and more fully by Greig. The result of a study by Henty, concerning unsuccessful keyword searching, indicates that the reasons for the users' search failures are, to some extent, due to the implications of variant forms of corporate names.

Some of the problems concerning the searching, retrieval and display of corporate headings in online systems are:

* It is particularly difficult to search under the exact form of corporate headings in online catalogues because the user has to key in the search string. How much of the heading should be keyed in by the searcher to initiate the search, since corporate names are usually long, often similar to one another and appear in different forms such as acronyms, initials and subordinations?
* In some cases, headings for subordinate bodies associated with the same parent body do not follow a uniform approach. While the 'World Health Organization' appears as the heading for this body, a number of subordinate bodies incorporating the acronym 'WHO' are treated as headings in the catalogue. for example, 'WHO Collaborating Centre on Environmental Pollution Control', 'WHO Commission on Health and Environment', 'WHO Expert Group on Pesticide Residues'. The same problem exists with the 'Food and Agriculture Organization of United Nations' and some of its subordinate bodies beginning with 'FAO'.
* Entering corporate bodies under the name of the higher body would often cause inconvenience for the

searcher, especially in large catalogues and shared systems. The use of indirect corporate headings is not innate and could appear meaningless to catalogue users. They "can be considerably distorted because of re-arrangement of the elements of the name and, in many codes, by translating the name of the jurisdiction".

* The addition of a geographic name to the heading for corporate bodies often does not make sense in the online environment. Exact searching and truncation on headings beginning with the name of the jurisdiction often result in too many hits. Headings like 'Australia. Australian Parliamentary Observer Group', 'Canada. Canadian High Commission' and 'Canada. Canadian Armed Forces' which are problematic for searching could be more straightforward if 'Australia' and 'Canada', were omitted from the heading.
* Truncation on the name of the parent body will usually retrieve too many records that are not easy to distinguish from one another, especially in brief displays where, because of screen limitation, the name of the parent body alone may fill the allotted space.
* Clustering of all the publications of different departments and divisions of a corporate body is not usually sought by searchers. Also, it does not make sense in brief displays where, because of screen limitation, only the first few elements of the heading are displayed thus obscuring the name of the actual issuing body. Consider, for example, how frustrating the retrieval of publications of different subordinates bodies of the United Nations would be in an online catalogue.

ABSTRACTING AND INDEXING SERVICES AND LIBRARY CATALOGUING: RECONCILIATION OF PRINCIPLES

Online and/or on-disk A & I databases are now a major component of the online environment. As indicated earlier, one of the aims of this research is to acknowledge the impact of the merging, integrating and accessibility of different types of bibliographic files, particularly library catalogues and A&I databases, on cataloguing principles and to see in what areas and how far similar principles might be applicable to the practices of the two communities.

Library cataloguing has over a century's history of establishing standards for the exchange of information whereas, due to the production of abstracts and indexes by publishers rather than by libraries, there is less standardisation within A&I services. Many indexing rules in the first half of the twentieth century were practically identical with those used in the preparation of library catalogues such as Cutter's *Rules for a Dictionary catalogue* and the *ALA Cataloguing rules for Author and Title Entries.*

Because of the introduction of new technologies, library cataloguing and indexing services now have more impact on one another than before largely due to three major factors:

* The extensive and powerful searching and retrieval capabilities that computer technology has introduced to library catalogues, such as keyword searching, truncation, Boolean searching and hypertext searching, were first introduced in A&I services. Consequently, the indexing of more data fields, which requires the addition of more data elements such as language, type of material and readership level, is another indication of the impact of A&I services on cataloguing practices.
* The accessibility of different online library catalogues and A&I databases through a single terminal and the increasing ability of the searcher to go from one bibliographic database/file to another and to navigate the whole bibliographic apparatus.
* The evolution of CD-ROM versions of many A&I databases which are now available to end users.

These factors have now become a cause for concern over the possible use of the same or compatible standards for the creation of bibliographic records. Because of technological advances in providing integrated access to different bibliographic files and databases, it is time to think as to whether bibliographical control of these different practices should be done based on a single standard. A first step in a study of the possible use of a single standard in both communities is to acknowledge the similarities and differences between library cataloguing and A&I practices. Library cataloguing has come to a set of principles which are internationally agreed upon and has provided bibliographic standards for description of and access to bibliographic items and for the communication of bibliographic data, whereas A&I services have not. There are differences within A&I services about their approaches to description and there are different standards.

Some of the major areas of differences/similarities between the two communities that have to be considered are:

* Objectives and functions of the catalogue/database,
* Structure of the catalogue/database and of the bibliographic record, and
* Choice and form of access points.

Objectives and Functions of the Catalogue/Database

Differences in the approaches of library cataloguing and A&I services towards creating bibliographic records are a result of different objectives which each of the two communities identifies for its bibliographic database. The major object of looking for an article's bibliographical citation in A&I databases is different from that of looking for bibliographic information in a library catalogue. While library cataloguing is traditionally concerned with the finding, identifying, collocating and organising of bibliographic entities, A&I services deal rather with the subject content of bibliographic entities and, to some extent only, the finding of works by a particular author.

In A&I databases, the assembling of all the works by a given author may be a common approach for some searchers, but there is usually no concept such as the assembling of all editions and manifestations of a work. Journal articles, patent documents, reports, dissertations and conference proceedings have fewer editions than books. Consequently, the concept of main entry, which is useful for bringing together different editions and manifestations of a work, has more justification in library catalogues than in A&I databases. A similar idea is present in the COSATI (the Committee on Scientific and Technical Information) standard with the policy of a main entry free environment: "The system works because only rarely are there technical reports that are about other technical reports and unrelated by contract number".

Structure of the Catalogue/Database and of the Bibliographic Record

Because of the differences in their objectives and functions, library catalogues and A&I databases differ from one another in terms of the structure of the bibliographic record and the structure of the database. There is no concept such as multiple entries in A&I databases.

However, in terms of the structure of the record, there are similarities in some of the data fields which can potentially conform to the same standard: headings for persons and corporate bodies associated with an item, date of publication, title of analytic, title of monograph, title of collection or series, language of the item, ISBN/ISSN, conference identification information, abstract/summary, country of publication, target audience and subject headings. These data fields can be treated similarly by the two communities by using identical terms/phrases. The searcher can approach the catalogue or the database with the same search string.

Choice and form of Access Points

This is one of the most important areas of possible reconciliation between cataloguing principles and indexing conventions. Because CD-ROM versions of A&I databases are becoming increasingly available to end users and have larger cumulations of citations in them, there is more need to reconcile variant names. Since there is usually no retrospective editing of headings when a CD-ROM is produced, such discrepancies are simply left alone.

Many A&I databases also include citations of monographs, such as conference proceedings, festschriften and books reviewed, that are duplicated in library catalogues. This also indicates the need for more consistency in name headings between library cataloguing and A&I practices.

In terms of the treatment of names for inclusion in the record for later retrieval, A&I conventions differ markedly both within themselves and from cataloguing conventions. In respect of the choice of names to be entered in the bibliographic record, A&I conventions usually provide author indexing in depth. They do not conform to principles such as main entry and the 'rule of three'. The names of persons associated with an item are entered as they appear on the item in hand. For example, the UNISIST *Reference Manual* prescribes that the names of all individual authors associated with a given item are to be entered in the record, unless there is a clear indication on the original that the chief responsibility for authorship lies with choosing only one or less than all of the persons cited, in which case only those indicated as chief contributors are to be entered.

There are other similarities or differences:

* Since A&I databases are not searched through the exact titles of items, title is not as common an access point as in library catalogues. Instead, a title keyword index is provided for title as well as subject searching.
* As a first principle in the indexing of names, both communities invert names of persons to secure alphabetic arrangement by family names.
* A&I conventions regard the names of editors of collections as an essential element for the identification of monographs whereas cataloguing conventions put less emphasis on the role of such contributors, in that they no longer consider editors and compilers as main entries.
* In terms of the names of persons associated with a monograph, A&I conventions regard the form derived from the item as essential and other forms as optional.

Since A&I services do not normally use name authority files and do not maintain references, many of them prefer to include other forms of the name with initials immediately after the complete form:

* Wendt, Richard P. Wendt, R. P.
* Atkinson, H Craig Craig Atkinson, H

Library cataloguing, on the other hand, treats names with initials differently. For example, AACR2R has the following approach:

* Wendt, R.P. (Richard P.)
* Eliot, T.S. (Thomas Stearns)

One reason why many A&I services do not conform to the principle of uniform heading may be that they are usually discipline-oriented and, therefore, the chance of similarity between the forms of names within a given discipline is not great. There are usually not many identical names with identical forenames or initials within a given A&I database. for example, there were only two authors with the surname 'Buckland' in the LISA database and three in ERIC but none with identical forename or initial.

* A&I conventions emphasise the addition to names of two other elements: 1) the 'role', *i.e.*, the type of intellectual responsibility, such as 'author', 'editor', 'compiler', 'translator', etc., and 2) the person's affiliation. Cataloguing rules, on the other hand, treat the role of persons in the statement of responsibility area and discard affiliations.
* With regard to corporate names, there are some similarities and differences between A&I conventions and cataloguing principles:
  - The full form of corporate names is entered by A&I services with the inclusion of an abbreviation or acronym of a corporate body as an optional element. AACR2R prescribes a similar approach without the optional inclusion of an abbreviation or acronym.
  - If the official or formal name of an organisation is usually quoted in the form of an acronym, this may be entered as the full form. AACR2R has the same approach.
  - The name of a corporate body should be entered in the language of the document, unless the name shown on the document is itself a translation, and the name in its original language is known, in which case the latter form should be entered if better known. AACR2R prescribes that the official language of the body should be used.

- Where several levels of an organisation are cited, they should be given in descending order of scale from the larger unit to the smaller. In terms of entering at the intermediate levels, if their inclusion does not add significant information to the entry, they may be omitted provided always that the most specific unit is cited and that the entry provides an unambiguous identification of the organisation. Similarly, AACR2R prescribes that a subordinate or related body should usually be entered as a subheading of the main body.

SUMMARY AND CONCLUSIONS

The following conclusions are derived from the examination of a number of cataloguing principles carried out in this chapter, in the light of the various capabilities of the online environment.

Functions of the catalogue:

* Conceptually, the objectives and functions of the catalogue are independent of its physical form and arrangement. Technology can, however, influence the way in which these functions are carried out: the more developments there are in the technology of catalogue construction and in the online environment, the more possibilities there are to achieve those objectives and functions.
* Due to the potential use of bibliographic records by a variety of users, the scope of catalogue functions should be expanded to encompass additional functions. The two basic functions remain valid in the online environment but the catalogue also can serve additional functions: to further identify entities, to choose one item over similar items, to locate items and copies of items and to maintain databases in terms of record updating.
* While the finding function is a general approach in almost all bibliographic databases, the collocating function is more important to library catalogues and, to some extent, to publishers' databases than to other

communities such as A & I services. However, in the online environment, with a variety of users, all the functions of the catalogue need to be considered important. It is therefore necessary to elaborate on this issue and arrive at an international agreement, since the delineation of the objectives and functions of the catalogue influences other cataloguing principles.

The concept of main entry:

* Rather than being the locus of complete information for the bibliographic record or the primary access point, main entry is an important concept that maintains some basic functions of the catalogue, that of identifying and collocating, in a uniform way, different editions and manifestations of a work. In other words, if a major function of the catalogue is to identify and collocate works as well as their editions and manifestations, there is a need for a concept such as main entry. The lack of such a concept could result in failure to place a publication in the context of its bibliographic relationships. Unless we devise new mechanisms for the uniform identification and collocation of the different manifestations and editions of a work, it would be unwise to abandon the concept of main entry.
* Nevertheless, in order to delineate the concept more clearly and to avoid confusion as to its functions, main entry is in need of re-definition. The new functional definition should address the validity of the concept in terms of its various functions, irrespective of the catalogue's physical environment. Main entry is particularly needed in the online environment for the useful retrieval, display and arrangement of search results.

The concept of uniform titles:

* Similarly to the concept of main entry, uniform titles are needed to perform some basic functions such as providing links between different editions and manifestations of a work and to distinguish among works with identical titles proper. Because of present

problems in the online retrieval of the various editions and manifestations of works, a concept such as a standardised form of the title of a work can serve to identify and collocate them. However, uniform titles need to be simplified in order to avoid online retrieval problems.

The principle of uniform headings:

* It is difficult to fulfil the collocating function of the catalogue/database without maintaining the principle of uniform headings. Uniformity of headings for authors and titles is especially important in network environments, where different catalogues and other bibliographic databases are accessible to the user through the same terminal. The principle is also of particular significance in shared cataloguing systems and union databases. Library cataloguing, book trade bibliographic databases and A&I services should at least be consistent or compatible in certain areas such as uniform headings. In effect, standardisation or compatibility in the form of headings is an essential requirement for *universal bibliographical control* (UBC), particularly in the global online environment.

Form of name headings:

* In terms of the form of personal and corporate name headings for effective searching, retrieval and display, online catalogues need a simpler approach. The form of headings needs to be reconsidered in terms of its suitability for different searching patterns and for display. For example, given adequate software, full forms of name should satisfy searchers seeking either that form, or only the surname plus initials. But searching under single letters, such as initials, is still a problem for many library systems. For subordinate corporate bodies direct headings are usually more responsive to online search/retrieval/displays.

Number of contributors:

* As a consequence of the potential of the online system to incorporate more names as access points, the 'rule

of three' is not sensible in the online environment. Removal of this outdated principle would add to the functionality of the catalogue, in that it would enhance access to and identification of works of all authors.

Wider application of the principles:

* Current cataloguing principles are not based on the overriding requirements of different users in a variety of environments. There are advantages if we can arrive at a body of principles which can serve to reconcile the bibliographical practices of publishers and booksellers with those of libraries, bibliographic utilities, national bibliographies and the archival community. It would also be advantageous if A&I services and library cataloguing practices could come closer in terms of providing consistent access to bibliographic information, particularly in terms of the form of name headings. Although the objectives and functions of book trade databases, A&I databases and library catalogues are different from one another, the entries created by each community need to be consistent or at least compatible for the purposes of record exchange and database searching. A possible solution is for each community to conform to national name authority files.

In terms of some fundamental questions such as the 'basic unit of description', 'the edition issue' and the display of bibliographic data, current cataloguing principles are not adequately responsive to the requirements of the new online environment. In considering basic concepts for further investigation, attention should be paid to a possible resolution of such questions.

5

Approaches to Evaluation for Library Catalogues

INTRODUCTION

This chapter presents a review of the different approaches to evaluation and in particular the data gathering methods which have been used in both traditional library catalogue use studies and in online catalogue research. It is suggested that the methodological shortcomings of the quantitative surveys in the evaluation of manual catalogues may have led to an incomplete picture of the search process and possible misinterpretation of user needs.

Online catalogue research has adopted a diversity of methods including comparative studies, prototyping, controlled experiments, transaction log analysis and protocol analysis. These take into account system performance through retrieval tests and user performance through diagnostic analysis.

EVALUATION AND TRADITIONAL LIBRARY CATALOGUES

The main objective of traditional catalogue use studies has been to collect data on the use or usage of the tool and then by inference to draw conclusions about user behaviour and user needs. The emphasis appears to have thus been placed on the means rather than on the end, *i.e.* the tool as opposed to the task. A closer examination of the data gathering methods applied illustrates some of the methodological shortcomings of these studies.

QUESTIONNAIRES AND INTERVIEWS

In traditional catalogue use studies, the survey method including questionnaires and interviews has been the dominant form of data gathering. The point at which the searcher was interrogated has varied and has to a large extent determined the type, amount and reliability of the data collected. In the U.K. catalogue use survey, library users were interviewed as they left the library and were asked to recall their last search as well as to generalise on how they would normally search. Lipetz in the Yale study, interviewed users before and after they had consulted the catalogue and focused on a more immediate and specific search.

In doing so he was able to ascertain to some extent, whether or not users really did what they set out to do and thus discovered that searchers' immediate and underlying objectives differed. Tagliacozzo went further by observing and questioning subjects about success and failure at different stages during their consultation. By identifying the different strategies adopted by searchers after their initial access to the catalogue, the progression of the search was thus partly followed.

This was achieved by the experimenter noting if the user moved from one entry point of the card catalogue to another, whereupon questions could then be asked about the different access points. The catalogue consultation was also followed up by questioning users when they returned from the shelves and it was found that subsequent shelf-browsing was widespread. By their very large scale, these studies aimed to gather quantitative data on use and by the very nature and breadth of the samples (over 2,000 cases), in-depth qualitative analysis of user activity was limited. In not observing the search at first hand, the indirect and partial approach resulted in an incomplete picture of catalogue searches. Consequently, little is revealed about searching as a process and the interactive nature of user searching behaviour at the catalogue.

PROTOCOL ANALYSIS

Experimenters avoided a more direct approach to eliciting information from the user on the grounds that it would interfere and possibly distort the search process. Ericsson and Simon's seminal paper on verbal reports as data has led to the use of protocols or spoken thoughts in task analysis and decision making processes in a number of other areas. Markey applied protocol analysis to study manual subject searching at the library catalogue.

With minimal prompting by the experimenter, the searcher was encouraged to talk aloud as the search was carried out. The proceedings were recorded on a tape recorder and from the transcript a flow chart of the different steps in the complete search was produced, indicating all the decision points and actions taken by the searcher. From the coded protocols, searching patterns of behaviour emerged and models of different types of searches were identified. It was found that the majority of searchers extracted a class of numbers from the catalogue and proceeded to continue their search at the shelves rather than at the catalogue.

This method of eliciting information from the user does generate a vast amount of data. It appears to be an effective way of obtaining a typography of searches but the transcription and subsequent coding are very cumbersome and time consuming. To circumvent some of the disadvantages of protocol analysis Hancock devised a combined observation and talk aloud technique to study searchers using a microfiche catalogue and printed subject index. Data were recorded on a highly structured dual purpose observation and questionnaire form incorporating some real time interpretation. Subjects were encouraged to talk aloud as they searched merely to give an indication of what they were looking for and to confirm whether or not they succeeded. The direct observation of searchers' actions provided the experimenter with the framework of the activity whilst the verbal data gave the details which could not be easily observed or which were not observable.

Searchers' actions thus confirmed what they said they were doing or *vice versa*. In order to get a more complete picture of the information seeking behaviour, a holistic approach was also adopted by including searching activity at the shelves following the catalogue consultation.

OUTLINE OF METHODOLOGICAL SHORTCOMINGS

Although the limitations in the performance of traditional library catalogues particularly for subject searching, had been recognized, Hafter in her review of catalogue use studies states:

"The major conclusion that emerges from these studies is that the card catalogue works. Even more importantly, users are skilful at manipulating it for their own purpose".

The general results of low usage and the dominance of the catalogue as a finding tool for specific item searching does not appear to support this conclusion. It could be argued that the apparent preference for specific item searching may have been more a function of the catalogue's limited subject access capability than a reflection of the user's information need. The very design of the tool could well have been encouraging a certain type of behaviour, that is the tool tailoring the task.

In the study of users and the usage of the library catalogue, a number of difficulties and constraints have been met in data gathering, namely:

* Observation of the user is difficult, the physical format being only one of the obstacles.
* The catalogue consultation is not a static process but consists of a series of events and the searcher's pattern of behaviour depends on what comes before and after the different stages. The links between each step of the searching process are just as much an integral part of the search as the individual steps.
* The structure of the catalogue influences user behaviour and does not necessarily reflect information needs, *i.e.* user performance is dependent on systems performance.

Moreover some of the methodological limitations have also stemmed from:

* A dependence on the catalogue consultation alone to inform on the information seeking process as a whole,
* A reluctance to use more direct or diverse means of eliciting information from users for fear of interfering with the search process,

* A reliance on users themselves to provide adequate information before and after the event.

EXPERIMENTAL AND ANALYTICAL METHODS FOR OPAC EVALUATION

Whereas traditional catalogue use studies have been dependent on the survey method and based on collecting data from the user in an operational setting, online catalogue studies have adopted a more experimental and controlled approach. Partly because of the technological environment, a number of different methods and combinations of methods for data gathering and evaluation have been used.

These can be divided into two groups. The first consists of more general testing methods which aim to measure system performance through retrieval tests, and include comparative studies, prototyping and laboratory type controlled experiments. The second group are more user orientated, diagnostic analytical methods, such as transaction log analysis, protocol analysis and talk-aloud techniques, as well as the other usual methods of eliciting information from users *i.e.* questionnaires and interviews.

The design of the evaluative component of an experimental study could include a combination of methods from both groups. We shall draw on the major online catalogue studies for a critical assessment of how each of these two categories of evaluative methods have been applied.

COMPARATIVE STUDIES

Several different types of comparative studies have been undertaken. Researchers compared searching for assigned titles on an online catalogue as well as on a card catalogue. The object was to assess user acceptability of the new medium. In spite of limitations in the performance of the online catalogue, users nevertheless expressed their preference for the computerized tool.

The trial test, the online catalogue at the National Library of Medicine, had a much more system defined objective in comparing the performance of two online catalogues. In an attempt to differentiate system dependent and independent variables, a combined methodology was devised. Two separate groups of library staff and users were assigned searches on either system.

In addition to this 'sample search experiment', a 'comparison search experiment' was also conducted whereby users searched both systems for topics of their choice. A survey using a self-administered questionnaire provided additional user data. The main drawback in this type of general comparison in an operational setting is the inability to control the variables across the two systems.

We are not comparing like with like. In this case the searching capability of Cite was far superior to that of its rived and so it was not surprising that it performed better and users preferred it. It may have been more valuable if it had been possible, to have tested the contribution of individual features to the overall result.

A similar disadvantage is to be found when Okapi'86 was compared with the operational system Libertas to determine:

* User preference for specific features,
* User assessment of performance and
* User attitudes to Okapi's recall improvement devices.

In this case however, evidence could be corroborated with other Okapi evaluative studies. The quantitative measure of recall was also correlated with the qualitative measure of user satisfaction.

Although satisfaction was measured in terms of number of references, there may have been other contributory factors which were not accounted for. In all of these comparative studies although system performance is the dominant interest, there is nevertheless some attempt to take the user into account to some extent particularly in the Okapi'86 evaluation.

PROTOTYPING

Prototyping as a methodology can be an effective way of developing and testing individual system design features. This is not an uncommon method in numerous other computer applications for example in manufacturing and processing.

Unfortunately this method as an evaluative method has only been used in the design of experimental systems.

In spite of the many in-house online catalogues and the commercial systems available, evaluative data on their different stages of development, if it does exist, has not been made available. The Okapi'84-86 projects funded by British Library are a major exponent of this approach. Each successive version built on the results of the former. Evaluation was carried out in an operational setting with real users and real searches.

Failure analysis of transactions logs of the first version Okapi'84 led to improvements of the combinational search mechanisms for partial matches and new devices to improve recall in the second version Okapi'86. These included automatic stemming or truncation, cross-reference tables and spelling corrections. To evaluate these features three catalogues were used.

EXP contained all the devices, including both weak stemming (*i.e.* plurals, ing and ed endings) and strong stemming (*i.e.* tion, ness, ist endings) and CTL included weak stemming only. The third catalogue, OSTEM, contained none of the new retrieval aids and was used as a control to repeat searches which had been identified from the transaction logs of the other two catalogues in the library trials.

Thus by isolating variables the retrieval effectiveness of the different devices was tested and compared. 50% of spelling errors were corrected with favourable results and weak stemming was found to increase recall without affecting precision. Strong stemming on the other hand was more tenuous. The Dewey Decimal Classification Online Project also produced a prototype system which was evaluated in four libraries in the form of two catalogues featuring different subject searching capabilities.

One included keyword access in titles and LCSH headings and the other was enhanced with the DDC classification schedules and the relative index. Retrieval tests were conducted using comparative as well as sample searches as with the CITE experiment and were followed by a post-search interview which provided some insight into user expectations and behaviour.

Comparative results of estimated recall and precision based on references displayed, showed that the more traditional keyword access performed better than the enhanced system, however the latter retrieved a different set of references. Moreover failure analysis revealed that the Dewey catalogue provided more relevant items for searches which were dependent on user-entered terms.

At the same time success was not dependent on user-entered terms alone in that the user also had the opportunity to further specify and search. Improvement in subject access can thus be seen in terms of quality and not simply quantity. Recall and precision alone do not appear to be adequate measures of success. In addition searchers expressed difficulties in choosing between all the different options.

Whether or not searching techniques should be transparent to the user remains problematic. The automatic implementation of the retrieval aids in Okapi'86 made it easier to test their effectiveness. In the Dewey project where the choice of options was left to the user and the search process was more interactive, results were less conclusive. This would depend not only on how search features are presented to the user at the interface but also on the type of retrieval aids being tested.

It may be easier to evaluate retrieval techniques based on the matching or partial matching principle than contextual aids where there is an attempt to place the user query in a subject context. The involvement of users at the different stages of the design process is an important part of the prototyping methodology. In addition the development of more interactive features does highlight the interdependence of user and system performance in the evaluative process.

CONTROLLED EXPERIMENTS

A third approach in OPAC research has been concerned with investigating the cognitive elements of searching behaviour. Through controlled laboratory type of experiments and searching performance tests, these studies aim to gain a better understanding of how users search in order to ascertain how they can be assisted to search more effectively.

Based on the theory that the user builds a mental model of how a system operates, Borgman investigated whether a user with a conceptual understanding of how a system works will perform better than a user with only a procedural knowledge. In comparing procedural and conceptual training (*i.e.* Boolean logic and operators), greater variance was found amongst individual subjects with different backgrounds (*i.e.* science/ engineering vs. humanities/social sciences) than between experimental variables.

Whether users with different characteristics require a different approach to training and how they can be trained to develop a 'correct' model of the system is unclear. A second study looked at procedural problems for first time users. Subjects were given access to both online or printed help to undertake five assigned searches. Twenty four out of thirty searchers called up the online help in the course of the searches but success rates ranged from 0% to 58%.

Some of the difficulties arose because searchers did not distinguish between procedural and conceptual instructions, *e.g.* type in 'author' was taken literally. Other problems were caused by not reading enough of the help screen which then made it difficult to recover from errors.

The naive user undoubtedly with experimentation and a more natural setting could overcome some of the procedural difficulties but the conceptual elements are proving to be much more problematic. Nielsen, Baker and Sandore experimented with more in-depth instruction provided by a workshop and a printed brochure.

Three groups of first year undergraduates were used, two provided with one type of instruction and a third, a control group received no instruction. All three were given written tests and online searches which were logged. Results showed that those who attended the workshop performed better on the written tests and marginally better on the online searches.

However those who read the brochure did not perform better than the control group. As with all exam type tests, questions can be raised as to whether the content or the method of instruction is being tested. In this case the learning objectives were very high and included selecting controlled vocabularies, truncation and Boolean logic. The authors concluded that some of the instruction would be more effective if it were 'embedded' in the system.

Clearly user training and instruction in the use of online catalogues, cannot be regarded as a substitute for system improvement. However user assistance designed as an integral part of the searching process within the information system could make a substantial contribution to overall performance.

NON-VERBAL DATA: TRANSACTION LOG ANALYSIS

With the advent of the online environment came the possibility of observing the user directly and unobtrusively without interrupting the search process. Automatic monitoring of activity on the computer system, *i.e.* logging transactions, was regarded as a powerful technique for evaluating user system interaction and performance.

However the type of quantitative global data elements recorded, that is search commands, occurrence of errors, number of hits and time factors, did not provide sufficient information or the right type of data to inform adequately on how or why users searched in the way they did. The method proved to have a number of more specific limitations.

Firstly not all systems have logging facilities. If they do, specifications for the data recorded will vary from system to system, making comparisons difficult. Secondly there are problems in identifying individual search sessions as users do not log on or off as with other online bibliographic systems. Thirdly the log usually records users' input in full but the system's displayed output is logged in a coded form so that it is not possible to ascertain the basis of users' decisions. Fourthly logs generate a lot of data, the sheer volume makes analysis a daunting task.

If spite of these limitations studies of transaction logs have produced some useful diagnostic evidence of procedural and conceptual problems. Using direct observation to determine search boundaries, Borgman analysed search commands, types of errors, and time factors on the Ohio State University online catalogue. One in three of all sessions were multiple search types which included at least one subject search command. 13% of all commands were errors.

Logs of the Melvyl system at the University of California collected in 1982 and in 1985, were compared and revealed changes in user behaviour. The call up of help screens had diminished. More searchers than previously were using the standard command search mode, as opposed to the menu search mode. Another study analysed the effectiveness of keyword access in titles and searching LCSH headings.

Failure analysis of transaction logs of three systems with different searching features revealed that searching LCSH or keywords in titles alone or a combination of both led to comparable failure rates (39% to 46%). Searchers did not use available search options (Boolean, browsing headings or class numbers) to expand their searches but tended to change search terms instead.

Two other log analysis studies by Dickson and by Henty revealed that most errors were due to miskeyings, mispellings or syntactic problems relating to initials, hyphens etc. Transaction logging as a data gathering method has potential both as a diagnostic tool to be used in combination with other evaluative approaches in experimental settings or as a monitoring device for operational systems in general. The development of transactions logs is central to the work undertaken by City and being reported here.

VERBAL DATA: PROTOCOL ANALYSIS

Protocol analysis has been used as a method of eliciting verbal data from users in two doctoral projects. Dalrymple used a combination of observation and protocol analysis to compare how users reformulated a set of assigned searches in a card catalogue and in an online catalogue. The study found that the online catalogue seemed to stimulate more reformulations but the card catalogue led to the retrieval of more items.

The author concluded that:

* It is not known how the internal cognitive reformulation process interfaces with the external system.

It appeared that the difficulty lay in isolating independent variables in the interaction and identifying the different types of feedback. In an attempt to define characteristics of searching behaviour, Sullivan adopted a type of simulation method. A search planning exercise was designed in which six expert and six novice users were asked to plan 32 assigned searches. From the verbal protocols, search plans were produced which the experimenter then used to carry out the searches.

The findings reveal significant differences in the planning process between experts and novices in terms of understanding the query, how they simulated the search and how they evaluate their likelihood of success.

Novices concentrated on starting rules whereas experts focused on setting goals and planning alternatives in case of failure. The work does point to some basic requirements for an 'expert' help system. However such a facility would need to be developed in parallel with improved features for a third generation system and not on the basis of current second generation catalogues.

OUTLINE OF EVALUATION METHODS APPLIED TO OPACS

It is evident that the methodological problems encountered in traditional catalogue use studies have not all been overcome in the online environment although some progress has been made.

The advances can be summarised as follows:

* Transaction logs present the possibility of recording searches in their entirety.
* Both system and user performance are starting to be taken into account.
* Corroborative data is being collected in the form of verbal and non-verbal data.
* A more systematic approach is being taken to isolate variables in testing new system features.

The state of the art in the evaluation of online catalogues is still at a diagnostic stage. It would appear that the development of more effective evaluation methods is dependent on being able to take full account of human factors at the interface.

6

Library Cataloguing and Classification

A.L.A. CATALOGUE

The A.L.A. Catalogue is the first general book selection guide cooperatively prepared for use by American public libraries. In the early stage of public libraries' development, book selection is the job of library committee composed of library director and trustees rather than librarians.

However, there might be problems for the committee to reach an agreement on which book should be include/exclude for their libraries due to the following two reasons:

* Firstly, the committee members might be different in terms of education background and personal interests, therefore, they might come up with "different theories of what the library shall be".
* Secondly, even without the disagreement of theories, it is impossible for committee members to have an adequate knowledge of "books, editions, and prices, outside of their own line of reading."

Thus they need the assistance from experts to revise and complete their booklist for libraries.

DEWEY AND THE CATALOGUE

The A.L.A. Catalogue, also known as the Catalogue of A.L.A. Library, as one of the most popular booklists developed by experts, is the "first general book selection guide cooperatively prepared for use by American public libraries." Before the development of the catalogue, Melvil Dewey first promoted the idea of a universal library collection guide in an article "The Coming Catalogue" in Library Journal in 1877.

He suggested a co-operative way for creating the collection guide among library committee, field specialist, as well as authors, for the reason that "no one person living unites in himself the wisdom necessary to make the best notes on all the books of the library", and "not one but many minds must contribute to the work." Dewey also suggested American Library Association (A.L.A) appoints a committee to take "entire charge" of the "coming catalogue". The primary usage of such catalogue would be "as a guide in the purchase of books for either private or public collection. as the main catalogue of many of these libraries."

Based on Dewey's article, A.L.A. began to take steps of creating such catalogue. In November 1878, A.L.A. appointed five people as the committee in charge of the catalogue. They decided to adopt a classified arrangement of the catalogue. The catalogue was planned to be about 250 pages with a fixed price of $2.50.

After years' cession of catalogue development, Dewey attempted to re-start his plan for A.L.A. catalogue when he worked at Columbia College as the "Librarian in Chief" in 1883. He tried to obtain suggestion from Columbia faculty members through their lectures on "bibliography and literature in their areas of expertise" when the School of Library Economy was established in 1887, and later Dewey moved to University of the State of New York in 1888, where he continued his work on catalogue by asking his library employees and students in Albany to compile the catalogue through scholarly journals.

The Catalogue was finally published and promoted in the A.L.A. annual conference in 1893 at the Chicago World's Fair. The 1893 Catalogue of A.L.A. library provides a list of 5000 "best reading selections" that were "approved by distinguished specialists in various lines and organized by librarians into two separate classification schemes".

EARLY ADOPTION IN LIBRARIES

After the Catalogue had been developed, more and more libraries began to adopt it as the guide for book selection. For instance, Mrs. Horace M. Towner, one of the trustee members of Iowa Library Commission in Corning, published a short paper "Trustees' Problems" in *Iowa Library Quarterly* in 1908 discussing the budget problem related to book purchasing.

Towner states that the general rules for books purchasing is depending on the specific situation within each library. In other words, there is no fixed rule for book purchasing. However, Towner discussed a lot about the "right" evaluation of fiction. In order to avoid unsuitable and vicious fiction in a library, trustees should rely on "best" book reviews, in addition to "Booklist" from ALA. Towner pointed out trustee members should read report from professional journals, like Library Journal and Public Libraries, to obtain knowledge from other library about the budget issue.

ANGLO-AMERICAN CATALOGUING RULES

The Anglo-American Cataloguing Rules (AACR) were first published in 1967. AACR2 stands for the *Anglo-American Cataloguing Rules, Second Edition*. It is published jointly by the American Library Association, the Canadian Library Association, and the Chartered Institute of Library and Information Professionals in the UK. The editor is Michael Gorman, a British-born librarian living in the Chicago area and honoured by both the ALA and CILIP. AACR2 is designed for use in the construction of catalogues and other lists in general libraries of all sizes. The rules cover the description of, and the provision of access points for, all library materials commonly collected at the present time.

Despite the claim to be 'Anglo-American', the first edition of AACR was published in 1967 in somewhat distinct North American and British texts. The second edition of 1978 unified the two sets of rules (adopting the British spelling 'cataloguing') and brought them in line with the International Standard Bibliographic Description. Libraries wishing to migrate from the previous North American text were obliged to implement 'desuperimposition', a substantial change in the form of headings for corporate bodies.

AACR2 exists in several print versions, as well as an online version. Gorman has edited several revisions of AACR2 including a concise edition. Print versions are available from the publishers. The online version is available only via Cataloger's Desktop from the Library of Congress. Various translations are also available from other sources.

Principles of AACR include cataloguing from the item 'in hand' rather than inferring information from external sources and the concept of the 'chief source of information' which is preferred where conflicts exist.

Over the years AACR2 has been updated by occasional amendments, and was significantly revised in 1988 and 2002. The 2002 revision included substantial changes to parts for non-book materials. A schedule of annual updates began in 2003 and ceased with 2005.

AACR2 has been succeeded by Resource Description and Access (commonly referred to as RDA), which was released in June 2010. This new code is informed by the Functional Requirements for Bibliographic Records and was conceived to be a framework more flexible and suitable for use in a digital environment.

In the fall of 2010, the Library of Congress, National Library of Medicine, National Agricultural Library, and several other institutions and national libraries of other English-speaking countries performed a formal test of RDA, the results of which were released in June 2011.

ACCESSION NUMBER (LIBRARY SCIENCE)

An accession number is a sequential number given to each new book, magazine subscription, or recording as it is entered in the catalogue of a library. If an item is removed from the collection, its number is usually not reused for new items. This numbering system is usually in addition to the library classification number (or alphanumeric code) and to the ISBN or International Standard Book Number assigned by publishers.

Accession numbers are also used by an arboretum, botanic garden, greenhouse, or museums to identify objects or plants by the order in which they entered the museum's collection. Typically, the accession number consists of the year acquired and a sequential number separated by a period.

In addition, departments or art classifications within the collection or museum may reserve parts of numbers. For example, objects identified by the numbers 11.000 through 11.999 may indicate objects obtained by the museum in 1911. the first 300 numbers may be used to indicate American art, while the next fifty (11.301-350) may be used for African art.

AgMES

The AgMES (Agricultural Metadata Element set) initiative was developed by the Food and Agriculture Organization (FAO) of the United Nations and aims to encompass issues of semantic standards in the domain of agriculture with respect to description, resource discovery, interoperability and data exchange for different types of information resources.

There are numerous other metadata schemas for different types of information resources.

The following list contains a list of a few examples:

* *Document-like Information Objects (DLIOs):* Dublin Core, Agricultural Metadata Element Set (AgMES)
* *Events:* VCalendar
* *Geographic and Regional Information:* Geographic information—Metadata ISO/IEC 11179 Standards
* *Persons:* Friend-of-a-friend (FOAF), vCard
* *Plant Production and Protection:* Darwin Core (1.0 and 2.0) (DwC)

AgMES as a namespace is designed to include agriculture specific extensions for terms and refinements from established standard metadata namespaces like Dublin Core, AGLS etc. Thus to be used for Document-like Information Objects, for example like publications, articles, books, web sites, papers, etc., it will have to be used in conjunction with the standard namespaces mentioned before. The AgMES initiative strives to achieve improved interoperability between information resources in agricultural domain by enabling means for exchange of information.

Describing a DLIO with AgMES means exposing its major characteristics and contents in a standard way that can be reused easily in any information system. The more institutions and organizations in the agricultural domain that use AgMES to describe their DLIOs, the easier it will be to interchange data in between information systems like digital libraries and other repositories of agricultural information.

USE OF AgMES

Metadata on agricultural Document-like Information Objects (DLIOs) can be created and stored in various formats:

* Embedded in a web site (in the manor as with the HTML meta tag)
* In a separate metadata database
* In an XML file
* In an RDF file

AgMES defines elements that can be used to describe a DLIO that can be used together with other metadata standards such as the Dublin Core, the Australian Government Locator Service. A complete list of all elements, refinements and schemes endorsed by AgMES is available from the AgMES website.

Creating Application Profiles

Application profiles are defined as schemas which consist of data elements drawn from one or more namespaces, combined by implementers, and optimized for a particular local application.

Application profiles share the following four characteristics:

* They draw upon existing pool of metadata definition standards to extract suitable application-or requirement oriented elements.
* An application profile cannot create new elements.
* Application profiles specify the application specific details such as the schemes or controlled vocabularies. An application profile also contains information such as the format for the element value, cardinality or data type.
* Lastly, an application profile can refine standardized definitions as long as it is "semantically narrower or more specific". This capability of application profiles caters to situations where a domain specific terminology is needed to replace a more general one.

Sample Application Profiles Using AgMES

* The AGRIS Application Profile is a standard created specifically to enhance the description, exchange and subsequent retrieval of agricultural Document-like Information Objects (DLIOs). It is a format that allows sharing of information across dispersed bibliographic systems and is based on well-known and accepted metadata standards.
* The Event Application Profile is a standard created to allow members of the Agricultural community to 'know' about an upcoming event and guide them to the event Web site where they can find further information. The information communicated is thus minimum yet interoperable across domains and organizations.

AgMES AND THE SEMANTIC WEB

One of the advantages of the AgMES metadata schema is the ability to link between the metadata element and controlled vocabularies. The use of controlled vocabulary provides a "known" set of options to the indexer (and the search programmer) as to how the field can be filled out. Often the values may come from a specific thesaurus (*e.g.* AGROVOC) or classification schemes (*e.g.* the AGRIS/CARIS classification scheme)etc. Thanks to the possibility to use controlled vocabularies for metadata elements, the user is provided with the most precise information. In this context, work is also being carried out on exploiting the power of controlled vocabularies expressed as using URIs and machine-understandable semantics.

In this context, FAO is promoting the Agricultural Ontology Service (AOS) initiative with the objective of expressing more semantics within the traditional thesaurus AGROVOC and build a Concept Server as a repository from which it will be always possible to extract traditional KOS.

ALA-LC ROMANIZATION

ALA-LC is a set of standards for romanization, or the representation of text in other writing systems using the Latin alphabet. The initials stand for American Library Association-Library of Congress. This system is used to represent bibliographic information by North American libraries and the British Library (for acquisitions since 1975), and in publications throughout the English-speaking world.

AUTHORITY CONTROL

Authority control is the practice of creating and maintaining index terms for bibliographic material in a catalogue in library and information science. Authority control fulfills two important functions. First, it enables catalogers to disambiguate items with similar or identical headings.

For example, two authors who happen to have published under the same name can be distinguished from each other by adding middle initials, birth and/or death (or flourished, if these are unknown) dates, or a descriptive epithet to the heading of one (or both) authors.

Second, authority control is used by catalogers to collocate materials that logically belong together, although they present themselves differently. For example, authority records are used to establish uniform titles, which can collocate all versions of a given work together even when they are issued under different titles.

Although theoretically any piece of information on a given book is amenable to authority control, catalogers typically focus on authors and titles. Subject headings fulfill a function similar to authority records, although they are usually considered separately.

AUTHORITY RECORDS

The most common way of enforcing authority control in a bibliographic catalogue is to set up a separate index of authority records, which relates to and governs the headings used in the main catalogue. This separate index is often referred to as an "authority file." It contains an indexable record of all decisions made by catalogers in a given library (or—as is increasingly the case—cataloguing consortium), which catalogers consult when making, or revising, decisions about headings.

It is to be remembered that the function of authority files is essentially organizational, rather than informational. That is to say, they (ideally) contain a sufficient amount of information to establish a given author or title as unique, while excluding information that, while perhaps interesting to a reader, does not contribute to this goal.

Although practices certainly vary internationally, in the English-speaking world, it is generally the case that a valid authority record must contain:

* Heading refers to the form of name (or title) that the cataloguer has chosen as the authorized form.
* Cross references are other forms of the name (or title) that might appear in the catalogue. There are two types of cross-references: *see* references, which reference forms of the name (or title) that have been deprecated in favour of the authorized form. and *see also* references, which point to other forms of the name (or title) that are authorized.
* Statement(s) of justification: In addition to providing a heading and applicable references, a valid authority record should also contain a reference to whatever sources of information the cataloguer used to determine both the authorized and any deprecated forms of the name. This is usually done by citing the title and publication date of the source, the location of the name (or title) on that source, and the form in which it appears on that source.

An example authority record, for author Flann O'Brien, taken from the United States Library of Congress authorities files, is reproduced below.

(The original record has been abbreviated somewhat for clarity):

```
O'Brien, Flann, 1911-1966
Na Gopaleen, Myles, 1911-1966
Knowall, George
Na gCopaleen, Myles, 1911-1966
His At Swim-Two-Birds...1939.
His The best of Myles, 1983: CIP t.p. (Myles na
```

```
Gopaleen (Flann O'Brien))
His Myles away from Dublin, 1985: t.p. (Myles na
Gopaleen (Flann O'Brien) selection from the
column written for...under the name of George Knowall)
Rhapsody in Stephen's green, 1994: t.p. (Flann O'Brien
(Myles na gCopaleen))
```

This example contains all the elements of a valid authority record: the first heading is the form of the name that the Library of Congress has chosen to be authoritative. In theory, every record in the catalogue that represents a work by this author should have this form of the name as its author heading.

These forms of the author's name will appear in the catalogue, but only as transcriptions, not as headings. If a user queries the catalogue under one of these variant forms of the author's name, she would receive the response: The final four entries in this record constitute the justification for this particular form of the name: it appeared in this form on the 1939 edition of the author's novel *At Swim-Two-Birds,* whereas the author's other *noms de plume* appeared on later publications.

ACCESS CONTROL

The act of choosing a single authorized heading to represent all forms of a name is often difficult, sometimes arbitrary and on occasion politically sensitive. An alternative is the idea of *access control,* where variant forms of a name are related without the endorsement of one particular form.

AUTHORITY CONTROL AND COOPERATIVE CATALOGUING

Before the advent of digital OPACs and the Internet, the work of creating and maintaining a library's authority files was generally carried out (if at all) by individual cataloguing departments. This meant that there could be a fair amount of disagreement among libraries over which form of a given name was considered authoritative. so long as a library's catalogue was internally consistent, differences between catalogs didn't much matter.

However, even before the Internet revolutionized the way libraries go about cataloguing their materials, catalogers began moving towards the establishment of cooperative consortia, such as OCLC and RLIN in the United States, in which cataloguing departments from libraries all over the world contributed their records to, and took their records from, a shared database. This development gave rise to the need for national standards for authority work.

In the United States, the primary organization for maintaining cataloguing standards with respect to authority work operates under the aegis of the Library of Congress, and is known as the Name Authority Cooperative Programme, or NACO Authority.

STANDARDS

* *ISAAR (CPF)*: International Standard Archival Authority Record for Corporate Bodies, Persons, and Families. Published by the International Council on Archives
* *MARC standards* for authority records in machine-readable format.
* *Metadata Authority Description Schema* (*MADS*), an XML schema for an authority element set that may be used to provide metadata about agents (people, organizations), events, and terms (topics, geographics, genres, etc.).
* *Encoded Archival Context*, an XML schema for authority records conforming to ISAAR(CPF)

BCM CLASSIFICATION

The British Catalogue of Music Classification (BCM Classification) is a faceted classification that was commissioned from E.J. Coates by the Council of the British National Bibliography to organize the content of the British Catalogue of Music. The published schedule (1960) was considerably expanded by Patrick Mills of the British Library up until its use was abandoned in 1998.

Entries in the catalogue were organized by BCM classmark from the catalogue's inception in 1957 until 1982. From that year the British Catalogue of Music was organized instead by Dewey Decimal Classification number, though BCM classmarks continued to be added to entries up to the 1998 annual cumulation.

The schedule is divided into two main parts: A-B representing Musical literature and C-Z representing Music—Scores and Parts. There are also seven auxiliary tables dealing with various sub-arrangements, sets of ethnic/locality subdivisions and chronological reference points.

The notation is retroactive using uppercase alphabetic characters omitting I and O, with the addition of slash/and parentheses which have specific anteriorizing functions. Retroactive notation requires that the classifier combines terms in reverse schedule order. This has the benefit of producing a compact notation by removing the need for facet indicators.

The schedule at A (Music Literature) parallels that from the Scores and Parts schedules thus Choral Music is at D while books about Choral Music are at AD. Harp Music is at TQ so books on harp music are at ATQ. The schedule at B accommodates books about specific composers and music in non-European traditions.

As a fully faceted scheme after the ideas of S.R. Ranganathan, BCM class numbers are capable of being chain-indexed, allowing index access to each step of the hierarchy. BCM classification had a strong influence on Russell Sweeney's so-called Phoenix Dewey 780 schedule which in turn influenced the 780 Music schedule in the 20th edition of Dewey Decimal Classification. The music schedule of the second edition of the Bliss Classification is also strongly influenced by BCM.

BIBLIOGRAPHIC CONTROL

In library and information science, bibliographic control (also known as information organization or bibliographic organization) is the process by which information resources are described so that users are able to find and select that information resource. An information resource could be a book, a movie, or an image, among other things.

By providing a name, title, and subject access to the description, a bibliographic record is created. This bibliographic record, which is essentially metadata, is indexed by an information retrieval tool (such as a database or a search engine) so that a user can find out whether or not the information resource is relevant to them.

SIX FUNCTIONS OF BIBLIOGRAPHIC CONTROL

Ronald Hagler identified six functions of bibliographic control:

* "Identifying the existence of all types of information resources as they are made available." The existence and identity of an information resource must be known before it can be found.
* "Identifying the works contained within those information resources or as parts of them." Depending on the level of granularity required, multiple works may be contained in a single package, or one work may span multiple packages. For example, is a single photo considered an information resource? Or can a collection of photos be considered an information resource?
* "Systematically pulling together these information resources into collections in libraries, archives, museums, and Internet communication files, and other such depositories." Essentially, acquiring these items into collections so that they can be of use to the user.
* "Producing lists of these information resources prepared according to standard rules for citation." Examples of such retrieval aids include library catalogs, indexes, archival finding aids, etc.
* "Providing name, title, subject, and other useful access to these information resources." Ideally, there should be many ways to find an item so there should be multiple access points. There must be enough metadata in the surrogate record so users can successfully find the information resource they are looking for. These access points should be consistent, which can be achieved through authority control.
* "Providing the means of locating each information resource or a copy of it." In libraries, the online public access catalogue (OPAC) can give the user location

information (a call number for example) and indicate whether the item is available.

HISTORY OF BIBLIOGRAPHIC CONTROL

While the organization of information has been going on since antiquity, bibliographic control as we know it today is a more recent invention. Ancient civilizations recorded lists of books onto tablets and libraries in the Middle Ages kept records of their holdings. With the invention of the printing press in the 15th century, multiple copies of a single book could be produced quickly.

Johann Tritheim, a German librarian, was the first to create a bibliography in chronological order with an alphabetical author index. Konrad Gesner followed in his footsteps in the next century as he published an author bibliography and subject index. He added to his bibliography an alphabetical list of authors with inverted names, which was a new practice. He also included references to variant spellings of author's names, a precursor to authority control.

Andrew Maunsell further revolutionized bibliographic control by suggesting that a book should be findable based on the author's last name, the subject of the book, and the translator. In the 17th century Sir Thomas Bodley was interested in a catalogue arranged alphabetically by author's last name as well as subject entries.

In 1697 Frederic Rostgaard called for subject arrangement that was subdivided by both chronology and by size (whereas in the past titles were arranged by their size only), as well as an index of subjects and authors by last name and for word order to in titles to be preserved based on the title page.

After the French Revolution, France's government was the first to put out a national code containing instructions for cataloguing library collections. At the British Museum Library Anthony Panizzi created his "Ninety-One Cataloguing Rules" (1841), which essentially served as the basis for cataloguing rules of the 19th and 20th centuries.

Panizzi's "91 Rules" are also the origins of ISBD and Dublin Core. Charles C. Jewett took Panizzi's "91 Rules" and used them at the Smithsonian Institution, thus bringing Americans into the mix of cataloguing, a domain where Europeans had traditionally had more influence.

‡BIBLIOS.NET

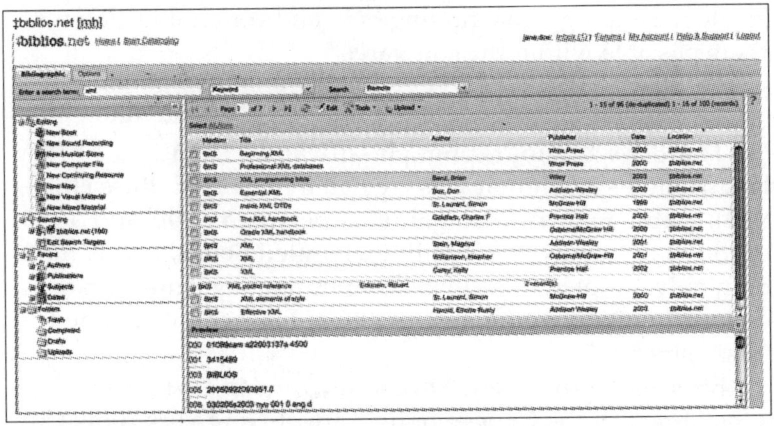

‡biblios.net is a free browser-based cataloguing service with a data store containing over thirty-million records. Records are licensed under the Open Data Commons Public Domain Dedication and License, making the service the world's largest repository of freely-licensed library records. The service was created and is maintained by LibLime.

FEATURES

‡biblios.net (pronounced 'biblios dot net') features a metadata editor with templates, macros, authority auto-completion and embedded context-sensitive help. The central record repository contains 25-million bibliographic records and just under eight-million authority records.

The data is maintained by ‡biblios.net users similar to the Wikipedia model. Catalogers can use and contribute to the database without restrictions because records in ‡biblios.net are freely-licensed under the Open Data Commons Public Domain Dedication and License.

‡biblios.net also includes a built-in federated search system allowing catalogers to find records from any Z39.50 target. Additionally, there is a central Search Target Registry, seeded

with over 2,000 Z39.50 servers, for catalogers to find, create and share Z39.50 targets.

In addition to offering a traditional cataloguing interface, ‡biblios.net offers social cataloguing features. Built-in forums and private messaging make finding help and communicating with others possible within the software.

BLISS BIBLIOGRAPHIC CLASSIFICATION

The Bliss bibliographic classification (BC) is a library classification system that was created by Henry E. Bliss (1870–1955), published in four volumes between 1940 and 1953. Although originally devised in the United States, it was more commonly adopted by British libraries than by American ones. A second edition of the system (BC2) has been developed in Britain since 1977.

Bliss was born in New York in 1870 and in 1891 began work in the library of the College of the City of New York (now City College of the City University of New York).

Bliss had a lifelong interest in the organization, structure and philosophy of knowledge and was very critical of the library classification systems that were available to him. He believed that because the popular Library of Congress system had been designed for a specific library (the Library of Congress) it had no use as a standard system outside that library. He also greatly disliked the Dewey Decimal system.

Bliss wanted a classification system that would provide distinct rules yet still be adaptable to whatever kind of collection a library might have, as different libraries have different needs. His solution was the concept of "alternative location," in which a particular subject could be put in more than one place, as long as the library made a specific choice and used it consistently.

In 1908 Bliss reclassified 60,000 of his library's books, and in 1910 he published an article with a rough scheme of his general ideas. But as he continued to develop his system he realised that it was going to be a much larger project than he had anticipated. The first of his four volumes appeared in 1940 (the year he retired) and the last in 1953, two years before his death.

Some of the underlying policies of the BC system were:

* Alternative location
* Brief, concise notation
* Organizing knowledge according to academic expertise
* Subjects moving gradually from topic to topic as they naturally related to one another.

ADOPTION AND CHANGE

BC was not used by many North American libraries. The system was not without its flaws (the result of being largely a one-person project), and the layout of Bliss's text was difficult to read. A few library schools sometimes taught the BC system to their students, but only in a minor way. The failure of the system to catch on in North America was partly because of its internal deficiencies but also because the Dewey Decimal and Library of Congress systems were already well established.

The City College library continued to use Bliss's system until 1967, when it reluctantly switched to the Library of Congress system. It had become too expensive to train new staff members to use BC, and too expensive to maintain in general. Much of the Bliss stacks remain, however, as no-one has recatalogued the books. The case was different, however, in Britain. BC proved more popular there and also spread to other English-speaking countries. Part of the reason for its success was that libraries in teachers' colleges liked the way Bliss had organized the subject areas on teaching and education. By the mid-1950s the system was being used in at least sixty British libraries and in a hundred by the 1970s.

In 1967 the Bliss Classification Association was formed. Its first publication was the *Abridged Bliss Classification* (ABC), intended for school libraries. In 1977 it began to publish and maintain a much-improved, revised version of Bliss's system, the Bliss Bibliographic Classification or BC2. This retains only the broad outlines of Bliss's scheme, replacing most of the detailed notation with a new scheme based on the principles of faceted classification. Fifteen of approximately 28 volumes of schedules have so far been published.

The top level organisation is:

* 2/9-Generalia, Phenomena, Knowledge, Information science and technology
* A/AL-Philosophy and Logic
* AM/AX-Mathematics, Probability, Statistics
* AY/B-General science, Physics
* C-Chemistry
* D-Astronomy and earth sciences
  - DG/DY-Earth sciences
* E/GQ-Biological sciences
* GR/GZ-Applied biological sciences: agriculture and ecology
* H-Physical Anthropology, Human biology, Health sciences
* I-Psychology and Psychiatry
* J-Education
* K-Society (includes Social sciences, sociology and social anthropology)
* L/O-History (including area studies, travel and topography, and biography)
  - LA-Archaeology
* P-Religion, Occult, Morals and ethics
* Q-Social welfare and Criminology
* R-Politics and Public administration
* S-Law
* T-Economics and Management of economic enterprises
* U/V-Technology and useful arts (including household management and services)
* W-The Arts
  - WV/WX-Music
* X/Y-Language and literature
* ZA/ZW-Museology

BRINKLER CLASSIFICATION

Brinkler Classification is the library classification system of Bartol Brinkler described in his article *"The Geographical Approach to Materials in the Library of Congress Subject Headings"*. The geographical aspect of a subject may be conveyed through three types of headings labelled A, B, and C. Heading A uses a primary topical description with geographical subdivisions (*e.g.* Art—Paris). Type B uses a place-name for the main heading with a topical subdivision (*e.g.* Paris—Description). While with C headings use a geographical description of a phrase (*e.g.* Paris Literature).

Brinkler explores what type of heading is more useful to a patron, and he finds that it depends on the level of familiarity a patron has with a topic and what approach they take when searching for resources on their topic. Ideally readers will either be looking for everything on a particular topic, or everything regarding a particular place.

Bartol Brinkler investigates a system of classification that will best serve these two ideal types of patrons. He finds working with Type A headings will best assist a patron who is more topic oriented, while using Type B headings is preferable for those who are primarily interested in one place.

However this is problematic in practice. One possibility is to assign Type A and Type B headings to every resource, but the cataloguing cost would be high. A system that aids readers regardless of their approach to a topic involves using cross-references. Admitting that see and see also references would require more work on the part of librarians, Bartol Brinkler notes that librarians must keep in mind "... readers do not have the same knowledge and do need all the help they can get ... "

CANADIAN SUBJECT HEADINGS

Canadian Subject Headings (CSH) is a list of subject headings in the English language, using controlled vocabulary, to access and express the topic content of documents on Canada and Canadian topics. Library and Archives Canada publishes and maintains CSH on the Web. Prior to the merger of the National Library of Canada and the National Archives of Canada, the National Library of Canada published a print version of CSH.

The headings are compatible with the United States Library of Congress Subject Headings, with modifications to include specifically Canadian content or to reflect a Canadian perspective. Library and Archives Canada also publishes Répertoire de vedettes-matière (RVM), a list intended to provide access to Canadian subject headings in the French language.

CATALOGUING IN PUBLICATION

In publishing and library science, Cataloguing in Publication (CIP, or Cataloguing in Publication) is basic cataloguing data for a work, prepared in advance of publication by the national library of the country where the work is principally published or by the library of a publishing organisation such as a government department.

The name reflects the usual practice of including that information in the corresponding publication-—in the case of books, near the bottom of the copyright page, and can be very useful for less experienced cataloguers when adding such items to their collections. The national libraries' CIP staffs restrict the range of publications that CIP will be prepared for, for instance requiring access to assistance from the publisher's staff.

An all too frequent problem with CIP is when publishers change bibliographic details, such as the wording of a title, after receiving the CIP data. The CIP data as published in the item will be incorrect and not able to be used by subsequent catalogue-uing agencies without manual amendment and if a pre-publication record has been entered onto a database it can be difficult to locate and edit to match the details on the item itself. Each national library maintains a database of the entries it writes.

COBISS

COBISS (abbreviation for *Co-operative Online Bibliographic System and Services*) is an organisational model used to join libraries in a uniform library information system with shared cataloguing. It has many functions of the so-called virtual library. It is currently in use in Slovenia (COBISS.SI), Bosnia and Herzegovina (COBISS.BH), Republic of Macedonia (COBISS.MK), Serbia (COBISS.SR) and Montenegro (COBISS.CG).

These information systems are autonomous, but share the platform. Over 350 libraries use COBISS software for the automation of their operations. COBISS.Net is the name of the network connecting the COBISS co-operative bibliographic systems of different countries. COBISS has been developed by the Institute of Information Science (Slovene: *Institut informacijskih znanosti, IZUM*) from Maribor. In March 2011, all the management of IZUM decided to step down from their positions, the stated reason being the dismissive attitude of the Slovenian Ministry of Higher Education, Science and Technology (led by Gregor Golobiè) towards IZUM.

COLLABORATIVE CATALOGUING

Collaborative Cataloguing is shared action of a group making bibliographic records available to its participants in order to prevent duplication of bibliographic records. Thusly, cooperative cataloguing has benefits such as cost effectiveness and availability of a ready cataloguing model

A notable example of collaborative cataloguing takes place at the National Transportation Library or NTL, which is administered by the U.S. Department of Transportation. NTL participates in a consortium called the National Transportation Knowledge Network (TKN), "which was establishe[d]...to help facilitate access to information in support of transportation development". Pursuing that goal, the TKN engages in cooperative cataloguing with other transportation libraries. For example, in early summer 2011, the TKN held a meeting on cataloguing standards that are used by transportation libraries nationwide.

More specifically, NTL uses cooperative cataloguing to examine subject headings that are used in transportation literature. NTL is a key player in the organization of subject headings and has made significant contributions to the Transportation Research Thesaurus. The Transportation Research Thesaurus, or TRT, is a controlled vocabulary that was developed to improve the indexing and retrieval of transportation information. The TRT is used by indexers, content managers and librarians in the transportation community and is an internationally recognized standard.

COLON CLASSIFICATION

Colon classification (CC) is a system of library classification developed by S. R. Ranganathan. It was the first ever faceted (or analytico-synthetic) classification. The first edition was published in 1933. Since then six more editions have been published. It is especially used in libraries in India.

Its name "colon classification" comes from the use of colons to separate facets in class numbers. However, many other classification schemes, some of which are completely unrelated, also use colons and other punctuation in various functions. They should not be confused with colon classification.

As an example, the subject "research in the cure of tuberculosis of lungs by x-ray conducted in India in 1950" results in a call number:

* L,45.421:6.253:f.44'N5

The components of this call number represent:

* *Medicine,Lungs.Tuberculosis:*Treatment.X-ray: Research.India'1950

ORGANIZATION

The colon classification uses 42 main classes that are combined with other letters, numbers and marks in a manner resembling the Library of Congress Classification to sort a publication.

Facets

CC uses five primary categories, or facets, to further specify the sorting of a publication.

Collectively, they are called PMEST:

* Personality
* Matter or property
* Energy
* Space
* Time

CONTROLLED VOCABULARY

Controlled vocabularies provide a way to organize knowledge for subsequent retrieval. They are used in subject indexing schemes, subject headings, thesauri, taxonomies and other form of knowledge organization systems. Controlled vocabulary schemes mandate the use of predefined, authorised terms that have been preselected by the designer of the vocabulary, in contrast to natural language vocabularies, where there is no restriction on the vocabulary.

IN LIBRARY AND INFORMATION SCIENCE

In library and information science controlled vocabulary is a carefully selected list of words and phrases, which are used to tag units of information (document or work) so that they may be more easily retrieved by a search. Controlled vocabularies solve the problems of homographs, synonyms and polysemes by a bijection between concepts and authorized terms. In short, controlled vocabularies reduce ambiguity inherent in normal human languages where the same concept can be given different names and ensure consistency.

For example, in the Library of Congress Subject Headings (a subject heading system that uses a controlled vocabulary), authorized terms—subject headings in this case—have to be chosen to handle choices between variant spellings of the same concept (American versus British), choice among scientific and popular terms (Cockroaches versus Periplaneta americana), and choices between synonyms (automobile versus cars), among other difficult issues.

Choices of authorized terms are based on the principles of user warrant (what terms users are likely to use), literary warrant (what terms are generally used in the literature and documents), and structural warrant (terms chosen by considering the structure, scope of the controlled vocabulary).

Controlled vocabularies also typically handle the problem of homographs, with qualifiers. For example, the term "pool" has to be qualified to refer to either swimming pool, or the game pool to ensure that each authorized term or heading refers to only one concept.

There are two main kinds of controlled vocabulary tools used in libraries: subject headings and thesauri. While the differences between the two are diminishing, there are still some minor differences.

Historically subject headings were designed to describe books in library catalogs by catalogers while thesauri were used by indexers to apply index terms to documents and articles.

Subject headings tend to be broader in scope describing whole books, while thesauri tend to be more specialized covering very specific disciplines.

Also because of the card catalogue system, subject headings tend to have terms that are in indirect order (though with the rise of automated systems this is being removed), while thesaurus terms are always in direct order.

Subject headings also tend to use more pre-coordination of terms such that the designer of the controlled vocabulary will combine various concepts together to form one authorized subject heading. (*e.g.*, children and terrorism) while thesauri tend to use singular direct terms. Lastly thesauri list not only equivalent terms but also narrower, broader terms and related terms among various authorized and non-authorized terms, while historically most subject headings did not.

For example, the Library of Congress Subject Heading itself did not have much syndetic structure until 1943, and it was not until 1985 when it began to adopt the thesauri type term "Broader term" and "Narrow term".

The terms are chosen and organized by trained professionals (including librarians and information scientists) who possess expertise in the subject area. Controlled vocabulary terms can accurately describe what a given document is actually about, even if the terms themselves do not occur within the document's text. Well known subject heading systems include the Library of Congress system, MeSH, and Sears. Well known thesauri include the Art and Architecture Thesaurus and the ERIC Thesaurus.

Choosing authorized terms to be used is a tricky business, the designer has to consider the specificity of the term chosen, whether to use direct entry, inter consistency and stability of the language. Lastly the amount of pre-co-ordinate (in which case the degree of enumeration versus synthesis becomes an issue) and post co-ordinate in the system is another important issue. Controlled vocabulary elements (terms/phrases) employed as tags, to aid in the content identification process of documents, or other information system entities (*e.g.* DBMS, Web Services) qualifies as metadata.

INDEXING LANGUAGES

There are three main types of indexing languages:

* Controlled indexing language-Only approved terms can be used by the indexer to describe the document
* Natural language indexing language-Any term from the document in question can be used to describe the document.
* Free indexing language-Any term (not only from the document) can be used to describe the document.

When indexing a document, the indexer also has to choose the level of indexing exhaustivity, the level of detail in which the document is described. For example using low indexing exhaustivity, minor aspects of the work will not be described with index terms. In general the higher the indexing exhaustivity, the more terms indexed for each document.

In recent years free text search as a means of access to documents has become popular. This involves using natural language indexing with an indexing exhaustively set to maximum (every word in the text is *indexed*). Many studies have been done to compare the efficiency and effectiveness of free text searches against documents that have been indexed by experts using a few well chosen controlled vocabulary descriptors.

Controlled vocabularies are often claimed to improve the accuracy of free text searching, such as to reduce irrelevant items in the retrieval list. These irrelevant items (false positives) are often caused by the inherent ambiguity of natural language. Take the English word *football* for example.

Football is the name given to a number of different team sports. Worldwide the most popular of these team sports is Association football, which also happens to be called *soccer* in several countries. The English language word football is also applied to Rugby football (Rugby union and rugby league), American football, Australian rules football, Gaelic football, and Canadian football.

A search for *football* therefore will retrieve documents that are about several completely different sports. Controlled vocabulary solves this problem by tagging the documents in such a way that the ambiguities are eliminated.

Compared to free text searching, the use of a controlled vocabulary can dramatically increase the performance of an information retrieval system, if performance is measured by precision (the percentage of documents in the retrieval list that are actually relevant to the search topic).

In some cases controlled vocabulary can enhance recall as well, because unlike natural language schemes, once the correct authorized term is searched, you don't need to worry about searching for other terms that might be synonyms of that term. However, a controlled vocabulary search may also lead to unsatisfactory recall, in that it will fail to retrieve some documents that are actually relevant to the search question.

This is particularly problematic when the search question involves terms that are sufficiently tangential to the subject area such that the indexer might have decided to tag it using a different term (but the searcher might consider the same). Essentially, this can be avoided only by an experienced user of controlled vocabulary whose understanding of the vocabulary coincides with the way it is used by the indexer.

Another possibility is that the article is just not tagged by the indexer because indexing exhaustivity is low. For example an article might mention football as a secondary focus, and the indexer might decide not to tag it with "football" because it is not important enough compared to the main focus. But it turns out that for the searcher that article is relevant and hence recall fails. A free text search would automatically pick up that article regardless. On the other hand free text searches have high exhaustivity (you search on every word) so it has potential for high recall (assuming you solve the problems of synonyms by entering every combination) but will have much lower precision.

Controlled vocabularies are also quickly out-dated and in fast developing fields of knowledge, the authorized terms available might not be available if they are not updated regularly. Even in the best case scenario, controlled language is often not as specific as using the words of the text itself. Indexers trying to choose the appropriate index terms might misinterpret the author, while a free text search is in no danger of doing so, because it uses the author's own words.

The use of controlled vocabularies can be costly compared to free text searches because human experts or expensive automated systems are necessary to index each entry. Furthermore, the user has to be familiar with the controlled vocabulary scheme to make best use of the system. But, the control of synonyms, homographs can help increase precision.

Numerous methodologies have been developed to assist in the creation of controlled vocabularies, including faceted classification, which enables a given data record or document to be described in multiple ways.

APPLICATIONS

Controlled vocabularies, such as the Library of Congress Subject Headings, are an essential component of bibliography, the study and classification of books. They were initially developed in library and information science. In the 1950s, government agencies began to develop controlled vocabularies for the burgeoning journal literature in specialized fields.

An example is the Medical Subject Headings (MeSH) developed by the U.S. National Library of Medicine. Subsequently, for-profit firms (called Abstracting and indexing services) emerged to index the fast-growing literature in every field of knowledge. In the 1960s, an online bibliographic database industry developed based on dialup X.25 networking.

These services were seldom made available to the public because they were difficult to use. specialist librarians called search intermediaries handled the searching job. In the 1980s, the first full text databases appeared. these databases contain the full text of the index articles as well as the bibliographic information.

Online bibliographic databases have migrated to the Internet and are now publicly available. however, most are proprietary and can be expensive to use. Students enrolled in colleges and universities may be able to access some of these services without charge. some of these services may be accessible without charge at a public library.

In large organizations, controlled vocabularies may be introduced to improve technical communication. The use of controlled vocabulary ensures that everyone is using the same word to mean the same thing. This consistency of terms is one of the most important concepts in technical writing and knowledge management, where effort is expended to use the same word throughout a document or organization instead of slightly different ones to refer to the same thing.

Web searching could be dramatically improved by the development of a controlled vocabulary for describing Web pages. the use of such a vocabulary could culminate in a Semantic Web, in which the content of Web pages is described using a machine-readable metadata scheme. One of the first proposals for such a scheme is the Dublin Core Initiative. An example of a controlled vocabulary which is usable for indexing web pages is PSH.

It is unlikely that a single metadata scheme will ever succeed in describing the content of the entire Web. To create a Semantic Web, it may be necessary to draw from two or more metadata systems to describe a Web page's contents. The eXchangeable Faceted Metadata Language (XFML) is designed to enable controlled vocabulary creators to publish and share metadata systems. XFML is designed on faceted classification principles.

CONTROVERSIAL LITERATURE (LIBRARY OF CONGRESS SUBJECT HEADINGS)

Controversial literature is a subdivision of the Library of Congress Subject Headings, used in the description of religious books.

In this context, it has the following narrow use:

- "Under names of individual religious and monastic orders, individual religions, individual Christian denominations, and uniform titles of sacred works for works that argue against or express opposition to those groups or works".

Prior to 1998 the subdivision was permitted for 'general religious and philosophical topics'.

CUTTER EXPANSIVE CLASSIFICATION

The Cutter Expansive Classification system is a library classification system devised by Charles Ammi Cutter. The system was the basis for the top categories of the Library of Congress Classification.

HISTORY OF THE EXPANSIVE CLASSIFICATION

Charles Ammi Cutter, inspired by the decimal classification of his contemporary Melvil Dewey, and with Dewey's initial encouragement, developed his own classification scheme for the Winchester Town Library and then the Boston Athenaeum, at which he served as librarian for twenty-four years. He began work on it around the year 1880, publishing an overview of the new system in 1882. The same classification would later be used, but with a different notation, also devised by Cutter, at the Cary Library in Lexington.

Many libraries found this system too detailed and complex for their needs, and Cutter received many requests from librarians at small libraries who wanted the classification adapted for their collections. He devised the Expansive Classification in response, to meet the needs of growing libraries, and to address some of the complaints of his critics. Cutter completed and published an introduction and schedules for the first six classifications of his new system (*Expansive Classification: Part I: The First Six Classifications*), but his work on the seventh was interrupted by his death in 1903.

The Cutter Expansive Classification, although adopted by comparatively few libraries, mostly in New England, has been called one of the most logical and scholarly of American classifications.

Library historian Leo E. LaMontagne writes:

> "Cutter produced the best classification of the nineteenth century. While his system was less "scientific" than that of J.P. Lesley, it's other key features – notation, specificity, and versatility – make it deserving of the praise it has received".

Its top level divisions served as a basis for the Library of Congress classification, which also took over some of its features. It did not catch on as did Dewey's system because Cutter died before it was completely finished, making no provision for the kind of development necessary as the bounds of knowledge expanded and scholarly emphases changed throughout the 20th century.

STRUCTURE OF THE EXPANSIVE CLASSIFICATION

The Expansive Classification uses seven separate schedules, each designed to be used by libraries of different sizes. After the first, each schedule was an expansion of the previous one, and Cutter provided instructions for how a library might change from one expansion to another as it grows.

SUMMARY OF THE EXPANSIVE CLASSIFICATION SCHEDULES

First Classification

The first classification is meant for only the very smallest libraries. The first classification has only seven top level classes, and only eight classes in all.

* A Works of reference and general works which include several of the following parts, and so could not go in any one.
* B Philosophy and Religion
* E Biography
* F History and Geography and Travels
* H Social sciences
* L Natural sciences and Arts
* Y Language and Literature
* YF Fiction

Further Classifications

Further expansions add more top level classes and subdivisions. Many subclasses arranged systematically, with common divisions, such as those by geography and language, following a consistent system throughout.

By the fifth classification all the letters of the alphabet are in use for top level classes, these are:

* A General Works
* B Philosophy
* C Christianity and Judaism
* D Ecclesiastical History
* E Biography

* F History, Universal History
* G Geography and Travels
* H Social Sciences
* I Demotics, Sociology
* J Civics, Government, Political Science
* K Legislation
* L Science and Arts together
* M Natural History
* N Botany
* O Zoölogy
* P Anthropology and Ethnology
* Q Medicine
* R Useful arts, Technology
* S Constructive arts (Engineering and Building)
* T Manufactures and Handicrafts
* U Art of War
* V Recreative arts, Sports, Games, Festivals
* W Art
* X English Language
* Y English and American literature
* Z Book arts

These schedules were not meant to be fixed, but were to be adapted to meet the needs of each library. For example, books on the English language may be put in X, and books on language in general in a subclass of X, or this can be reversed. The first option is less logical, but results in shorter marks for most English language libraries.

HOW EXPANSIVE CLASSIFICATION CALL NUMBERS ARE CONSTRUCTED

Most call numbers in the Expansive Classification follow conventions offering clues to the book's subject. The first line represents the subject, the second the author (and perhaps title), the third and fourth dates of editions, indications of translations, and critical works on particular books or authors. All numbers in the Expansive Classification are (or should be) shelved as if in decimal order.

Size of volumes is indicated by points (.), pluses (+), or slashes (/or//). For some subjects a numerical geographical subdivision follows the classification letters on the first line. The number 83 stands for the United States—hence, F83 is U.S. history, G83 U.S. travel, JU83 U.S. politics, WP83 U.S. painting. Geographical numbers are often further expanded decimally to represent more specific areas, sometimes followed by a capital letter indicating a particular city.

The second line usually represents the author's name by a capital letter plus one or more numbers arranged decimally. This may be followed by the first letter or letters of the title in lower-case, and/or sometimes the letters a, b, c indicating other printings of the same title. When appropriate, the second line may begin with a 'form' number—*e.g.*, 1 stands for history and criticism of a subject, 2 for a bibliography, 5 for a dictionary, 6 for an atlas or maps, 7 for a periodical, 8 for a society or university publication, 9 for a collection of works by different authors.

On the third line a capital Y indicates a work about the author or book represented by the first two lines, and a capital E (for English—other letters are used for other languages) indicates a translation into English. If both criticism and translation apply to a single title, the number expands into four lines.

Cutter Numbers

One of the features adopted by other systems, including Library of Congress, is the Cutter number. It is an alphanumeric device to code text so that it can be arranged in alphabetical order using the fewest characters. It contains one or two initial letters and Arabic numbers, treated as a decimal. To construct a Cutter number, a cataloguer consults a Cutter table as required by the classification rules. Although Cutter numbers are mostly used for coding the names of authors, the system can be used for titles, subjects, geographic areas, and more.

DEWEY DECIMAL CLASSIFICATION (DDC)

Dewey Decimal Classification (also called the Dewey Decimal System) is a proprietary system of library classification developed by Melvil Dewey in 1876. It has been greatly modified and expanded through 23 major revisions, the most recent in 2011. This highly organized system categorizes books on library shelves in an efficient, specific and repeatable order that makes it easy to find any book and return it to its proper place on the library shelves. The system is used in 200,000 libraries in at least 135 countries. A designation such as *Dewey 16* refers to the 16th edition of the DDC.

DESIGN

The DDC attempts to organize all knowledge into ten main classes. The ten main classes are each further subdivided into ten divisions, and each division into ten parts, giving ten main classes, 100 divisions and 1000 parts. DDC's advantage in using decimals for its categories allows it to be purely numerical, while the drawback is that the codes are much longer and more difficult to remember as compared to an alphanumeric system.

Just as an alphanumeric system, it is infinitely hierarchical. It also uses some aspects of a faceted classification scheme, combining elements from different parts of the structure to construct a number representing the subject content (often combining two subject elements with linking numbers and geographical and temporal elements) and form of an item rather than drawing upon a list containing each class and its meaning.

Except for general works and fiction, works are classified principally by subject, with extensions for subject relationships, place, time or type of material, producing classification numbers of at least three digits but otherwise of indeterminate length with a decimal point before the fourth digit, where present (for example, 330 for economics +.9 for geographic treatment +.04 for Europe = 330.94 European economy. 973 for United States +.05 form division for periodicals = 973.05 periodicals concerning the United States generally).

Books are placed on the shelf in increasing numerical order of the decimal number, for example, 050, 220, 330, 330.973, 331. When two books have the same classification number the second line of the call number (usually the first letter or letters of the author's last name, the title if there is no identifiable author) is placed in alphabetical order.

The DDC has a number for all books, including fiction: American fiction is classified in 813. Most libraries create a separate fiction part to allow shelving in a more generalized fashion than Dewey provides for, or to avoid the space that would be taken up in the 800s, or simply to allow readers to find preferred authors by alphabetical order of surname.

Some parts of the classification offer options to accommodate different kinds of libraries. An important feature of the scheme is the ability to assign multiple class numbers to a bibliographical item and only use one of them for shelving. The added numbers appear in the classified subject catalogue (though this is not the usual practice in North America).

For the full benefit of the scheme the relative index and the tables that form part of every edition must be understood and consulted when required. The structure of the schedules is such that subjects close to each other in a dictionary catalogue are dispersed in the Dewey schedules (for example, architecture of Chicago quite separate from geography of Chicago).

Classes Listed

The system is made up of seven tables and ten main classes, each of which is divided into ten secondary classes or subcategories, each of which contain ten subdivisions.

The tables are:

* Standard subdivision
* Areas
* Subdivision of individual literatures
* Subdivisions of individual languages
* Racial, ethnic, national groups
* Languages
* Persons

The classes are:

* *000*: Computer science, information and general works
* *100*: Philosophy and psychology
* *200*: Religion
* *300*: Social sciences
* *400*: Language
* *500:* Science (including mathematics)

* *600*: Technology and applied science
* *700*: Arts and recreation
* *800:* Literature
* *900*: History and geography

ADMINISTRATION AND PUBLICATION

While he lived, Melvil Dewey edited each edition himself: he was followed by other editors who had been very much influenced by him. The earlier editions were printed in the peculiar spelling that Dewey had devised: the number of volumes in each edition increased to two, then three and now four.

The Online Computer Library Center (OCLC) of Dublin, Ohio, United States, acquired the trademark and copyrights associated with the DDC when it bought Forest Press in 1988. OCLC maintains the classification system and publishes new editions of the system.

The editorial staff responsible for updates is based partly at the Library of Congress and partly at OCLC. Their work is reviewed by the Decimal Classification Editorial Policy Committee (EPC), which is a ten-member international board that meets twice each year. The four-volume unabridged edition is published approximately every six years, the most recent edition (DDC 23) in mid 2011. The web edition is updated on an ongoing basis, with changes announced each month.

Linked to each full edition is the single volume abridged edition designed for libraries with 20,000 titles or fewer. Abridged 14 was published in 2004, Abridged 15 is due early 2012.

The work of assigning a DDC number to each newly published book is performed by a division of the Library of Congress, whose recommended assignments are either accepted or rejected by the OCLC after review by an advisory board. to date all have been accepted.

In September 2003, the OCLC sued the Library Hotel for trademark infringement. The settlement was that the OCLC would allow the Library Hotel to use the system in its hotel and marketing. In exchange, the Hotel would acknowledge the Centre's ownership of the trademark and make a donation to a nonprofit organization promoting reading and literacy among children.

INFLUENCE

DDC's numbers formed the basis of the more expressive but complex Universal Decimal Classification (UDC), which combines the basic Dewey numbers with selected punctuation marks (comma, colon, parentheses, etc.). Adaptations of DDC for specific regions outside the English-speaking world include the Korean Decimal Classification, the New Classification Scheme for Chinese Libraries and the Nippon Decimal Classification (Japanese).

COMPARISON WITH LIBRARY OF CONGRESS CLASSIFICATION

Besides its frequent revision, DDC's main advantage over its chief American rival, the Library of Congress Classification system developed shortly afterward, is its simplicity. Thanks to the use of pure notation, a mnemonics system and a hierarchical decimal place system, it is generally easier to use.

DDC and UDC are more flexible than Library of Congress Classification because of greater use of facets (via auxiliary tables) while Library of Congress Classification is almost totally enumerative.

DDC's decimal system means that it is less hospitable to the addition of new subjects, as opposed to Library of Congress Classification, which has 21 classes at the top level. DDC notations can be much longer compared to other classification systems.

Another disadvantage of DDC is that it was developed in the 19th century essentially by one man and was built on a top-down approach to classify all human knowledge, which makes it difficult to adapt to changing fields of knowledge. The Library of Congress Classification system was developed based mainly on the idea of literary warrant. classes were added (by individual experts in each area) only when needed for works owned by the Library of Congress.

As a result, while the Library of Congress Classification system was able to incorporate changes and additions of new branches of knowledge, particularly in the fields of engineering and computer science (the greater hospitability of the Library of Congress Classification was also a factor), DDC has been criticized for being inadequate in covering those areas.

It is asserted that, as a result, most major academic libraries in the US do not use the DDC because the classification of works in those areas is not specific enough, although there are other reasons that may truly be more weighty, such as the much lower expense of using a unique "pre-packaged" catalogue number instead of having highly skilled staff members engaging in the time-consuming development of catalogue numbers.

The Library of Congress Classification system is not without problems. For example, it is highly US-centric because of the nature of the system, and it has been translated into far fewer languages than DDC and UDC.

DICKINSON CLASSIFICATION

The Dickinson classification is a library classification scheme used to catalogue and classify musical compositions. It was developed by George Sherman Dickinson (1886-1964), and is used by many music libraries, primarily those at University at Buffalo, Vassar, and Columbia Universities.

FACETED CLASSIFICATION

A faceted classification system allows the assignment of an object to multiple characteristics (attributes), enabling the classification to be ordered in multiple ways, rather than in a single, predetermined, taxonomic order. A facet comprises "clearly defined, mutually exclusive, and collectively exhaustive aspects, properties or characteristics of a class or specific subject". For example, a collection of books might be classified using an author facet, a subject facet, a date facet, etc.

Faceted classification is used in faceted search systems that enable a user to navigate information along multiple paths corresponding to different orderings of the facets. This contrasts with traditional taxonomies in which the hierarchy of categories is fixed and unchanging. The colon classification developed by S. R. Ranganathan is an example of faceted classification applied to the physical world, specifically for the purpose of organizing library materials. In the colon classification system, a book is assigned a set of values from independent facets.

It differs from traditional library classification schemas like the Dewey Decimal System and Library of Congress classification system, in which each document has a unique assignment in a single, hierarchically organized classification system. Faceted classification systems are also distinct from folksonomies or other tagging systems that do not break out the tags into independent facets.

FREINET CLASSIFICATION

The Freinet classification ("To organise everything") is used in the libraries of some elementary schools, and was invented by Célestin Freinet to facilitate the easy finding of documents, and the use of the "Bibliothèque de Travail". The principles are simple: Everything is split into 12 major divisions. 12 subdivisions along the principles of the Dewey decimal system are then divided into 10, and then 10 again.

Because of its logical classifications based on school work, this classification is seen by some educators to be more natural and more logical to students than official classifications based on organizational criteria. The last revision took place in 1984. It is still used, in addition to keywords, in IT and some data information organization systems.

THE 12 DIVISIONS

* 0. Reference:
  - 00 General
  - 01 English Dictionaries
  - 02 Dictionaries in foreign languages
  - 03 Bilingual, trilingual... dictionaries
  - 04 Other Dictionaries (proper names, places...)
  - 05 Encyclopedias
  - 06 Repertory, bibliographies
  - 07 Reference works (textbooks)
* 1. Natural Environment:
  - 11 Land (geology)
  - 12 Relief

- 13 Freshwater
- 14 The oceans and seas
- 15 The climates and vegetation
- 16 Heaven (astronomy)
- 17 Nature and Life (ecology)

* 2. Plants:
- 21 Study of the plant
- 22 The flowering plants
- 23 The plants without flowers or seeds
- 24 The microscopic beings

* 3. Animals:
- 30 General study of the body (in humans and animals)
- 31 The health of humans
- 32 Mammals (except humans)
- 33 Birds
- 34 Reptiles and amphibians
- 35 Fish
- 36 Insects (articulated)
- 37 Other articulated
- 38 Shellfish
- 39 Other animals

* 4. Other sciences:
- 41 Mathematics
- 42 Physical Sciences
- 43 Chemistry
- 44 Technology

* 5. Food and Agriculture:
- 51 Working the earth
- 52 Cultures
- 53 Livestock
- 54 Forestry
- 55 Fishing
- 56 Hunting
- 57 Food industry
- 58 Foods
- 59 Drinks

* 6. Labour and Industry:

- 60 General
- 61 Sources of energy and engines
- 62 Mining and quarrying
- 63 Metals
- 64 Chemical Industry
- 65 Textile and clothing industry
- 66 Building industry, housing and furniture
- 67 Other Industries

* 7. The city and stock exchanges:
  - 71 The city, the municipality
  - 72 Trade
  - 73 Road Transport
  - 74 Rail transport
  - 75 Inland waterway transport
  - 76 Maritime Transport
  - 77 Air transportation and space
  - 78 Post, Telecommunications and IT
  - 79 Travel and Tourism
* 8. Society:
  - 81 People
  - 82 Contracts (environmental and social issues)
  - 83 Administrative organization of society
  - 84 Organisation of social policy
  - 85 Reports from nations
* 9. Culture and Recreation:
  - 91 Education and instructions
  - 92 Languages
  - 93 Literature and Philosophy
  - 94 Religions
  - 95 Arts and Entertainment
  - 96 Sports and Games
* G. Geography:
  - G0 The study of geography
  - G1 General Geography
  - G2 Geography locally and regionally
  - G3 Our country
  - G4 Europe
  - G5 Asia

- G6 Africa
- G7 America
- G8 Oceania
- G9 The Polar World

* H. History:
  - H1 Prehistory
  - H2 The East, Greece
  - H3 Rome and the early Middle Ages (from "700 to 987)
  - H4 Middle Ages (from 987 to 1492)
  - H5 Absolute monarchy (1492 to 1789)
  - H6 Struggles for Democracy (1789 to 1848)
  - H7 Organization of the Republic (1848 to 1914)
  - H8 Contemporary history (1914–present)

FRSAD

Functional Requirements for Subject Authority Data (FRSAD), previously known as Functional Requirements for Subject Authority Records, or FRSAR is a conceptual entity-relationship model currently being developed by a workgroup International Federation of Library Associations and Institutions (IFLA).

It is a continuation of the work done on the FRBR model, further explaining how the Group 3 entities, that consists of "entities that serve as subjects of intellectual or artistic endeavour" can be related and controlled within the bibliographic universe.

The model is meant to ease global sharing and use of subject authority data. The final draft of the report is to be presented in the spring of 2009 at the 75th IFLA General Conference and Council in Milan.

THE CONCEPTUAL MODEL

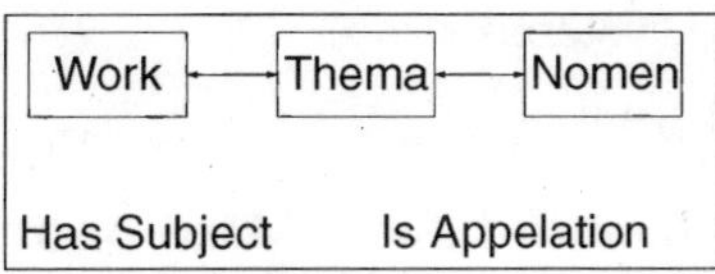

* *Work:* Work is a "distinct intellectual or artistic creation.
* *Thema:* Is anything that can be the subject of a work. This is the abstract idea of the aboutness of a given work. Thema is independent of language and disciplines.
* *Nomen:* Any alphanumeric, sound, visual, or any other symbol, sign or combination of symbols by which a thema is known, referred to or addressed. A nomen can be any expression of a thema. Ideally there will exist an authority file with every possible subject/thema. This means that it should be possible to exchange subject authority data between systems. If a user looks up a specific subject in a catalogue and wants to look in other places, he or she should not have to worry about translating the query, since the system would be able to recognize the underlying thema and automatically translate it into the relevant nomen. One way to understand this is to think about how a subject can be described in different ways. For example, if one looks at a work about the city Stockholm, the capital of Sweden, there are many ways to describe Stockholm. First, one must distinguish between the city Stockholm and the many other meanings of the word. for example, Stockholm is also the name of other cities, a record label, and a syndrome. When the thema is established in an authority file, it is possible to translate across systems. The nomen for Stockholm could be anything from "Stockholm", "Stockholm (City)", "Tukholma"-the Finnish spelling of Stockholm-or a range of Zip-codes, or the longitude and latitude, or a picture of the city, or a sound. FRSAR, if implemented, enables users to perform specific and precise subject searching across multiple systems.

RELATIONSHIPS

Works and themas have a Many-to-many (data model) relationship, meaning that any work can have more than one subject, and any subject can be expressed in one or more works. The same is true for the relationship between thema and nomen. A thema can be expressed in many different ways and a nomen can express many different themas, all depending on the given system.

Besides these relationships, the workgroup has so far identified several other thema-thema and nomen-nomen relationships. Two nomens can, for example, be said to have an equivalence relationship, if they both are appellations of the same thema.

USER TASKS

The workgroup conducted two user studies in 2006 and 2007, and based on the results of these studies, four subject authority data user tasks were defined:

* *Find:* To find an entity (thema or nomen) or set of entities corresponding to stated criteria
* *Identify:* To identify an entity (thema or nomen) based on certain attributes/characteristics
* *Select:* To select an entity (thema or nomen)
* *Explore:* To explore any relationships between entities (thema or nomen), correlations to other subject vocabularies and structure of a subject domain

FUNCTIONAL REQUIREMENTS FOR BIBLIOGRAPHIC RECORDS (FRBR)

Functional Requirements for Bibliographic Records (FRBR), sometimes pronounced is a conceptual entity-relationship model developed by the International Federation of Library Associations and Institutions (IFLA) that relates user tasks of retrieval and access in online library catalogues and bibliographic databases from a user's perspective.

It represents a more holistic approach to retrieval and access as the relationships between the entities provide links to navigate through the hierarchy of relationships. The model is significant because it is separate from specific cataloguing standards such as AACR2 or International Standard Bibliographic Description (ISBD).

FRBR ENTITIES

FRBR comprises groups of entities:

* Group 1 entities are work, expression, manifestation, and item (WEMI). They represent the products of intellectual or artistic endeavour.
* Group 2 entities are person and corporate body, responsible for the custodianship of Group 1's intellectual or artistic endeavour.
* Group 3 entities are subjects of Group 1 or Group 2's intellectual endeavour, and include concepts, objects, events, places.

Group 1 entities are the foundation of the FRBR model:

* *Work* is a "distinct intellectual or artistic creation." For example, Beethoven's Ninth Symphony apart from all ways of expressing it is a work. When we say, "Beethoven's Ninth is magnificent!" we generally are referring to the work.
* *Expression* is "the specific intellectual or artistic form that a work takes each time it is 'realised.'" An expression of Beethoven's Ninth might be the musical score he writes down.
* *Manifestation* is "the physical embodiment of an expression of a work. As an entity, manifestation represents all the physical objects that bear the same characteristics, in respect to both intellectual content and physical form." The recording the London Philharmonic made of the Ninth in 1996 is a manifestation. When we say, "The recording of the London Philharmonic's 1996 performance captured the essence of the Ninth," we are generally referring to a manifestation.
* *Item* is "a single exemplar of a manifestation. The entity defined as item is a concrete entity." Each of the 1996 pressings of that 1996 recording is an item. When we say, "Both copies of the London Philharmonic's 1996 performance of the Ninth are checked out of my local library," we are generally referring to items.

RELATIONSHIPS

FRBR is built upon relationships between and among entities. "Relationships serve as the vehicle for depicting the link between one entity and another, and thus as the means of assisting the user to 'navigate' the universe that is represented in a bibliography, catalogue, or bibliographic database." Examples of relationship types include, but are not limited to:

Equivalence Relationships

Equivalence relationships exist between exact copies of the same manifestation of a work or between an original item and reproductions of it, so long as the intellectual content and authorship are preserved. Examples include reproductions such as copies, issues, facsimiles and reprints, photocopies, and microfilms.

Derivative Relationships

Derivative relationships exist between a bibliographic work and a modification based on the work.

Examples include:

* Editions, versions, translations, summaries, abstracts, and digests
* Adaptations that become new works but are based on old works
* Genre changes
* New works based on the style or thematic content of the work

Descriptive Relationships

Descriptive relationships exist between a bibliographic entity and a description, criticism, evaluation, or review of that entity, such as between a work and a book review describing it. Descriptive relationships also includes annotated editions, casebooks, commentaries, and critiques of an existing work.

ICONCLASS

Iconclass is a specialized library classification designed for art and iconography. It was originally conceived by Henri van de Waal, and was further developed by a group of scholars after his death.

The Iconclass system is probably the largest classification system for cultural content. Initially designed for historical imagery, it is now also used to create subject access to texts and to classify a wide range of images, including modern photography. At the moment it contains over 28,000 unique concepts (classification types) and has an entry vocabulary of 14,000 keywords. It can be consulted with the help of the freely available Iconclass 2100 browser.

Iconclass was developed in the Netherlands as a standard classification for recording collections, with the idea of assembling huge databases that will allow the retrieval of images featuring particular details, subjects or other common factors. For example, the Iconclass code "71H7131" is for the subject of "Bathsheba (alone) with David's letter", whereas "71" is the whole "Old Testament" and "71H" the "story of David".

A number of collections of different types have been classified using Iconclass, notably many types of old master print, the collections of the Gemäldegalerie, Berlin and the German Marburger Index. These are available, usually on-line or on DVD. The system can also be used outside pure art history, for example on sites like Flickr. The content of Iconclass is currently maintained by the Rijksbureau voor Kunsthistorische Documentatie (Netherlands Institute for Art History). The online Iconclass browser is developed by the Henri van de Waal Foundation.

INTERNATIONAL STANDARD BIBLIOGRAPHIC DESCRIPTION

The International Standard Bibliographic Description (ISBD) is a set of rules produced by the International Federation of Library Associations and Institutions (IFLA) to create a bibliographic description in a standard, human-readable form, especially for use in a bibliography or a library catalogue.

A consolidated edition of the ISBD was published in 2007 and revised in 2011, superseding earlier separate ISBDs for monographs, older monographic publications, cartographic materials, serials and other continuing resources, electronic resources, non-book materials, and printed music. IFLA's ISBD Review Group is responsible for maintaining the ISBD.

One of the original purposes of the ISBD was to provide a standard form of bibliographic description that could be used to exchange records internationally. This would support IFLA's programme of universal bibliographic control.

INVENTORY

Libraries need methods, such as inventories, to determine whether their collections are in good shape, or whether some preservation or conservation activities are necessary. How do libraries identify which particular items sitting on their shelves that may not have crossed the circulation desk in a number of years need special attention?

ROLE OF INVENTORY IN THE MISSION OF LIBRARIES

Libraries have thousands of books. large academic libraries may have millions of books. therein lies our problem. Doing an annual (or less frequent) physical inventory with the laying on of hands on each individual item may not be financially feasible, employees required may not have extra time to devote to such an inventory, and there are no financial rewards for the Library for completing an inventory—essentially we are out looking for our problem books and missing items when we conduct an inventory.

The solutions to solving the problems that are discovered (books in need of repurchase, rebinding, repair, or digitization) are expensive and labour intensive. Inventories may not take place for decades, if ever, at large academic institutions because of these restraints.

Although collecting new materials is viewed as a central mission of the library, maintaining the condition of library collections, which includes less satisfactory activities such as weeding, book repair, shifting and counting what libraries think they have on their shelves, are also a vital part of the library's mission to provide access to current patrons, as well as those people who will use the library at some point in the future.

Adelphi University Libraries in 2004 completed a complete physical inventory of its collections (465,629 volumes) as part of its strategic planning process utilizing the Association of College and Research Libraries Standards for Libraries in Higher Education. Examining item by item with a barcode scanner and a laptop, the objective is to adjust bibliographic and item records in theirs and OCLC's WorldCat databases.

Complete inventory or stocktaking is often a regular part of the school library media specialist's job at K-12 institutions, where inventory may be a legal requirement that shows that the libraries are accountable for the money they have spent throughout the year. Checking for lost books and materials can be similarly compared to auditing. We are trying to guarantee that our collections as listed in our OPACs and Finding Aids do not lack integrity.

School libraries use the inventory to assess the collection (numbers, age and ratio:student) against benchmarks of accrediting institutions, and also to examine each resource and determine its future in the collection based on age, relevance, currency and condition—which may include repair, replacement, disposal or cleaning to ensure that attractive, up-to-date resources are available for patrons. Inventory can also identify anomalies in the catalogue and provide an opportunity to correct catalogue records and labeling of items. This is also a time when shelves can be rearranged to minimize overcrowding to prevent damage.

SAMPLING

Sampling is a compromise measure, which can be an important management tool. Random sampling of library collections can give a quick and clear assessment measure of a collection—whether the books are present, and whether those books present are in good physical condition.

In 1982, the California State University libraries, suggested inventory procedures to insure that the 19 campus collections were secure and intact. They recognized that a complete regular inventory was too expensive, and decided that the best method of assessing book loss would be to use sampling. Every three years, a sample was to be taken of an identified number of items in each Library of Congress letter classification. If loss rates were more than 1% for two years in a row, this would indicate that a full inventory was needed.

A random sampling of the collection serves as an indicator for the rest of the collection. If all the items are accounted for in a random sampling, then it can be assumed that rest of the collections' records is just as reliable. However, a complete inventory provides the institution with the knowledge that the entire collection can be accounted for. the random sampling is used to check the consistency of the collections' records.

DETERMINING THE SAMPLE SIZE AND ITEMS

First, it must be determined if the entire collection, including stacks, reference and special collections will be sampled together or if just a particular area will be analysed. At the University of Illinois, their bookstacks included government publications and the Asian library, but these special holdings were not included in their study. Unbound items may also be excluded.

Next, the Library needs to decide upon the size of its sample. More datapoints, of course result in more accurate data about the collection. There are two types of errors possible in sampling: tolerance and confidence.

Tolerance is the unexact percentage, a maximum deviation from the nominal error value, for example, a survey question may be accurate for 85-95% of the population, it could also be stated 90% ±5. in this case, the tolerance is five. Confidence is the second error, measuring the certainty of a true answer within the limits stated in the tolerance. If there is a 90 per cent confidence, it is predicted that if the sample study is repeated ten times using different samples, but with the same tolerance, then the results would be accurate for nine of those studies out of ten.

In Table 6.1, for a tolerance of ±5%, the sample sizes for a collection of more than 50,000 books would be 381 items for 95% confidence, and 648 items for 99% confidence. To achieve a lower tolerance of ±1% one would have to sample thousands of books, which might stretch the resources available for even a sample inventory. Surveying 270 to 655 volumes is much more reasonable for the average-sized library staff.

Table 6.1: Necessary Sample Sizes for various Library Collection

	Confidence Level/Confidence Interval/Sample Size							
Collection Size	95% Confident				99% Confident			
(Population)	10%	5%	2%	1%	10%	5%	2%	1%
1,000	88	278	706	906	143	400	806	943
10,000	95	370	1936	4899	164	624	2,938	6,246
50,000	96	381	2,291	8,057	166	648	3,841	12,486
100,000	96	383	2,345	8,763	166	657	3,994	14,267
250,000	96	384	2,345	8,057	166	661	4,092	15,602
500,000	96	384	2,378	9,249	166	665	4,126	16,105
1,000,000	96	384	2,395	9,513	166	665	4,143	16,369

An alternative for counting hundreds of books in a given random sample is to count until you know that you do or do not have a problem. The Prescott Memorial Library at Louisiana Tech employed sequential analysis in the late 1980's when working on automation of the collections.

Random selection of the books can take place in a couple of different ways. If in addition to the physical condition of items, a library also wants to know whether items are missing from shelves, random samples should be generated from the library's integrated library system (ILS).

If librarians are just accessing the collection for preservation purposes, they can easily count ranges, columns, shelves and books and use Microsoft Excel or other spreadsheet software to create random samples. It should be noted, however, that misplacement of books on shelves does have associated costs—in the patron's satisfaction with the library's services and in staff time trying to locate missing books. It may be well worth the extra time to figure out how to extract random items from your library's ILS to complete your sample.

MANAGEMENT OF SAMPLING SURVEYS

Once librarians are laying hands on individual books in their sample, what do they look for? They should check the cover of the book for discoloration, peeling, damage. Then they should open the book and look at the pages of the text—are they yellowing, brittle? An archival marking pen may be used to determine whether a book is acidic. How is the binding? Are the pages intact? This data can be recorded in a spreadsheet for use of later analysis of the entire sample.

Include the item's call number, place of publication, place of production, publication date, measurements (spine height, cover width, depth of back to front cover, the amount of shelving space surrounding the item, horizontally and vertically). describe the case style, leaf attachment and binding condition, text attachment, acidity, paper strength, and text contrast. list the damaged pages and describe the enclosure type and condition. record any additional notes that will be useful for future reference and analysis.

Costs for sampling 384 random items at the University of Illinois at Urbana-Champaign in 1987 were less than $5000. The UIUC Library employed eleven graduate students from the school of library and information science, who received training and supervision. Each surveyor collected forty samples, 90% of the surveys were completed on the first day in 5.5 survey hours.

ANALYSIS OF RESULTS

Information from samples can easily be recorded in Excel or some other spreadsheet programme, where simple analysis can be performed. For preservation purposes, librarians want to know the condition of their collections: what percentage of the books are acidic? What percentage of the collection is damaged? Does more damage take place on cramped shelves? Does the library need to be concerned with books printed in Eastern Europe? Etc. After identifying the issues of primary concern in the collection, preservation measures should be considered.

What needs to happen as soon as possible to preserve the collection? What choices can be delayed for some time? Does the library have a preservation plan in its collection management policy? Is there a budget for maintaining the collections? What can be extrapolated from the data about what might happen to the collection in ten to twenty years?

Using the results of the library's collection assessment, budgetary requests can be substantiated by data. The library needs an increase in budget to care for aging collections, or the library needs an increase in funding to add new materials for our students to meet deficiencies and weaknesses. This strategy was employed by the Joyner Library at East Carolina University after an inventory and shelf-analysis project in 2005.

OTHER USES OF SAMPLING IN LIBRARY COLLECTION MANAGEMENT

Sampling can also be used to calculate optimum intervals for shelf reading. Average misplacement of books on a shelf in a university library is 5.6%. Sixty-five per cent of the books were located on the correct shelf, but not in the right order. Cooper and Wolthausen developed equations indicating that the optimal shelf-reading interval is a function of the number of books in a part, the likelihood that a book in one part will migrate to another, checking and users costs, and the error rate of the shelf reader.

LIBRARY OF CONGRESS CLASSIFICATION

The Library of Congress Classification (LCC) is a system of library classification developed by the Library of Congress. It is used by most research and academic libraries in the U.S. and several other countries. for example, Australia and Taiwan, R.O.C. It is not to be confused with the Library of Congress Subject Headings or Library of Congress Control Number. Most public libraries and small academic libraries continue to use the Dewey Decimal Classification (DDC).

The classification was originally developed by Herbert Putnam in 1897, just before he assumed the librarianship of Congress. With advice from Charles Ammi Cutter, it was influenced by his Cutter Expansive Classification and by the DDC, and was designed specifically for the purposes and collection of the Library of Congress.

The new system replaced a fixed location system developed by Thomas Jefferson. By the time Putnam departed from his post in 1939, all the classes except K (Law) and parts of B (Philosophy and Religion) were well developed. It has been criticized as lacking a sound theoretical basis. many of the classification decisions were driven by the practical needs of that library, rather than epistemological considerations.

Although it divides subjects into broad categories, it is essentially enumerative in nature. It provides a guide to the books actually in the library, not a classification of the world. The National Library of Medicine classification system (NLM) uses the classification scheme's unused letters *W* and *QS–QZ*. Some libraries use NLM in conjunction with LCC, eschewing LCC's R (Medicine). Others prefer to use the LCC scheme's *QP–QR* schedules and include Medicine *R*.

LIBRARY OF CONGRESS CONTROL NUMBER

The Library of Congress Control Number or LCCN is a serially based system of numbering cataloguing records in the Library of Congress in the United States. It has nothing to do with the contents of any book, and should not be confused with Library of Congress Classification.

The LCCN numbering system has been in use since 1898, at which time the acronym LCCN originally stood for Library of Congress Card Number. It has been variously called the Library of Congress Catalogue Card Number. The Library of Congress prepared cards of bibliographic information for their library catalogue and would sell duplicate sets of the cards to other libraries for use in their catalogs. This is known as centralized cataloguing. Each set of cards was given a serial number to help identify it.

Although most of the bibliographic information is now electronically created, stored and shared with other libraries, there is still a need to identify each unique record, and the LCCN continues to perform that function.

Librarians all over the world use this unique identifier in the process of cataloguing most books which have been published in the United States. It helps them reach the correct cataloguing data (known as a cataloguing record), which the Library of Congress and third parties make available on the Web and through other media. In February 2008, the Library of Congress created the LCCN Permalink service, providing a stable URL for all Library of Congress Control Numbers.

FORMAT

In its most elementary form the number includes a year and a serial number. The year has two digits for 1898 to 2000, and four digits beginning in 2001. The three ambiguous years are distinguished by the size of the serial number. There are also some peculiarities in numbers beginning with a "7" because of an unsuccessful experiment applied between 1969 and 1972. Serial numbers are six digits long and should include leading zeros. The hyphen that is often seen separating the year and serial number is optional. More recently, the Library of Congress has instructed publishers not to include a hyphen.

MARC STANDARDS

MARC (MAchine-Readable Cataloguing), is an international standard digital format for the description of bibliographic items developed by the Library of Congress during the 1960s to facilitate the creation and dissemination of computerized cataloguing from library to library within the same country and between countries. By 1971, the MARC format had become the national standard for dissemination of bibliographic data and by 1973, an international standard. There are several versions of MARC in use in the world, the most predominant being MARC 21, created in 1999 as a result of the harmonization of U.S. and Canadian MARC formats, and UNIMARC, widely used in Europe. The MARC 21 family of standards now includes formats for authority records, holdings records, classification schedules, and community information, in addition to formats for the bibliographic record.

MARC RECORD STRUCTURE AND FIELD DESIGNATIONS

The MARC standards define three aspects of a MARC record: the record structure, the field designations within each record, and the actual content of the record itself.

Record Structure

ISO 2709

MARC records are typically stored and transmitted as binary files, usually with several MARC records concatenated together into a single file. MARC uses the ISO 2709 standard to define the structure of each record. This includes a marker to indicate where each record begins and ends, as well as a set of characters at the beginning of each record that provide a directory for locating the fields and subfields within the record.

MARC-XML

In 2002, the Library of Congress developed the MARC-XML schema as an alternative record structure, allowing MARC records to be represented in XML. Libraries typically expose their records as MARC-XML via a web service, often following the SRU or OAI-PMH standards.

Field Designations

Each field in a MARC records provides information about the item the record is describing. Since it was first developed at a time when computing power was low, and space precious, MARC uses a simple three-digit numeric code (from 001-999) to identify each field in the record. The bibliographic standard, for example, defines 100 as the primary author of a work, 245 as the title, 260 is used for publisher information, and so on.

Fields above 008 are further divided into subfields using a single letter or number designation. The 260, for example, is further divided into subfield 'a' for the place of publication, 'b' for the name of the publisher, and 'c' for the date of publication.

Content

MARC is a metadata transmission standard, not a content standard. Other than a handful of fixed fields defined by the MARC standards themselves, the actual content a cataloger will place in each MARC field is usually governed and defined by standards outside of MARC.

The Anglo-American Cataloguing Rules, for example, define how the physical characteristics of books and other item should be cataloged. The Library of Congress Subject Headings (LCSH) provides a list of authorized subject terms to describe the main content of the item. Other cataloguing rules, subject thesauri, and classification schedules can also be used.

MARC 21 allows the use of two character sets, either MARC-8 or Unicode encoded as UTF-8. MARC-8 is based on ISO 2022 and allows the use of Hebrew, Cyrillic, Arabic, Greek, and East Asian scripts. MARC 21 in UTF-8 format allows all the languages supported by Unicode.

MARC 21

MARC 21 is a result of the combination of the United States and Canadian MARC formats (USMARC and CAN/MARC). MARC21 is based on the ANSI standard Z39.2, which allows users of different software products to communicate with each other and to exchange data. MARC 21 was designed to redefine the original MARC record format for the 21st century and to make it more accessible to the international community. MARC 21 has formats for the following five types of data: Bibliographic Format, Authority Format, Holdings Format, Community Format, and Classification Data Format. Currently MARC 21 has been implemented successfully by The British Library, the European Institutions and the major library institutions in the United States, and Canada.

MARC 21 allows the use of two character sets, either MARC-8 or Unicode encoded as UTF-8. MARC-8 is based on ISO 2022 and allows the use of Hebrew, Cyrillic, Arabic, Greek, and East Asian scripts. MARC 21 in UTF-8 format allows all the languages supported by Unicode.

MARC FORMATS

Name	Description
Authority records	Provide information about individual names, subjects, and uniform titles. An authority record establishes an authorized form of each heading, with references as appropriate from other forms of the heading.
Bibliographic records	Describe the intellectual and physical characteristics of bibliographic resources (books, sound recordings, video recordings, and so forth).

Table Contd...

Classification records	MARC records containing classification data. For example, the Library of Congress Classification has been encoded using the MARC 21 Classification format.
Community Information records	MARC records describing a service providing agency. For example, the local homeless shelter or tax assistance provider.
Holdings records	Provide copy-specific information on a library resource (call number, shelf location, volumes held, and so forth).

MARCXML

MARC XML is an XML schema based on the fairly common MARC21 standards. MARCXML was developed by the US Library of Congress and adopted by it and others as a means of easy sharing of, and networked access to, bibliographic information.

Being easy to parse by various systems allows it to be used as an aggregation format, as it is in software packages such as MetaLib, though that package merges it into a wider DTD specification.

The MARC XML primary design goals included:

* Simplicity of the schema
* Flexibility and extensibility
* Lossless and reversible conversion from MARC
* Data presentation through XML stylesheets
* MARC records updates and data conversions through XML transformations
* Existence of validation tools

FUTURE

The future of the MARC formats is a matter of some debate among libraries. On the one hand, the storage formats are quite complex and are based on outdated technology. On the other, there is no alternative bibliographic format with an equivalent degree of granularity. The billions of MARC records in tens of thousands of individual libraries (including over 50,000,000 belonging to the OCLC consortium alone) create inertia.

VIRTUAL INTERNATIONAL AUTHORITY FILE

The Virtual International Authority File (VIAF) is an international authority file. It is a joint project of several national libraries and operated by the Online Computer Library Center (OCLC). The project was initiated by the German National Library and the American Library of Congress.

The aim is to link the national authority files (such as the German Name Authority File) to a single virtual authority file. In this file, identical records from the different data sets are linked together. A VIAF record: receives a standard data number. contains the primary, "see", and "see also" records from the original records. and refers to the original authority records. The data are made available online and are available for research and data exchange/sharing. Data set updating uses the Open Archives Initiative protocol.

UNIVERSAL DECIMAL CLASSIFICATION

The Universal Decimal Classification (UDC) is a bibliographic and library classification developed by the Belgian bibliographers Paul Otlet and Henri La Fontaine at the end of the 19th century. The UDC provides a systematic arrangement of all branches of human knowledge organized as a coherent system in which knowledge fields are related and inter-linked.

Originally based on the Dewey Decimal Classification, the UDC was developed as a new analytico-synthetic classification system with a significantly larger vocabulary and syntax that enables very detailed content indexing and information retrieval in large collections.

In its first edition in 1905, the UDC already included many features that were revolutionary in the context of knowledge classifications: tables of generally applicable (aspect-free) concepts-called common auxiliary tables. a series of special auxiliary tables with specific but re-usable attributes in a particular field of knowledge. An expressive notational system with connecting symbols and syntax rules to enable coordination of subjects and the creation of a documentation language proper. Although originally designed as an indexing and retrieval system, due to its logical structure and scalability, UDC has become one of the most widely used knowledge organization systems in libraries, where it is used for either shelf arrangement, content indexing or both.

UDC codes can describe any type of document or object to any desired level of detail. These can include textual documents and other media such as films, video and sound recordings, illustrations, maps as well as realia such as museum objects.

Since the first edition in French "Manuel du Répertoire bibliographique universel" (1905), UDC has been translated and published in various editions in 40 languages. UDC Summary, an abridged Web version of the scheme is available in over 45 languages. The classification has been modified and extended over the years to cope with increasing output in all areas of human knowledge, and is still under continuous review to take account of new developments.

THE APPLICATION OF THE UDC

The UDC is used in around 150,000 libraries in 130 countries and in many bibliographical services which require detailed content indexing. In a number of countries it is the main classification system for information exchange and is used in all type of libraries: public, school, academic and special libraries.

The UDC is also used in national bibliographies of around 30 countries. Examples of large databases indexed by UDC include: NEBIS (The Network of Libraries and Information Centers in Switzerland)-2.6 million records, COBIB.SI (Slovenian National Union Catalogue)-3.5 million records.

Hungarian National Union Catalogue (MOKKA)-2.9 million records. VINITI RAS database (All-Russian Scientific and Technical Information Institute of Russian Academy of Science) with 28 million records. Meteorological and Geoastrophysical Abstracts (MGA) with 600 journal titles. PORBASE (Portuguese National Bibliography) with 1.5 million records etc. The UDC has traditionally been used for the indexing of scientific articles which was an important source of information of scientific output in the period predating electronic publishing. Collections of research articles in many countries covering decades of scientific output contain UDC codes.

Examples of journal articles indexed by UDC:

* *UDC Code 663.12:57.06 in the Article "Yeast Systematics:* From Phenotype to Genotype" in the journal Food Technology and Biotechnology (ISSN: 1330-9862)
* UDC code 37.037:796.56, provided in the article "The game method as means of interface of technical-tactical and psychological preparation in sports orienteering" in the Russian journal "Pedagogico-psychological and medico-biological problems of the physical culture and sport" (ISSN 2070-4798).
* UDC code 621.715:621.924:539.3 in the article Residual Stress in Shot-Peened Sheets of AIMg4.5Mn Alloy-in the journal Materials and technology (ISSN 1580-2949).

The design of UDC lends itself to machine readability, and the system has been used both with early automatic mechanical sorting devices, and modern library OPACs. From 1993, a standard version of UDC is maintained and is distributed in a database format: UDC Master Reference File (UDC MRF) which is updated and released annually. The 2010 version of the MRF contains over 69,000 classes. In the past full printed editions used to have around 220,000 subdivisions.

UDC STRUCTURE AND CONTENT

Notation

A notation is a code commonly used in classification schemes to represent a class, *i.e.* a subject and its position in the hierarchy, to enable mechanical sorting and filing of subjects. UDC uses Arabic numerals arranged decimally. Every number is thought of as a decimal fraction with the initial decimal point omitted, which determines the filing order. An advantage of decimal notational systems is that they are infinitely extensible, and when new subdivisions are introduced, they need not disturb the existing allocation of numbers. For ease of reading, a UDC notation is usually punctuated after every third digit:

Notation	Caption (Class Description)
539.120	Theoretical problems of elementary particles physics. Theories and models of fundamental interactions
539.120.2	Symmetries of quantum physics
539.120.22	Conservation laws
539.120.222	Translations. Rotations
539.120.224	Reflection in time and space
539.120.226	Space-time symmetries
539.120.23	Internal symmetries
539.120.3	Currents
539.120.4	Unified field theories
539.120.5	Strings

In UDC the notation has two features that make the scheme easier to browse and work with:

* *Hierarchically Expressive*: The longer the notation, the more specific the class: removing the final digit automatically produces a broader class code.
* *Syntactically Expressive*:When UDC codes are combined, the sequence of digits is interrupted by a precise type of punctuation sign which indicates that the expression is a combination of classes rather than a simple class *e.g.* the colon in 34:32 indicates that there are two distinct notational elements: 34 Law. Jurisprudence and 32 Politics. the closing and opening parentheses and double quotes in the following code 91(574.22)"19"(084.3) indicate four separate notational elements: 913 Regional geography, (574.22) North Kazakhstan. "19" 20th century and (084.3) Maps (document form)

Basic Features and Syntax

The UDC is an anlytico-synthetic and/or faceted classification. It allows an unlimited combination of attributes of a subject and relationships between subjects to be expressed. UDC codes from different tables can be combined to present various aspects of document content and form, *e.g.* 94(410)"19"(075) History *(main subject)* of United Kingdom *(place)* in 20th century *(time)*, a textbook *(document form)*. Or: 37:2

Relationship between Education and Religion. Complex UDC expressions can be accurately parsed into constituent elements.

The UDC is also a disciplinary classification covering the entire universe of knowledge. This type of classification can also be described as *aspect* or *perspective,* which means that concepts are subsumed and placed under the field in which they are studied. Thus, the same concept can appear in different fields of knowledge. This particular feature is usually implemented in UDC by re-using the same concept in various combinations with the main subject, *e.g.* a code for language in common auxiliaries of language is used to derive numbers for ethnic grouping, individual languages in linguistics and individual literatures. Or, a code from the auxiliaries of place, *e.g. (410) United Kingdom,* uniquely representing the concept of United Kingdom can be used to express *911(410) Regional geography of United Kingdom* and *94(410) History of United Kingdom.*

Organization of Classes

Concepts are organized in two kinds of tables in UDC:

* Common auxiliary tables (including certain auxiliary signs). These tables contain facets of concepts representing, general recurrent characteristics, applicable over a range of subjects throughout the main tables, including notions such as place, language of the text and physical form of the document, which may occur in almost any subject. UDC numbers from these tables, called common auxiliaries are simply added at the end of the number for the subject taken from the main tables. There are over 15,000 of common auxiliaries in UDC.
* The main tables or main schedules containing the various disciplines and branches of knowledge, arranged in 9 main classes, numbered from 0 to 9 (with class 4 being vacant). At the beginning of each class there are also series of special auxiliaries, which express aspects that are recurrent within this specific class. Main tables in UDC contain more than 60,000 subdivisions.

Main Classes

* 0 Science and Knowledge. Organization. Computer Science. Information. Documentation. Librarianship. Institutions. Publications
* 1 Philosophy. Psychology
* 2 Religion. Theology
* 3 Social Sciences
* 4 *vacant*
* 5 Mathematics. Natural Sciences
* 6 Applied Sciences. Medicine, Technology
* 7 The Arts. Recreation. Entertainment. Sport
* 8 Language, Linguistics, Literature
* 9 Geography, Biography, History

The vacant class 4 is the result of a planned schedule expansion. This class was freed by moving linguistics into class 8 in 1960s to make space for future developments in the rapidly expanding fields of knowledge. primarily natural sciences and technology.

Common Auxiliary Tables

Common auxiliaries are aspect-free concepts that can be used in combination with any other UDC code from the main classes or with other common auxiliaries. They have unique notational representations that makes them stand out in complex expressions.

Common auxiliary numbers always begin with a certain symbol known as a facet indicator, *e.g.* = (equal sign) always introduces concepts representing the language of a document. (0...) numbers enclosed in parentheses starting with zero always represent a concept designating document form.

Thus (075) Textbook and =111 English can be combined to express, *e.g.*(075)=111 Textbooks in English, and when combined with numbers from the main UDC tables they can be used as follows: 2(075)=111 Religion textbooks in English, 51(075)=111 Mathematics textbooks in English etc.

* =... Common auxiliaries of language.
* (0...) Common auxiliaries of form.
* (1/9) Common auxiliaries of place.

* (=...) Common auxiliaries of human ancestry, ethnic grouping and nationality.
* "..." Common auxiliaries of time.
* -0... Common auxiliaries of general characteristics: Properties, Materials, Relations/Processes and Persons.
* -02 Common auxiliaries of properties.
* -03 Common auxiliaries of materials.
* -04 Common auxiliaries of relations, processes and operations.
* -05 Common auxilaries of persons and personal characteristics.

UNION CATALOGUE

A union catalogue is a combined library catalogue describing the collections of a number of libraries. Union catalogs have been created in a range of media, including book format, microform, cards and more recently, networked electronic databases. Print union çatalogs are typically arranged by title, author or subject (often employing a controlled vocabulary). electronic versions typically support keyword and Boolean queries.

Union catalogs are useful to librarians, as they assist in locating and requesting materials from other libraries through interlibrary loan service. They also allow researchers to search through collections to which they would not otherwise have access, such as manuscript collections.

The largest print union catalogue ever published is the American *National Union Catalogue Pre-1956 Imprints* (NUC), completed in 1981. This achievement has since been superseded by the creation of union catalogs in the form of giant electronic databases, of which the largest is OCLC's WorldCat. Another example is Copac provided by Research Libraries UK. A third example is Amicus, provided by Library and Archives Canada.

UNIFORM TITLE

A uniform title in library cataloguing is a title assigned to a work which either has no title or has appeared under more than one title. It is part of authority control. The phrases *conventional title* and *standard title* are sometimes used. the forthcoming Resource Description and Access uses *preferred title*. and the 2009 Statement of International Cataloguing Principles deprecates it in favour of *authorized access point*.

There are many instances in which a uniform title can be used. Anonymous works such as sacred texts and folk tales may lack an obvious title: for instance, the Bible, *Epic of Gilgamesh, Beowulf* or the *Chanson de Roland*. Works of art and music may contain no text that can be used for reference. A uniform title allows all of the works to fall under one title and will reference all of the items to which the uniform title applies.

For example, if a library had 10 copies of *Crime and Punishment* but each copy was in a different language, an online library catalogue can display all of the copies of the book together under the chosen uniform title.

The library could also list any copies of *Crime and Punishment* in other mediums, such as film adaptations or abridged editions, under the same uniform title. This can help a library patron when searching the online catalogue find all of the versions of *Crime and Punishment* at once instead of searching for each foreign title or film individually.

Uniform titles are particularly useful when cataloguing music, where pieces of music are often known by multiple valid titles and those titles are known in multiple languages, or when an individual work has been adapted as a contrafactum.

The Library of Congress provides an example of how books of the New Testament are referred to in the Anglo-American Cataloguing Rules:

* Bible. N.T. Acts
* Bible. N.T. Colossians
* Bible. N.T. Corinthians, 1st
* Bible. N.T. Corinthians, 2nd
* Bible. N.T. Ephesians.

The complementary situation occurs with a single work that exists with more than one title, especially when translated into another language, excerpted or collected with other works. In this case, the name of the language or a phrase such as 'Selections' is added to distinguish works with the same uniform title. The

MARC 21 standard uses fields 240, 243, 630, 730 and 830 for uniform titles.

SUBJECT ACCESS

Subject access refers to the methods and systems by which books, journals, and other documents are accessed in a given bibliographic database (*e.g.* a library classification system). The single records in a bibliographic file is structured in fields and each field can be searchable and combined with other fields.

Such searchable data from fields of records are termed access points. Some of these access points contain information such as author name, number of pages, language of publication, name of publisher etc. These are in library jargon termed "descriptive data". Other kinds of access points contains information such as title words, classification codes, indexing terms etc. They are termed subject access points.. However, a subject access point is defined as any access point useful for subject searching. There is no precise border between descriptive access points and subject access points. In theory any access point may hypothetically be used for subject searching.

PUBLIC INFORMATION NETWORK FOR ELECTRONIC SERVICES

The Public Information Network for Electronic Services (or PINES) is the statewide library consortium and its online library catalogue of the Georgia Public Library Service. By February 2010, the catalogue consisted of books from 282 library facilities in over 140 counties across the state of Georgia with a total item count of around 10 million, all of which are searchable by anyone with a PINES library card which can be obtained free of charge from any PINES-participating library.

The PINES system effectively turns most of the state of Georgia into one huge library. PINES cardholders are able to request that a copy of a specific book which is only available at a library out of town be shipped to their local library for them to check out-free of charge-all through the online catalogue.

In addition, PINES users can check out a book from one PINES-participating library and turn it into any other PINES-participating library without penalty. Another feature of the PINES network is that it allows members to place holds on items that they would like to check out from the library. PINES developed the open-source software, called Evergreen, which it and other library consortia use to manage their online catalogs.

OPEN CATALOGUE

Open catalogue is an open content catalogue or free content catalogue, *i.e.*, a structured database with information about products or other stored items in a standardized format. A catalogue implies categorization or classification of the items involved, and database normalization to increase the usability of the catalogue for searching and finding, and comparing items within the same category on their main attributes.

The term is first used by Prof. Dr. Martijn Hoogeveen of the Open University (Netherlands) for the Open ICEcat project, which resulted in an open catalogue for product information, often used by merchants as input for their mail-order catalogue. A DTD for the Open Catalogue Exchange Format is developed by Sergey Shvets and Dimitry Mitko.

NUCMC

NUCMC is the abbreviation for the National Union Catalogue of Manuscript Collections. It is a national-level programme based at the Library of Congress that seeks to promote free access to the documentary heritage of the United States. It does this by providing cataloguing for archives and historical societies around the country that do not have access to national online databases.

The programme started in 1959 and published bound volumes of cataloguing records until 1993. As of 1986, the cataloguing records were input into RLIN, the Research Libraries Information Network, an international online database. As of September 2007, all cataloguing records in RLIN have been migrated into the OCLC database (WorldCat), since RLIN was merged into OCLC. All cataloguing since that time has been input into OCLC. It is not related to the NUC Pre-1956 volumes.

NIPPON DECIMAL CLASSIFICATION

The Nippon Decimal Classification (NDC, also called the Nippon Decimal System) is a system of library classification developed for mainly Chinese and Japanese language books maintained by the Japan Library Association since 1956. It is based on the Dewey Decimal System. The system is based upon using each successive digit to divide into nine divisions with the digit zero used for those not belonging to any of the divisions.

NEWGENLIB

NewGenLib is an integrated library management system developed by Verus Solutions Pvt Ltd. Domain expertise is provided by Kesavan Institute of Information and Knowledge Management in Hyderabad, India. NewGenLib version 1.0 was released in March 2005. On 9 January 2008, NewGenLib was declared Open Source Software under GNU GPL Licence by Verus Solutions.

Currently NewGenLib 3.0.3 U2 is the latest version running. It is estimated that 2,500 libraries across 58 countries are using NewGenLib as their Primary integrated library management system.

FEATURES

The software modules are:

* Acquisitions
* Cataloguing
* Serials management
* Circulation
* Administration
* OPAC-Support for VuFind is also available
* MIS Reports
* End-of-day process (daily scheduler)

The system allows the creation of open access (OA) institutional repositories compliant with OAI-PMH. It is web-based software and has a multi-tier architecture using Java (a Swing-based librarian's GUI) and JBoss (J2EE-based application server). The default backend database is the open source PostgreSQL.

NewGenLib is compliant with MARC 21 format, has a MARC editor, and allows seamless bibliographic and authority data import into cataloguing templates. Form letter templates are configurable using OpenOffice 2.0 as ODT and htm.

SMTP mail servers can be configured for e-mails that can be sent from functional modules. NewGenLib servers are SRU/W compliant supporting MARC-21 and MODS 3.0 metadata formats. CQL (level 1) with both Bath and Dublin Core Profiles are supported. NewGenLib is Unicode 3.0 compliant and is RFID ready.

NewGenLib can be installed on Linux and Windows operating systems. It is an internationalized application (I18N) because it is Unicode 3.0 compliant, has an Arabic version available, is asily extensible to support other languages, and may use data entry, storage, retrieval in any (Unicode 3.0) language.

TYPES OF LIBRARIES

NewGenLib can be used for any type of library. In fact it is used by all types of libraries. This is because NGL is targeted towards public libraries.

The type of libraries in which NewGenLib can be used are:

* University libraries
* College/School libraries
* Public libraries
* Libraries in Research Institutes
* Church libraries
* Libraries in Offices/Corporates

COMMUNITY

Librarians and Library managers using NewGenLib Open Source for their libraries are part of this social network. Social networks are created on basis of geography so that the members of the social network can leverage a maximum benefit.

TECHNOLOGIES USED

* Java SE
* Apache Tomcat server
* Spring framework

* Hibernate and Solr
* JDOM for XML messaging
* Java Servlets, JavaServer Pages and Apache Struts
* Java Mail
* OpenOffice for form letters
* Jasper reports

7

Cataloguing in the Internet and Digital Era

This chapter explores those issues in greater detail. It begins by describing the motivations underlying the reuse of the term "library" to describe the new digital information research area. As will be described, those motivations reflected the expedient interests of each participant community and their respective definitions of a library.

It next describes the influence of that term on the architectures and applications that were produced by the digital library research programme over the subsequent years. The chapter continues with an explanation of how the architecture of those digital library applications impacts the technical coexistence of digital libraries with the mainstream web.

Finally, the chapter describes how the evolution of the web from Web 1.0 to Web 2.0 has not only increased the technical incompatibilities between the two information environments, but has led to a fundamental conceptual difference in their information models.

ORIGINS OF THE "DIGITAL LIBRARY"

The decision in the early 1990's to extend the notion of the library forward into the emerging digital information context was the result of the collective and distinctive assumptions of three stakeholder communities: the funders, the technology-focused researchers, and the practitioner library community.

Each community responded to the opportunities offered by emerging networked computing technologies in a unique, opportunistic (and sometimes myopic) fashion. While they all agreed that "digital libraries" was an appropriate term for the new endeavour, they each had a different idea of the meaning of the term and different allegiances to the components of what they considered a library. The following parts demonstrate this "interpretive flexibility" by describing the different meanings attributed to digital libraries by the three major communities involved in the research effort.

PERSPECTIVE OF THE DIGITAL LIBRARY FUNDERS

The primary funders of digital library research in the U.S. were the NSF, within the Directorate for Computer and Information Science (CISE), DARPA, NASA, and NIH, with lesser contributions from NEH, IMLS (Institute of Museum and Library Services), and the Library of Congress. The notable characteristic of all the primary funders is their focus on technology-oriented science, in contrast to social science, humanities, or arts.

This focus is reflected in a research programme that funded mainly core computer science and its applications to networked information, with very little attention to network information as a sociotechnical phenomenon. In fact, the first phase of Digital Library Initiative (DLI) funding was exclusively technical.

This was moderated somewhat in the second phase. Influenced by the results of a 1996 NSF workshop that called for increased research on the social aspects of digital libraries, the NSF included social science research in the DLI-2 solicitation. An examination of documents published early in the digital library effort reveals the underlying assumptions and biases of the lead agencies that shaped the nature of the funding programmes and their vision of the digital libraries that would emerge from it.

Although it appeared in a visionary 1988 document from Kahn and Cerf, the term "digital libraries" was introduced into the national research agenda in February 1994 in a report from a task force on Information Infrastructure Technologies and Applications (IITA). This report was commissioned by the newly funded High Performance Computing and Communications programme, which was formed to leverage advances in computing and networking for the general social benefit.

The report defines digital libraries as follows:

> "[Digital libraries are] both technologies and applications which will lead to significant advances in the generation, storage, and use of digital information of different kinds across high speed networks. A digital library is a knowledge center without walls, open 24 hours a day and accessible by way of a network. Research areas range from advanced mass storage, online capture of multimedia data, intelligent filtering, knowledge navigation, effective user interfaces, system integration, to prototyping and technology demonstration".

The list of research areas enumerated in this statement is notable for its omission of the implications of eliminating the "walls", or a being open "24 hours a day." Clearly, the impression of the task force, or at least the only concern, was that the transfer of information to an online form raised only technical issues and that the larger social issues raised by this transfer were either inconsequential, unforeseen, or not worthy of study.

Another report from the same era, authored by Gladney and Fox, demonstrates prevailing thinking of the time that perhaps underlies this decision by the funders to focus only on technical issues:

> "The concept "library" has been refined over several centuries. It would be injudicious to depart from what people expect merely because a digital service is replacing a material one. Except where explicit reasons suggest an improvement that is easily explained to ordinary users (*e.g.*, in query services), library services should implement a familiar model".

Implicit in this text is the assumption that the nature of the institution and the information model it entails should remain as a stable overlay on a changed technical foundation. A digital library should, by nature, imply the same notions of integrity, trust, and quality, historically associated with libraries.

Books might turn into bits, the catalogue might become an online database, and shelves might turn into repositories, but the values, structures, and practices of the "institution" should be based on a "familiar model." Even as the web continue to grow in importance and scale, the notion that digital libraries were the focus for "serious" information-oriented activities persisted.

The web was relegated to a more lowbrow status–an unfiltered mishmash of questionable and frequently objectionable content. For example, a 2001 (U.S.) President's Information Technology Advisory Committee report called the web a "rudimentary" information environment that "only hint[s] at the future of digital libraries".

Even if the funding agencies had decided that the broader implications of the transfer of information to the online environment deserved investigation, it is doubtful whether they were structurally configured to handle such investigations.

In a retrospective on the Digital Libraries Initiatives, Griffin takes note of the problem that agencies such as the NSF have with research that is by nature long-term: "The programme funding models did not work optimally, particularly for the mid-size, longer-term, interdisciplinary research and test bed projects."

PERSPECTIVE OF THE COMPUTER SCIENCE RESEARCH COMMUNITY

The computer science research community had every incentive to follow the funding agencies in this selective interpretation of digital library research. The DL initiatives were a new and relatively large stream of funding for extending their pre-existing database and information retrieval research into a new application area.

As stated by researchers: "The computer scientists] could see, or at least imagine, *how current library functions would be moved forward by an injection of computing insight*". The computer scientists who dominated DL research had little interest in examining the nature of "current library functions" or in understanding how the "injection of computing insight" might affect the foundations of these functions. The library was really only a convenient platform for technically focused work.

Indeed as researchers noted the computer science researchers had little patience for the less technically manageable aspects, and "nagging downsides" of digital library research. For example, issues related to copyright and intellectual property were perceived as an annoyance that interfered with work on more interesting technical problems.

Furthermore, the work often required collaboration with librarians who seemed overly focused on metadata "that the computer scientists felt would be replaceable by just another clever search algorithm improvement".

In hindsight, the attraction of the computer science research community to the field of digital libraries was really not based on special allegiance to the library notion, but was just a case of following the funding. When the funding disappeared and it became obvious that the web was a more attractive, and less restrictive environment for studying and exercising emerging computer science techniques such as machine learning, many of the former prominent members of the digital library community disappeared.

PERSPECTIVE OF THE LIBRARY COMMUNITY

The "real" librarians, those with over a century-long tradition collecting, curating, and preserving books and other materials, entered the realm of digital libraries with a considerably more institutionally-focused definition of the library and vision of what the digital library would look like.

From their perspective the library, as an institution, had successfully managed previous transitions to new media (the transition of the printed form from scrolls to the codex book to the printed book, the inclusion of recordings, etc.) and had a track record of incorporating new technology into established practices, such as the computer-based catalogue.

The "digital" library would be just another library and through all, the venerable institution would prevail:

* The functions of the librarian have always been to select the material that his constituents will require. to catalogue it so that those who would use it can know what is available and where it is. and to preserve

> it so that both contemporary readers and those who will follow will be able to use it...none of these tasks will disappear with the emergence of the electronic library. Somebody will have to perform them: if not the librarian, then his replacement. The anarchy of the Internet may be daunting for the neophyte, but it differs little from the bibliographic chaos that is the result of five and a half centuries of the printing press.

Because of this allegiance to the institutional basis of the library and the belief that it was a necessary component of a useful information environment, librarians vigourously resisted the encroachment of the web on the domain formally dominated by the library. For librarians the intrusion of the web into the work on digital libraries was much more difficult to integrate.

Initially, they were largely dismissive and disdainful of the web as a serious information space, declaring that the "web is not a library" and likening it to a bookstore in which "the entire stock is just piled up in the middle of the floor". As the amount of valuable content increased on the web, they responded with efforts to fold the web into standard operations, such as cataloguing.

While these efforts to catalogue the web were ultimately abandoned, they demonstrate how persistent traditional practices can be even in the face of a rapidly changing technical landscape. In summary, the application of the library concept to the uncharted and unruly context of networked information reveals the distinctly narrow and flawed assumptions of the three parties responsible for its origin and use.

The funding agencies mistakenly assumed that they could fund (and shape) the development of a new information infrastructure as a mainly technical endeavour. The computer scientists followed suit by framing digital libraries by-and-large as applications of familiar distributed database problems in which "predictable, repeatable ... access and retrieval is a prime value."

In fact, the unpredictability of the web and its seemingly autonomous dynamism has not only affected our perceptions of information use and management, but it has had a far-reaching effect on computer science shifting it from its deterministic, algorithmic foundations to a more probabilistic and socially-oriented focus.

Finally, the librarians assumed that they could safely wrap radically new technology and traditional organizational values and structures in the same embrace. In combination, these flawed assumptions lead to a research area that by and large treads the middle ground.

At a fine granular level, it produced a number of interesting research results and applications of those results. But, at the higher level, it failed to explore the more far-reaching questions of how putting information online and giving people power over their information might change the nature of the information and the way people use it.

It is useful in closing this part to quote Agre who, "Information and institutional change", spoke of the dangers of naively mixing historical forms with innovations:

> A concept of "library" that is too fully rooted in past historical forms will make innovation impossible, but a superficial concept of "library" that draws out only a few aspects of those past historical forms (for example, a library as a big container of documents) will pass over phenomena whose absence in a newly designed system may be fatal. The middle ground between the maximal and simplistic conceptions of "library" is enormous and is not easily mapped.

INFLUENCE OF THE LIBRARY ON DIGITAL LIBRARY TECHNOLOGY

The previous part described the set of assumptions about libraries and networked information that led to the choice of the term "digital libraries." This part describes the manner in which that term and the presumptions underlying it have affected the nature of the technical artifacts produced by digital library research. This effect is reflected in both the overall architectural framework and on the individual architectural components of that framework.

Table 7.1: Comparison of Digital Library and Web Architectures

	Digital Libraries	Web Architecture
Core Architecture	Repository-centric	Resource-centric
User Model	Portal Searching	Browsing
Content Model	Digital Objects	Resources
Indexing Model	Surrogates	Full-text and links
Identification	Persistent IDs	URIs
Federation Model	Federated Search, Metadata Harvesting	Centralized Indexing

CORE ARCHITECTURE: REPOSITORY-CENTRIC VERSUS RESOURCE-CENTRIC

Digital library systems are by and large based on the notion of the institutionallymanaged *repository* as the central architectural entity. The repository acts as the container for storage of and access to "digital objects", the content "within" the library. In this manner, the repository is a virtual boundary defining the locus of institutional management, curation, and preservation of the contained digital objects.

This virtual boundary is the functional equivalent of the physical boundary in the "bricks and mortar" library in which the physical structure defines the limits of library curation and stewardship of the information resources within it. In contrast, the *resource* is the central entity in the web architecture.

Uniquely identified resources are the nodes in a virtual directed graph, in which the edges are the hyperlinks that connect resources. Notably absent from this graph model is the notion of containment or location. There is no first-class entity that corresponds to the repository in digital architecture. Although repositories are sometimes compared to websites, the comparison is incorrect due to the nature of the latter.

A website is an ambiguously defined, second-class technical artifact – it may be all the web pages served within the same DNS domain, or those accessible through a single server. Technically, it has no identity (URI) and therefore it cannot be the target of any protocol requests. Conceptually, it does not imply control or management in the same manner as a repository. The remainder of this part describes the major components of digital library systems that support this repository-centric architectural core.

PORTALS

The portal, or the "front door of the digital library", serves the same purpose as the physical entry to the traditional library. It provides the user with the clear notion of being "inside" the digital library. Services and content within the portal are thereby blessed with the imprimatur of the library, endowing them with a level of trust and integrity. This is commonly known as "branding".

Correspondingly, most digital library applications clearly indicate to the user when they are "leaving the library", for example by traversing a hyperlink to a page outside the boundary of the library. The focus of a portal is usually a search interface, that in most cases is field-based, providing more functionality than the single text box search paradigm employed by most web search engines.

This allows users to search on specific bibliographic fields such as title, author, or subject. This search paradigm reflects the influence of the library cataloguing tradition, which eschews simple keyword searching that is predominant in mainstream crawler-based search engines (*e.g.*, Google) in favour of more targeted search capabilities.

Metadata, which is the basis of this field-based searching. In contrast to this "front-door" paradigm, the web user metaphorically "surfs" among linked information resources without regard for their location on the network. The informal notion of a "homepage" for a website does exist, but there is no presumption or enforcement of this as the uniform entry point to the collection of pages of that site.

The notion of uniform, location-independent sources has proven to be quite powerful. In its simplest form it makes it possible to aggregate information from multiple sources in a single webpage, in the manner that a page may include an image that is stored in some other location on the net. As I will describe later, location independence is leveraged in Web 2.0 in a much more powerful manner in the form of "mash-ups."

METADATA–CATALOGUING IN THE DIGITAL CONTEXT

The shaping effect of the library tradition on digital libraries is perhaps most evident in the focus on descriptive metadata. This focus has its roots in cataloguing, one of the core functions of the modern library. The traditional catalogue developed for a number of reasons. At the simplest level, in a library of physical resources it gave users an easy and compact tool for finding information resources without having to traverse the shelves.

However, describing the catalogue as merely a compact shelf list trivializes its complexity and intellectual content. Underlying cataloguing is the concept of information entities having uniform attributes, such as author, title, or subject classification, and the utility of those attributes for logical organization of those entities. This organization presents multiple *access points* based on those uniform attributes, and allows users to search and browse within those access points.

For example, a user may search for information by author name and then traverse the resources associated with that author, or alternatively they may search for information by subject classification and traverse the resources associated within that class. As a result, the organization of the catalogue and the manner in which it is made available to the user (*e.g.*, cards in drawers or screens in an electronic catalogue) is independent of the manner in which the physical, or digital, resources are organized on shelves, or in repositories.

Furthermore, an individual information resource (*e.g.*, a book) may have multiple catalogue instances, each accessible through specific access points (*e.g.*, title, author, subject, etc.). Efforts to extend the practice of cataloguing into the context of online information reflects an ongoing belief that in a world where even the books that are part of library collections have been digitized and are available for full-text search, structured search over surrogates is more functional and ultimately preferred by users.

This is despite empirical evidence that users seem to prefer the "one text box" search paradigm of Google to the fielded-search paradigm employed in most digital library portals and online catalogs, and decades-old evidence of the frequent superiority in recall and precision of automated full-text search to human-assisted indexing and cataloguing.

Traditional library cataloguing is both complex and expensive, especially when applied to the rapidly expanding and diverse set of digital resources. The notion of metadata emerged as a simpler and less expensive alternative to traditional cataloguing records, perhaps making it possible for nonprofessionals to create structured bibliographic information.

The predominant digital library metadata effort is the Dublin Core Metadata Initiative. Ironically, the origins of Dublin Core lie in improving search and retrieval on the general web. However, this effort to develop easy-to-use bibliographic standards for networked information objects has been deemed irrelevant, ill-conceived, or even counterproductive by the mainstream web community and most notably the search engines that dominate it.

As I describe later, the attempts to translate the benefits of cataloguing to the online domain via metadata have been compromised by problems with ensuring the quality of the metadata records that are produced by non-professionals and preventing so-called "metadata spamming" by unscrupulous agents trying to falsely lead information consumers to their sites.

DIGITAL OBJECTS — CONTAINERS FOR COMPLEX DATA AND METADATA

The content model of most digital library architectures is based on the notion of a *digital object*. an identified (first-class) information resource that is an aggregation of multiple information units consisting of multiple formats, multiple subsidiary units, versions, or document components (*e.g.*, the text, data, images, etc. of a scholarly paper).

These are generally known as *compound objects*. These object models reflect an ongoing effort by the library community to account for the complexity of information in both its abstract form and the physical or digital manifestations of it.

These efforts have focused on mechanisms to represent the various relationships among information resources. and to describe those resources at multiple levels of granularity, for various purposes, and in various descriptive formats. Access to compound objects and their components is frequently mediated by protocols unique to the particular repository architecture.

These protocols are usually embedded in the URLs that carry user requests from the digital library portal to the repository. These protocols allow operations such as access a digital object in a specific form, access a portion of a digital object such as its descriptive metadata, and the like.

The proliferation of these architecture-specific access protocols has spawned a virtual cottage industry of repository interoperability initiatives in the digital library community. In contrast, the web architecture includes a quite simple information model based on the atomic resource.

"Interoperability" is defined in the simple terms of the web architecture–resources, URIs, and HTTP. There is no architectural notion of a compound object, or aggregation of resources. Ad hoc and de facto aggregations exist, for example a logical document split into a set of interlinked web pages.

However, these aggregations are not first-class objects. they do not have a unique identity and are essentially ephemeral. There is, in fact, an increased awareness in the web community that more complex information models are appropriate in a number of instances. for example, scholarly publishing.

FEDERATION

The issue of federation arises because digital library systems are conceived as discrete institutionally-managed entities with distinct boundaries accessible to the user through branded portals. Sometimes, a user might want to search across multiple digital libraries when a selected resource is not available in their "local" library. In the physical library domain, this problem is solved by union catalogs such as WorldCat and by interlibrary loan.

Digital library applications employ two mechanisms to allow users to search for and access information outside the confines of a single digital library. The first is federated searching or meta-searching, in which a single search query is multicast to several digital library search engines.

The query is then individually processed at those search engines. the individual result sets are then returned and integrated at the site from which the original query was multicast. Federated searching was the subject of substantial work in the early years of digital library research describes our own work in this area.

Although instances of federated search still exist, the technique has fallen into some disfavour because of problems with dependence on the reliability of multiple search sites and the problems with the ranking of search results from several sources. The second is metadata harvesting, in which bibliographic records from several distributed institutional sources are combined at a single indexing site, which provides a search interface across the resulting "union catalogue".

The most widely deployed mechanism for metadata harvesting is the Open Archives Protocol for Metadata Harvesting (OAI-PMH). That same chapter describes complications with metadata harvesting. Neither of these techniques has achieved widespread deployment in the general web information space.

Boundaries and the repositories that implement them are not a part of the web architecture. Web search engines such as Google crawl the web via graph traversal, ignoring the notion of the location of a webpage, except as a tool for optimizing graph traversal strategies. In addition, ranking algorithms such as PageRank are designed to operate over a centralized index, and are difficult if not impossible in the context of distributed methods such as federated search,

PERSISTENT IDENTITY FOR NETWORK INFORMATION

A final example of the difference between digital library and web architecture is the notion of "persistent identity" for information stored in digital repositories. The attention to this issue in the digital library contexts reflects concerns about both preservation and control of intellectual property. The Handle System is the best known of this class of technologies.

Like many persistent naming systems, the Handle System depends on a hierarchy of identity resolvers, and therefore the notion of a central *root* name server. These efforts have gained little traction in the mainstream web community, which has historically resisted centralization and has comfortably adapted to the fragility of URLs, deeming identity persistence as a policy problem rather than a technical problem.

COEXISTENCE OF DIGITAL LIBRARIES AND THE WEB

The previous part described the distinction between the repository-centric digital library architecture and resource-centric web architecture. In addition, it described how these different core architectural principles affected the technical components of each architecture.

The digital library applications that have been assembled from these components are indeed quite powerful and include advanced searching capabilities, complex information models, and rich user interfaces.

Ironically, the same architectural features that enhance their functionality have often interfered with the interoperability of digital library applications with the mainstream web and thereby mitigated the impact of these applications in the broader web context.

The problem comes from the fact that the specialized, repository-specific access protocols that provide access to these digital library resources often do not follow the conventions of mainstream HTTP access methods. For example, in many cases the URLs used to access objects are conflated with query predicates, the syntax of which is unique to the digital library and is hardcoded into portal/repository interaction.

This is not a problem when access to the digital library resources occurs through the "front door" portal and through its respective search user interface that generates these query-based access URLs. However, mainstream crawler-based search engines, such as Google, do not access objects through the front door, but rely on generalized graph traversal.

The nature of the access URLs in digital libraries and their interdependence on the respective digital library search interface often makes these URLs unreachable via these graph traversal techniques. This is because the URLs of the digital objects in the repository are not explicitly linked to, but are generated by the digital library based on search engine queries.

These query-generated URLs are not visible in the web graph traversed by mainstream search engines and, as a result, the digital library resources are not crawled and are subordinated to an information black whole–the so-called "deep web". They fail to appear in result lists returned by main-stream search engines, which have emerged as the universal tool for discovery of information (much to the chagrin of the library community).

In an effort to increase search engine visibility, digital library providers frequently generate special link pages that expose the individual URLs of repository contents to crawlers as conventional hyperlinks. Digital library resources then appear as search results in Google and similar search engines.

As a result, a steadily expanding amount of access to digital library resources occurs through these commercial providers. But this reverse engineering to increase visibility of contained resources subverts the role of the digital library as a control zone, and the intention of the portal as a branded entry to that control zone

The "digital library collection" becomes just another set of web resources, with no joint identity or imprimatur. The digital library becomes "invisible infrastructure", barely evident through a web-dominated information paradigm.

DIGITAL LIBRARIES AND THE EVOLVING WEB

In addition to the technical incompatibilities between the digital library and web architectures that were described in the previous part, there is a widening gap between their underlying information models. The web that Tim Berners-Lee invented in 1989 has undergone an explosive growth in scale, measured in terms of number of URLs, servers, and traffic.

At the same time, it has experienced a radical change in form and impact, referred to as Web 2.0. In contrast to the relatively passive and transactional search/access paradigm characteristic of the library and Web 1.0 in which the delineation between authors and consumers was relatively distinct, information interactions in Web 2.0 are highly interactive and participatory.

Rather than just browsing and reading web pages, web users, acting as both authors and readers are writing reviews on Amazon, annotating and tagging pictures on Flickr, writing and updating articles on Wikipedia, publishing observations and research results in blogs, and mashing up online content into new content. This part examines the evolving web and the coexistence of digital libraries within that context.

The metaphor of versions – Web 1.0, Web 2.0, and the recently coined Web 3.0–is obviously artificial and overly simplistic. However, it is a useful rhetorical device. The predominant "features" of these versions are as follows. *Web 1.0*–called the document web, the "web of cognition", or the "read-only" web.

The time span of this version roughly extends from the invention of the web until 2000. It primarily consisted of hyperlinked, semi-static, atomic documents (HTML, PDF, GIF or JPEG images). Interaction and collaboration were minimal except for document authoring and querying. Content creation required specialized tools and, as a result, was restricted to a small subset of web users. *Web 2.0*-called the "web of communication" or the "read/write" web.

This "version" includes participation-oriented tools such as wikis, blogs, social applications like Flickr, and instant communication tools like Twitter. Another prominent feature is the notion of a "mash-up" whereby new information objects are created via the dynamic combination of existing information resources.

These features enable a phenomenon that Engestrom calls "object-centered sociality", in which information objects, people, and social exchanges are linked together in web space. This has effected a phase transition in the web's impact on economics, scholarship, learning, and most recently politics.

The effect of this impact on national politics is exemplified by the recent observation that "... Barack Obama's victories in the Democratic primary and in the presidential election would not have been possible without Internet-empowered fund-raising and social networking". *Web 3.0*–called the "web of meaning" or the "contextual web", this currently emerging web functionality incorporates concepts of the semantic web, the underpinnings of which Tim Berners-Lee and the W3C have been developing since the late 1990's.

The key features of the semantic web include machine readability and interpretation of web data and the ability to reason over that data. The technological foundation of the semantic web is the Resource Description Framework (RDF) a data model for expressing statements about entities (web resources) and their properties (ontologically defined relationships).

Raffl *et al.* adopt the language of Evolutionary Systems Theory to illustrate how the features of these versions are cumulative: "[E]ach new layer is built upon a preceding one and ...the new stage comprises not only the new layer, but parts of the old one". Figure illustrates the changing nature of the web through these versions.

As shown, Web 1.0 was primarily a one-way channel from producers to consumers. In Web 2.0, the bifurcation of web participants blurs into consumer/producers who collaboratively author, manage, and annotate content. This is enhanced in the Semantic Web (Web 3.0) in which machines (agents) process and interpret this collaboratively produced content and contribute new content back on the web.

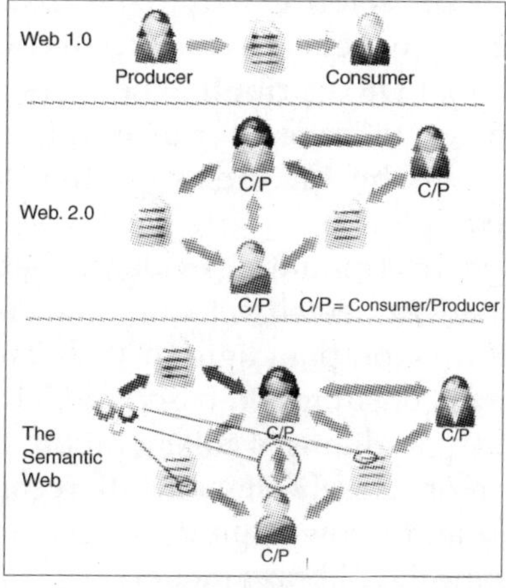

Fig. Expansion of Web Functionality

The participatory nature Web 2.0 should not be dismissed as just a popular phenomenon, manifested in increased use of mainly social sites like FaceBook. Many experts in the field, we are witnessing a fundamental change in the prevailing information paradigm that is transforming all aspects of our culture. Notably, this impact extends to the nature of scholarly research and communication, one of the backbones of the research library.

As pointed out by Paul Ginsparg, who create arXiv and is considered one of the icons of Internet-based scholarship:

> ...There are...objective reasons to believe that we are witnessing an essential change in the way information is accessed, the way it is communicated to and from the general public, and among research professionals-fundamental methodological changes that will lead to a terrain 10-20 years from now more different than it was 10-20 years ago than in any comparable time period.

Timo Hannay of Nature, one of the most prestigious scientific journals, makes the following observation of the impact of the current and future of the web on science scholarship:

> For all but a very small number of widely read titles, the day of the print journal seems to be almost over. Yet to see this development as the major impact of the web on science would be extremely narrow-minded–equivalent to viewing the web primarily as an efficient PDF distribution network... Though it will take longer to have its full effect, the web's major impact will be on the way that science itself is practiced.

In addition, there is mounting evidence that, for a number of important informationoriented activities such as education, the participatory information paradigm in Web 2.0 has advantages over the traditional consumption-based model. Fuchs and Raffl argue that Web 2.0 paradigms of collaboration, construction, and participation are more closely aligned with recognized models of human cognition and knowledge development than the more restrictive and controlled library model.

Downes and Ullrich describe the utility of the Web 2.0 model for education because of the manner in which it facilitates activities such as group collaboration, exploration, and manipulation that are key to learning according to cognitively-oriented constructivist theories.

Gee argues that the "affinity spaces" facilitated by the Web 2.0 environment are powerful tools for learning. Black identifies the notion of "beta-reading" in online fan communities where contributors grow as readers and writers based on mutual feedback. Finally, others see the general benefits of the "wisdom of crowds" that is enabled by the collaborative nature of Web 2.0.

8

Historical Development of Modern Library Catalogues and Cataloguing Codes

INTRODUCTION

This chapter reviews the historical development of basic concepts in descriptive cataloguing and provides an analytical overview of selected cataloguing codes affecting the evolution of cataloguing principles. The main purpose is to explore the basic concepts underlying different codes of cataloguing rules and to provide an understanding of how these codes have developed in accordance with forms of the catalogue.

A clear grasp of the historical development of modern cataloguing codes and an understanding of the evolutionary growth of catalogues are both essential to an understanding of the relevance of cataloguing codes to the new electronic environment. In this context, another aim of this chapter is to acknowledge the role of the catalogue environment on the cataloguing rules and principles, *i.e.*, to see how far the environment in which a catalogue is constructed might influence cataloguing principles.

This chapter is intended to be an introduction to later chapters concerning the conceptual analysis of theories and principles of descriptive cataloguing with regard to the possible influences of the online environment on them. To understand the historical background and to examine the past is very important to any study of cataloguing principles and rules and to the future of code revision.

To quote Svenonius:

> "A well-founded philosophy of catalogue code develop-ment must take cognizance of the past, particularly of those factors which have affected and may continue to affect code design".

Although cataloguing codes have a history as long as the history of libraries, the focus of the present chapter is on the development of codes in the Anglo-American context throughout the nineteenth and twentieth centuries. Two non Anglo-American codes are also introduced to illustrate some other cataloguing traditions which have been different in some basic aspects.

DEVELOPMENTS IN THE NINETEENTH CENTURY

The nineteenth century has been characterised as the formative era of modern catalogues and cataloguing codes. It was a time that revealed a keen interest in catalogues and the involvement of individual libraries and librarians in the compilation of cataloguing codes.

> The transformation of library cataloguing to its present form occurred in the nineteenth century, when it was argued that simple author access was not enough and that a different, more sophisticated, and more elaborate approach was needed.

Although the printed book catalogue was widely in use throughout the nineteenth century, the slip catalogue which was primarily created for the preparation of the printed book catalogue, was gradually found to be more flexible and more suitable. Book catalogues, which were found to be inflexible and in need of constant updating and reprinting, grew less popular in a short space of time.

In addition, the limited number of access points per entry was a major disadvantage of book catalogues. By the end of the nineteenth century the printed card catalogue, although not in a standard form, became the alternative to the printed book catalogue and its use became widespread in the twentieth century throughout the United States as well as in many other countries.

The two most common catalogue forms in the nineteenth century were the classified catalogue and the alphabetical catalogue. The classed or classified catalogue, which was a type of subject catalogue depending on a systematic classification, was used in many British, French and American libraries. In this form of the catalogue, entries were arranged in a systematic order to group together books with subject proximity.

Authors and titles made up accompanying alphabetical indexes. Although the classified catalogue continued its development during the nineteenth century, the difficulties of maintaining it limited its application to a relatively small number of libraries.

On the other hand, a major reason for the development of the alphabetical catalogue lies in the fact that alphabetical order has long been common knowledge and best suited for finding items in the catalogue. Most cataloguing codes developed by individuals or national agencies in modern times have been formulated for alphabetical catalogues rather than classified catalogues.

The nineteenth century was a time when the objectives of the catalogue became more clearly defined. As library catalogues had to be developed in accordance with the users' needs, a first step was to clarify the functions of the catalogue. Thus an essential principle on which rules for entries had to be based was the formulation of objectives for the catalogue.

The concept of one full record per book which was dominant in classified and alphabetical catalogues evolved into multiple entries in the dictionary catalogue. Although the dictionary catalogue had been first introduced by Andrew Maunsell in 1595 in the form of a simple list including authors, added entries and subjects in a single alphabetical sequence, it had its flourishing in the nineteenth century, particularly through the works of Charles Ammi Cutter. In effect, the development of our current cataloguing codes has its roots in the landmark works of a few librarians who formed the theoretical foundations of descriptive cataloguing:

ANTHONY PANIZZI AND THE BRITISH MUSEUM RULES

The beginning of the development of modern cataloguing codes is generally attributed to Sir Anthony Panizzi whose influence in descriptive cataloguing in general, and the theory of cataloguing in particular, is well known to the profession. The British Museum code of 1841 had its roots in preceding rules, and in fact continued practices common in libraries of medieval monasteries. Panizzi took the most useful principles, reshaping and widening them to offer solutions to most of the cataloguing problems of his time.

The *Ninety-One Rules* were drafted by Panizzi for the printed book catalogue of the British Museum and were modified substantially by the Trustees of the British Museum. The rules were a monumental achievement, as they represented the first attempt to codify rules for the compilation of an author catalogue with the inclusion of logical guides for cross references. This system was suited to book catalogues in which only one full entry was provided for each book and other entries were in the form of cross references.

Panizzi's *Letter* to the Earl of Ellesmere which defined the alphabetical catalogue. the concept of 'heading' as the most important bibliographical element in alphabetical catalogues under which other bibliographic data was subsumed in the catalogue. and the objectives and problems of the catalogue of a large library such as that of the British Museum are considered as the first theoretical foundations of descriptive cataloguing.

Throughout his *Letter* Panizzi emphasised the concept of uniformity, whether in the form of author heading, the alphabetical order of headings or in the form of slips or cards, and warned of the difficulties resulting from the lack of uniformity in a catalogue. Panizzi's approach to this concept can be seen in his rules for choice and form of a name.

The focus of Panizzi's code was primarily on the creation of entries based on the information found on the title-page. He selected the title-page as the authoritative source of cataloguing data in the sense that it would offer the same information to all cataloguers.

This was the first approach to standardisation in descriptive cataloguing and has been continued through some of the subsequent codes. Title-page cataloguing was also an indication of the focus of the code on the concept of 'bibliographic unit' and on the finding-list function of the catalogue in that it made for easier retrieval of the item for the user who searched the catalogue with information already obtained from the title page.

The principle of authorship was emphasised as the principal 'organising element' in the catalogue and entries were filed alphabetically by author. When compared to older codes, the treatment of various conditions of authorship that appear on the title-page is, to a considerable extent, complete in Panizzi's code. The principle of *multiple authorship*, although without any differentiation between *joint* and *collective authorship*, is apparent in the code. In fact, the type of publications of that time did not require a clear distinction. however, the 'Anglo-American Code of 1908' and the 'American Library Association Code of 1949' later found this to be necessary. In terms of cataloguing of publications by corporate bodies, the 91 rules do not envision corporate authorship. Instead, corporate entries could be used as a default or as an organising element.

Rule 80:

> All acts, memoirs, translations, journals, minutes, andc., of academies, institutes, associations, universities, or societies learned, scientific, or literary, by whatever name known or designated, as well as works by various hands, forming part of a series of volumes edited by any such society, to be entered, according to the English name of the country and town at which the sittings of the society are held, in the following order... .

In contrast to Needham, Carpenter states that this is a misconception to consider the 91 Rules as the first code which explicitly recognised the possibility of corporate authorship. Panizzi suggested the use of *form headings* as the main entry for certain types of publications. Publications such as acts, memoirs, transactions, and minutes published by institutes, universities and learned societies were entered under Academies.

Newspapers, magazines, and annuals under the heading Periodical Publications. and dictionaries under Dictionaries. These form headings, which can be regarded as akin to today's form subject headings, were a means for the bringing together of works of a common nature.

Panizzi used form headings also for anonymous works, which he entered under some catchword from the title. for example, in his rule 33, he prescribed that: "Anonymous publications relating to any act, or to the life of a person whose name occurs on the title of a work, are to be catalogued under the name of such person".

It is generally agreed that Panizzi's *Ninety-One Rules* for the construction of the British Museum catalogue became the source for all subsequent Anglo-American codes. Hyman

"All later catalogers started with Panizzi to compose their codes, and though the debates of his time are still with us, suggested solutions are largely expansions or refinements of the Ninety-One Rules."

CHARLES C. JEWETT AND HIS THIRTY-THREE RULES

It was Panizzi's code that influenced American cataloguers to compile their own codes of cataloguing rules. The rapid growth of libraries in the United States brought the same need for compiling cataloguing codes. Charles Coffin Jewett, then the librarian of the Smithsonian Institution, prepared the first distinct code of cataloguing rules in the United States.

Jewett's code of 1852 entitled *On the Construction of Catalogues of Libraries and of a General Catalogue, and Their Publication By Means of Separate Stereotype Titles. With Rules and Examples* consisted of thirty-three rules, mainly based upon Panizzi's code.

Through minor modifications to Panizzi's rules, Jewett attempted to compose a code of cataloguing rules which would be useful for all American libraries. Another distinct feature of Jewett's code was that it was to be used to prepare both an author listing and an alphabetical listing of subjects.

Jewett continued the work of Panizzi and laid the foundation for the later Anglo-American concept of authorship based upon the principle of intellectual responsibility. Unlike Panizzi, who did not envision corporate authorship, the concept of corporate authorship was reinforced and established more clearly in Jewett's Code. For example, rule 22 prescribed that:

> Academies, institutes, associations, universities, colleges. literary, scientific, economical,

> eleemosynary and religious societies. national and municipal governments, boards, corporations, and other bodies of men...issuing publications . . . are to be considered and treated as the author of all works issued by them, and in their name alone.

However, this rule implies that corporate bodies are not authors but should be considered as such. Carpenter has a similar interpretation. To provide effective access to the author/title catalogue, Jewett composed rules for the choice of headings. An interesting and new concept was that, in rule 13, he prescribed that the heading was to be written the transcribed title.

Tait, what makes Jewett modern and in line with cataloguing codes of recent times, such as CCR and AACR is in the extent to which he separated rules for titles from those for headings.

Another departure from Panizzi is in the entering anonymous works under the first word of the title rather than under catchwords contained in the title. Unlike Panizzi, Jewett did not use form headings for anonymous works. He suggested that anonymous works should be entered under the first word of the title, not an article or preposition.

Jewett emphasised uniformity as an essential issue in cataloguing and suggested all libraries should adhere to same set of rules. Jewett's contribution to author/title cataloguing and the idea of centralised and cooperative cataloguing was in his proposal to prepare stereotype entries for a printed book catalogue. The stereotype blocks that Jewett proposed could be used to print book catalogues for other libraries. In addition to being economically advantageous, this scheme necessitated uniformity in bibliographic description and an agreed code of cataloguing rules.

A technological advance that promises to reduce cataloguing effort tends to be accompanied by a concern for standardization. If the bibliographic records of one institution are to be used by another, they must be constructed according to a uniform style. For Jewett, a code of cataloguing rules exists to promote uniformity, and he formulated what might be called a principle of standardization.

CHARLES AMMI CUTTER AND HIS RULES FOR A DICTIONARY CATALOGUE

The year 1876, besides being the year in which the American Library Association was established, is also a significant date in the Anglo-American history of descriptive cataloguing. in this year Charles Ammi Cutter published his famous *Rules for a Dictionary Catalogue,* a landmark in the continuum of the Anglo-American cataloguing code tradition. Cutter's Rules are undoubtedly the most comprehensive set of rules ever produced by an individual.

Cutter's influence on descriptive cataloguing can be seen in the later design, objectives and principles of cataloguing codes. In his "Preface to the Fourth Edition" of *Rules for a Dictionary Catalogue,* Cutter illuminated cataloguing theory by considering the principle that "The convenience of the public is always to be set before the ease of the cataloger". Svenonius, *"Unlike Jewett, Cutter preferred to view cataloguing as an art needing only a few high-level rules or principles that could be applied by analogy to a variety of situations."* Through his 'Objectives of the catalogue' Cutter reinforced the contention that the catalogue should not only function as a finding list of what exists in a library, but also should assemble 'literary units' by showing what the library has under a given author.

Cutter formulated the objectives of the catalogue as:

* 1. To enable a person to find a book of which either
  - (A) the author
  - (B) the title is known
  - (C) the subject
* 2. To show what the library has
  - (D) by a given author
  - (E) on a given subject
  - (F) in a given kind of literature
* 3. To assist in the choice of a book
  - (G) as to its edition (bibliographically)
  - (H) as to its character (literary or topical)

To achieve these objectives, Cutter offered as practical means:

* Author-entry with necessary references

* Title-entry or title-reference
* Subject-entry, cross-references and classed subject table
* Form-entry and language entry
* Giving edition and imprint, with notes when necessary
* Notes

Cutter anticipated a need to go beyond the limits of the finding-list function and assumed that a library catalogue should assemble all the editions of a work. This can be considered to be an evolutionary step towards the further development of the concept of the functions of the catalogue.

> We find in Cutter, fixed for all time, I believe, the two fundamental principles of the modern author catalogue:
>
> – The author catalogue is more than a finding list of separate and particular books. It deals with literary unit and its function is to assemble under a convenient heading all issues or forms of the same literary unit.
>
> – The most satisfactory method of doing this is through the attribution of authorship, using as heading the name, of the person, or corporate body responsible for the work, or using as a substitute for author heading, a conventional name not derived from the title-page but from the literary source of the book or document.

Rules for a Dictionary Catalogue was a relatively comprehensive code that included provision for author, title, subject, form headings, description, and filing. Cutter made one of the most significant contributions to the development of the author catalogue and the establishment of the authorship principle.

He enriched the concept of authorship by using 'main entries' for the fullest bibliographic record and 'added entries' in abbreviated detail. 'Main' and 'added entries' would fulfil both the finding and the assembling functions of the catalogue. To Cutter, the assembling or collocating function of the catalogue, which brought together all works of an author and all editions of a work, was as important as the finding function.

A significant feature of Cutter's *Rules* was that he extended the concept of corporate authorship. This is an indication of the flexibility of the code towards changing conditions in the authorship concept.

Due to an increase in the number of corporate bodies and consequently the number of publications created under their responsibility, it was natural for the code to provide rules for them. Corporate bodies were considered as the authors of works that were published by them: "Bodies of men are to be considered as authors of works published in their name or by their authority".

This concept is a restatement of what Jewett embodied in his Rule 22. Carpenter identifies Cutter as the first theoretician of corporate authorship. Cutter's principle of corporate authorship, as Lubetzky points out, dominated all subsequent Anglo-American codes up to AACR2, which attempted to restrict it to only a few specified categories.

Cutter made no use of form headings for main entry but rather transferred this type of heading to the area of subjects. Like Jewett, he entered anonymous works under the first word of the title, but with an interesting exception in the case of biographies, which he entered not under the first word of the title but under the subject.

Cutter's Rules were designed for the construction of a dictionary book catalogue suited for small and medium-size public libraries with a collection of materials mainly in monographic format. His approach to the dictionary catalogue was to design a code consistent with the dominant printed book catalogues of the time.

Thus, the types of entries he proposed and the kinds of access points he prescribed were relevant to this form of catalogue. The use of a full main entry with abbreviated added entries for the retrieval of bibliographic information was suited to the printed book catalogue. In a book catalogue, the complete bibliographic record would be identified under the main entry and added entries would refer the user to the main entry.

The added entry function before Cutter was performed by cross-references which referred the reader to the main entry record. From the fourth edition of Cutter's rules onward the boundary between the use of added entries and cross references became clearer: added entries to provide added access to a bibliographic record, and cross references for name variations.

Another significant feature of Cutter's Rules was in the provision for short, medium and full entries. This was a requirement that Cutter considered necessary for different library catalogues of that time. It should be noted that a library could choose one option and construct its catalogue according to only one of the prescribed levels of entries.

Cutter took a pragmatic approach towards rules and suggested alternative rules based on the nature and size of the library and the physical form of the catalogue. The three styles of cataloguing that he formulated were a response to such considerations.

Rules for a Dictionary Catalogue became the chief source for later codes in the English language. Lubetzky, like many others, was influenced by Cutter and the principles he proposed in his Code of Cataloguing Rules and to the International Conference on Cataloguing principles are an indication of this influence. Tait, *"The principles laid down by Cutter in 1876 remained almost without challenge until almost the present decade—a testimony to their value."*

THE DEVELOPMENT OF THE CARD CATALOGUE IN THE LATE NINETEEN CENTURY

Parallel to the development of cataloguing codes in the nineteenth century in the Anglo-American countries, an innovation — the introduction of cards for the construction of library catalogues — changed the whole face of American libraries.

Although the idea of using slips and cards as a basis for creating the catalogue is not an American invention and goes back to the eighteenth century, when Abbé Rozier employed cards for the compilation of an index of publications of the Paris Académie des sciences in 1775, it was only much later and in the United States that card catalogues became common in libraries for public use. It should be added that slip or hand-written card catalogues were used for the preparation of book catalogues, but not for public use.

After a number of scattered attempts to use printed slips in public catalogues in the second half of the nineteenth century, the card catalogue became commonplace in the United States in the late nineteenth century.

In 1898, the Library of Congress began to provide printed catalogue cards for distribution. Although the service became available to all American libraries by 1898, it was not widely accepted by librarians, due to the various approaches and practices of individual libraries towards author headings, the size of the card, and long delays in shipment. In the last edition of his rules in 1904, Cutter recognised the card catalogue as the way of the future.

By the late nineteenth century, the dictionary card catalogue had been universally accepted as a practical and responsive catalogue. Researchers state:

"By the end of the nineteenth century the pattern of catalogue construction was well defined with subject headings, main entry, literary unit principle, dictionary catalogue, classification, unit cards, added entries, and adequate bibliographical descriptions all well-developed elements".

DEVELOPMENTS IN THE TWENTIETH CENTURY

Cataloguing in the second half of the nineteenth century was characterised by the compilation of a great number of codes which followed more or less the same trend in establishing principles for the construction of library catalogues. There was agreement on a number of general principles, particularly entry under author.

In the twentieth century, a number of significant factors have affected libraries in their operations and practices, including descriptive cataloguing. These factors are: the steady growth in the number of libraries and the size of collections, as an indirect indication of social and technological change.

A rapid increase in the number of publications in book and non-book form which led to the 'information explosion' in the twentieth century and the tendency to, and need for, more and closer international relations. There was a strong trend towards international cooperation and the exchange of ideas in the early twentieth century. The role of national libraries and library associations in formulating bibliographic standards is considered to have been a significant factor in the development of cataloguing codes and the move towards national as well as international standardisation. In the Anglo-American world, the move towards closer cooperation and formulation of joint codes is a clear expression of such trends in the cataloguing community.

Also, availability of printed catalogue cards from the Library of Congress, which was considered by Cutter as ". . . a great change . . . the status of cataloguing in the United States" was an important move towards bibliographic uniformity at the national, and later at the international, level.

ANGLO-AMERICAN CODE: CATALOGUE RULES. AUTHOR AND TITLE ENTRIES

As the first attempt at joint compilation of a code of cataloguing rules at an international level, the Anglo-American Code, known as AA or the *Joint Code,* was a response to the common interests and problems in descriptive cataloguing that existed in the United States and the United Kingdom in the late nineteenth and early twentieth centuries.

It was the result of cooperation between the [British] Library Association and the American Library Association in the production of ". . . a joint code which would bring uniformity into the cataloguing practice of the English-speaking countries". Although the idea came first from Melvil Dewey in 1900, the proposal was made by the [British] Library Association to ALA in 1904.

Unlike most older codes, AA was not formulated for an individual library, rather it was designed for larger libraries of scholarly character. It was, therefore, naturally influenced by other codes, such as Cutter's *Rules,* the *Prussian Instructions,* the *British Museum* code and also the Library of Congress rules, as shown in its preface and throughout the text. Daily, the code:

". . . was a largely successful effort to rationalize the rules of several different libraries into one readily followed standard".

It can be said that the Anglo-American Code of 1908 was designed for the construction of author/title card catalogues. The printed card service of the Library of Congress, started in 1898, is considered to have been a significant factor in the rapid proliferation of card catalogues among libraries of different sizes and types. In this situation, the compilation of a joint code which would bring uniformity to the catalogues of different libraries was a welcome event, particularly in the United States.

The code recognised the 'literary unit' as the basis for cataloguing. In this regard, the code preferred as the heading the full, real, baptismal name of the author rather than accepting the name by which the author was identified most commonly on the title pages of works or in reference sources.

A lack of definition of the concept of corporate authorship and also the undefined distinction and inconsistent treatment of institutions and societies were among some of the criticisms made of the code. For example, a difficulty with the rules concerning corporate entry was that buildings and ships were considered as authors?? Most importantly, the principles on which it was formulated were not stated in the code itself. In addition to some inconsistencies and many omissions, its numerous rules made it difficult to understand and use.

ALA CATALOGUE RULES. AUTHOR AND TITLE ENTRIES (ALA DRAFT CODE 1941)

Due to a perceived need for a more detailed and comprehensive code which would cover the various problems encountered by cataloguers, there was increasing demand for the revision of the 1908 code. In 1930 the Library of Congress appointed a subcommittee to study its revision.

Based on cataloguers' experiences in the actual use of the code, work was begun by ALA with the cooperation of the [British] Library Association. Because of the outbreak of World War II, the British could not continue their cooperation. A preliminary edition was published in 1941 and a second American edition was published in the same year as: *ALA Catalogue Rules. Author and Title Entries.* However, because of its adherence to American perspectives and cataloguing tradition, ALA is not considered an international code.

An extremely complex code with an enumeration of cases and what many regard as an over-elaboration of rules, ALA was not welcomed by the cataloguing community. Rather than defining principles, it supplemented and amended the 1908 Code. For example, the definition and the treatment of corporate entry are almost identical to AA 1908. the code was so severely criticised that the situation encouraged Andrew Osborn to write his famous article entitled *"The crisis in cataloguing"*.

This article is considered a classic within the cataloguing community and is very much cited in the literature. Osborn criticised the code's approach towards the provision of various rules for the coverage of different cataloguing cases. Daily restates Osborn's criticism of the code that "What is needed is a set of guiding principles, worked out for the most common cases, which accomplish the basic task of cataloguing without formalistic constraints that perplex the user without adding materially to precise description".

A.L.A. CATALOGUING RULES. AUTHOR AND TITLE ENTRIES (ALA 1949)

Due to the severe criticisms of ALA, a new edition, *i.e.*, the rules for entry was published by the American Library Association in 1949. The Library of Congress had already decided to prepare its own rules for descriptive cataloguing.

Therefore, ALA requested its Catalogue Code Revision Committee to deal only with the revision of part 1 of ALA, taking into account all the criticisms which had been made of it. Thus, the 1949 code covered only rules for entries. In this respect, the code was basically influenced by Cutter's rules for main entry, and his theory that "...the catalogue user was the final arbiter of the form that any specific rule should take".

Although ALA basically followed AA and ALA, it had some new features such as:

* The code chose 'work' as the basis for description. In this regard, it followed AA and took the concept of 'literary unit' from Cutter's rules.
* With regard to the choice of main entry, the code prescribed that the entry was to be made under "...the person or body chiefly responsible for the intellectual content of the book, literary, artistic or musical".

Intellectual responsibility was not confined to title page information, rather, the author was usually to be chosen from either the work itself or other sources. In this regard, the concept of principal responsibility was a new idea in ALA.

* It emphasised the concept of corporate versus personal authorship by giving more guidance on the construction of corporate headings. For example, Rule 1 prescribed that: "Enter a work under the name of its author whether personal or corporate".

In the introduction to the code it is stated that, as the dictionary card catalogue was the dominant form of the catalogue in most American libraries, the rules were prepared with that type of catalogue in mind. The main thrust of the Code's rules was the choice of main entry for the author, personal or corporate, who was considered to be chiefly responsible for the intellectual or artistic content of the work.

Added entries were to be made "to enable the user of the catalogue to find a work when incomplete knowledge or imperfect memory of the work, or unfamiliarity with the rules of entry, would prevent ready access to the main entry". References were to be used to provide uniformity and effectiveness in the catalogue.

ALA was criticised for not continuing the trend towards internationalism which AA had tried to achieve at the beginning of the century, especially as the time was more convenient for the code to approach international uniformity and the postwar condition also seemed to be more in need of international cooperation. By abandonment of the agreement reached in 1908 and by adherence to a national tradition, ALA missed a good opportunity for getting closer to uniformity and standardisation.

In his *Headings and Canons. Comparative Study of Five Catalogue Codes,* Ranganathan criticised the ALA Code more than other codes because of redundancies and inconsistencies in its rules. In relation to the lack of sufficient answers to different cataloguing problems, there were many objections to the ALA rules.

The criticism of Osborn did not seem to have a great deal of effect on ALA 1949, for the rules in this code, in the opinion of many, are as pedantic, elaborate, and often arbitrary, as those in the preliminary edition of 1941. The code was constructed on the same formula as AA and ALA but lacked a clear statement of basic principles.

Among major critiques of the code was Lubetzky's report, *Cataloguing Rules and Principles: A Critique of the A.L.A. Rules for Entry and a Proposed Design for their Revision, 1953*. Lubetzky stated that a major shortcoming of the code was that it was "vague in design and weak in structure." Tait Lubetzky criticised the code because of its "proliferation of rules to cover specific cases, and almost complete absence of any principles of entry, in spite of the statement in the introduction. The result is that proliferation also results in inconsistencies".

CODE OF CATALOGUING RULES (CCR 1960)

Lubetzky's *Cataloguing Rules and Principles* which was prepared for the Board of Cataloguing Policy and Research of the American Library Association received general approval. Because of his approach towards the design of an effective code of cataloguing rules, Lubetzky was invited by the ALA Catalogue Code Revision Committee to prepare a new edition of *ALA*. Being influenced by Cutter's 'Objectives', Lubetzky produced his *Code of cataloguing rules, author and title entry: an unfinished draft, 1960,* known as *CCR.*

Lubetzky stated the objectives on which the rules were formulated as follows:

The objectives which the catalogue has to serve are two:

* To facilitate the location of a particular publication, *i.e.*, a particular edition of a work which is in the library.
* To relate and display together the editions which the library has of a given work and the works which it has of a given author.

The two functions are complementary, but both are essential to the effectiveness of the catalogue. Lubetzky adopted Cutter's 'Objectives' with minor changes. Here, the word 'Book' is replaced by the words 'Work' and 'Edition' to give priority to the literary unit concept and to cater for the inclusion of various types of 'non-book' items in the code.

By a clear definition of the main entry concept, Lubetzky tried to remove inconsistencies within Cutter's Code, AA, and ALA in which "the main entry sometimes represents 'work' and sometimes 'edition'". His emphasis was on the 'work' and he considered that a major function for the main entry was the assembling of the editions of a certain work by a certain author.

To Lubetzky, the 'work', rather than the 'edition,' was the primary unit. He assumed that ". . . the catalogue user is interested in the work represented by the particular publication rather than in its embodiment in any particular edition". In determining the basic principles of his rules, Lubetzky followed Cutter's "convenience of the public" and considered the reader's approach to be an important factor.

As CCR was written primarily for the construction of a card catalogue using the concept of a unit cataloguing method, added entries carried far more information than in older Anglo-American codes. Main entry was not considered as the most important entry for a work and lost its importance significantly in the sense that the code avoided the use of the term "main entry". Instead, it used terms like "entry is made under . . ." or ". . . is entered under the person..." However, the significance of the main entry concept in single-entry catalogues, such as union catalogues in hard copies, could not be disregarded. In comparison to the older Anglo-American cataloguing codes, the concept of authorship was broadened and extended to all types of materials in CCR. The utility of such an approach to authorship in the case of non-book materials has been challenged. In this regard, Tait pointed out that:

Certain types of material may not be amenable to or require author entry as such, and one has the impression that CCR occasionally forces author entry, presumably for the sake of consistency.... This would appear to be pushing the authorship concept rather too far, but is almost inevitable within the general framework of the philosophy of CCR.

The code emphasised the concept of corporate authorship. Rule 22 was a general rule for works of corporate bodies. Another concept emphasised in the code was a reliance on title-page information in providing standard cataloguing data. In this respect, Lubetzky followed Panizzi, who was the first to recognise the importance of the title-page. This is in line with the users' knowledge of or familiarity with books as known or seen by them.

In this regard, it is generally said that the cataloguer can avoid the difficulty of determining the intellectual responsibility of the item in hand. However, this approach may be in conflict with the uniformity which is necessary in the assembling of different editions of a work under one form of heading. In relation to the discussion it should be added that, unlike ALA, CCR avoided the subjective judgements required of the cataloguer in distinguishing between different types of multiple authorship. As noted earlier, this was possible by relying on title-page criteria. Because of its logical consistency and its compilation on a solid theoretical basis, CCR received favourable reaction. However, in terms of the alterations that would result in catalogues from the possible implementation of the code, it was criticised by reference librarians who claimed that they would find answering reference questions difficult and by library administrators who preferred the simplification of cataloguing rules and less costly practices.

The CCR was very influential at the time and Lubetzky was hailed as one of the great theoreticians in descriptive cataloguing. Suffice it to say that the principles adopted and internationally agreed upon at the International Conference on Cataloguing Principles, Paris, 1961 were to a large extent influenced by CCR.

THE PARIS PRINCIPLES (ICCP 1961)

As one of the most important events in the history of descriptive cataloguing, the International Conference on Cataloguing Principles (ICCP), Paris, 1961 has had a great impact on the development of current cataloguing codes. ICCP was a response to the need for international agreement on the principles of cataloguing. The conference aimed at providing basic agreement for the compilation of national bibliographies and national codes.

In this regard and in order "to facilitate the international communication of knowledge by achieving the widest possible uniformity in library catalogues and other means of bibliographical communication", the Paris Conference has been considered to be one of the most effective attempts in the direction of universal bibliographical control and international standardization in cataloguing.

Due to a number of conflicting issues in different cataloguing codes and practices, which made the exchange and understanding of bibliographic information difficult at an international level, there was a strong need for some kind of uniformity in national bibliographies and, at a higher level, in the bibliographic universe at large.

The ICCP Report, the Conference intended:

* *... to take the necessary action to ensure:*
  - That cataloguing rules in their countries are established or revised as soon as possible in conformity with the principles laid down by the Conference, and put into practice.
  - That the same principles are taken into account in the compilation of national bibliographies.

Although the physical form of the catalogue was not directly specified in the Principles, it can be concluded that they and their allied recommendations were based on the concept of the card catalogue, the most widely used form of catalogue at the time. It should be added that, by this time, the card catalogue had become an internationally accepted form for the construction of library catalogues. The principles discussed and agreed upon at the ICCP applied mainly to the choice and form of headings and entry words as the most important organising elements in author/title catalogues, which needed uniformity at an international level. The ICCP continued the principles of the older codes in the sense that the emphasis was on alphabetical author/title catalogues and lists of books.

As the first issue in the Statement of Principles the functions of the catalogue were agreed upon as:

* *Functions of the Catalogue:* The catalogue should be an efficient instrument for ascertaining

- Whether the library contains a particular book specified by
  a. Its author and title, *or*
  b. If the author is not named in the book, its title alone, *or*
  c. If the author and title are inappropriate or insufficient for identification, a suitable substitute for the title. and
- Which works by a particular author and
- Which editions of a particular work are in the library.

In relation to the functions of the catalogue and their influence on other cataloguing principles two working papers were presented at ICCP. The two papers, in fact, illustrate the two contradictory approaches which have their root in the long history of cataloguing codes in relation to the functions of the catalogue and the choice and form of main and added entries.

In his working paper, Lubetzky emphasised the second function as the principal element for bringing together different editions of the same work. He considered the 'literary unit' as the basis for description. In this context, different editions and translations of a work should be found together rather than under their own titles. The name of an author must be uniform to bring together all publications by that author. In terms of titles, Lubetzky put emphasis on entering publications under the title as found in the first publication of the work, or where this was not possible, under the accepted 'conventional title.' This would bring together different appearances of exactly the same work.

This approach, of course, has some problems particularly for public library users who usually look for a specific edition or translation of a work and not the original work with a different title they are not familiar with. Verona, who presented the second approach to the function of the catalogue, emphasised the publication in hand as the basis for description.

She stressed that the function of main entries is:

* To represent particular publications, and
* To bring together in the catalogue all publications by one author.

In this context, a certain form of the author's name would group together all publications by the author. To Verona, not the main entries, but added entries would link all editions of a certain literary unit.

In Statements 3 to 12, the ICCP specified the structure of the catalogue and the kinds and forms of entries that were necessary for the effective discharge of the catalogue's functions. Although Principle 2.1 considered the single item important, Principle 2.2 put emphasis on the work. This was a contradictory situation to which the ICCP did not offer an effective solution and to which there were objections.

A significant improvement of the ICCP over AA and ALA was in the definitions that it provided for personal and corporate authorship. In this respect, ICCP put the emphasis on the intellectual responsibility concept of authorship. As opposed to some European traditions, Principles 9.1 to 9.3, that regarded corporate bodies as authors, approached the Anglo-American practice and were accepted by a majority of the national cataloguing committees.

Representing the point of view of Hungarian cataloguers, Domanovszky argued against this practice and considered it to be opposed to common practice in everyday speech. The German cataloguing tradition also rejected the concept of corporate authorship in most cases and accepted it only when there was no personal author named in the work and when the title of the work was explicitly related to the corporate body as the originator. On the other hand, Verona was one of the proponents of corporate authorship and later stated that:

A work should be considered to be of corporate authorship if it may be concluded by its character or nature that it is necessarily the result of the creative and/or organizational activity of a corporate body as a whole, and not the result of an independent creative activity of the individual(s) who drafted it.

An interesting issue in the list of topics discussed at ICCP that was not fully acknowledged at the time was the potential impact of electronic information systems upon the process of cataloguing. In his working paper presented at the Conference,

Gull discussed the potential impact of electronics, such as machine readable texts and the concept of 'automatic authorship' on cataloguing rules and suggested that the issue be addressed in the design of cataloguing codes.

For example, Gull anticipated that the concept of main entry would be influenced by electronic texts and main entry headings would not be needed for machine readable texts. Gull concluded that: ". . . cataloguers must fit cataloguing rules to human capabilities and adapt them to changes in technologies.

Indeed, they must enlist the aid of new technologies to assure that cataloguing rules are based on substance rather than form." In the early 1960s, however, the issue was far from clear and did not arouse much comment within the profession. Most subsequent current national cataloguing codes have been compiled on the basis of the ICCP Statements. Although ICCP was regarded as being highly successful in its resolutions and objectives at the time, it was later criticised for some inconsistencies and vagueness. As reported by national cataloguing committees, full conformity to the Statements proved not to be practical, due to variations in cataloguing traditions and practices.

ANGLO-AMERICAN CATALOGUING RULES (AACR 1967)

After ICCP it was time for the English-speaking world to prepare a new set of rules, a second Anglo-American joint code, which could provide for greater uniformity both in library catalogues and in the exchange of bibliographic information between libraries in the English-speaking countries. Based on ICCP and their own cataloguing traditions, the library associations of the United States, Canada and the United Kingdom, with the collaboration of the Library of Congress, provided the groundwork for the compilation of a new joint code which would be applicable at an international level.

Due to some variations in cataloguing practices, the code was published in 1967 in two separate texts: North American and British. One difference between these texts was the departure of the American text from the Paris Principles in its rejection of the entry of a collection under title when such a work had a collective title.

Furthermore, due to the recommendations and requirements of the Association of Research Libraries (ARL) the impact of the Paris Principles on existing entries for corporate bodies was reduced and there were a few cases in which the code departed from those principles.

The most significant departure was the exemption of certain bodies of an institutional nature from the principle of entry under name and a substitution of a rule of entry under the place in which the institution was situated.

Based on the American cataloguing tradition of entering a work under author rather than title, AACR1 gave entry of collections under compiler when the compiler's name was on the title-page. These exceptions, however, were changed in 1974 and 1975 to bring the code into line with the Paris Principles and to provide uniformity between the two versions.

Unlike AA and ALA, AACR1 was primarily drawn up to respond to the needs of general research libraries and had some features that distinguished it from its predecessors. The needs of smaller public libraries were addressed by the provision of alternative rules as well as more direct headings. Because of a basic difference in approach to the practice of cataloguing, the character of the rules for entry and heading was considerably different.

These differences were summarised as:

* The rules were based on internationally agreed principles,
* Choice of entry and construction of heading were treated as separate problems, except when form subheadings were involved,
* Choice of entry was treated as a problem of determination of authorship responsibility, and
* Construction of heading was treated as a problem of name.

A thorough examination of the code reveals that the rules for entry and heading are substantially based on ALA, Lubetzky's CCR, and ICCP. However, rules for description in AACR1 were formulated on the basis of *Rules for description in the Library of Congress* and its supplementary rules.

The principle of authorship was more clearly enunciated in AACR1, where the primary criterion for determining authorship was 'intellectual responsibility'. As will be discussed later, its handling of this issue was based on conditions of authorship rather than on types of work. Lubetzky, "*. . . the governing principle in AACR1 is that entry is to be based not on type of publication or work but on the varying conditions of authorship.*" With regard to corporate bodies, as can be seen from the AACR's definition, they were considered as authors in an explicit way.

Although the title-page was chosen as the chief source for determining entries, AACR1 chose the 'work' as the basis for cataloguing. This was apparent throughout the statements of the rules in part I. Lubetzky criticised the definition of authorship in AACR1 in that it based the chief responsibility for a work on its intellectual or artistic content rather than considering the producer as the person chiefly responsible for a work.

Through their emphasis on entries under uniform headings and the use of references, the rules were oriented to multiple-entry alphabetical catalogues. However, AACR1 still distinguished between main and added entries.

In explaining the significance of this concept, the framers of the code stated that, both for identification of a single-entry work in multiple entry catalogs as well as for the general needs of libraries and bibliographical and book-trade activities, a standard mode of identifying bibliographical entities was necessary. This standard mode is one of the often stated justifications for the use of main entries in such situations as single-entry bibliographies, book lists, order lists and bibliographic citations.

At the time that AACR1 was compiled, the card catalogue was the dominant form of library catalogue and the framers of the code did not take into account the potential impact of automation on library operations, particularly the application of the computer in providing public catalogues.

Daily believed that it was the fate of the code that it was designed for practices of that time and even previous years and not for the coming decades and for the computerised listing of entries. It is worth noting that in the 1960s, the attitude of most librarians towards computerised catalogues was limited to a superficial understanding of the concept of automation, *e.g.*, the ability of computers to perform repetitive tasks with much more precision and speed.

An important factor that disappointed cataloguers in the full adoption of AACR1 was the policy of 'superimposition', declared by the Library of Congress, of continuing the usage of headings which had been constructed according to ALA rules. This policy made trouble for some cataloguing departments in maintaining their catalogues and resulted in numerous inconsistencies in name headings.

Soon after the adoption of AACR1 in large libraries, it became apparent that the code was in need of a number of additions and changes. The Library of Congress and the ALA's Division of Cataloguing and Classification approved the need for the addition or change of a number of rules.

The British did not welcome the continuous revisions of the rules that were being undertaken in the United States. However, cataloguing trends in the 1970s, such as the introduction of the International Standard Bibliographic Description (ISBD), necessitated that the code should be brought into line with these new trends.

INTERNATIONAL STANDARD BIBLIOGRAPHIC DESCRIPTION (ISBD) (1971)

As one of the major products of the train of activity set in motion by ICCP and elaborated by a Working Group set up by the International Meeting of Cataloguing Experts, ISBD was developed to specify requirements for the description of publications for the purpose of international communication. The standard assigns an order to the descriptive elements, and specifies a system of punctuation for the description.

It is designed primarily as an instrument for the international communication of bibliographical information not only in library cataloguing but also in book trade activities. ISBD is not a set of cataloguing rules: it does not deal with access points and "does not include any prescription for the heading underwhich a description should appear in a catalogue or other bibliographical list". In addition to the General International Standard Bibliographic Description, IFLA has developed specialised ISBDs for specific types of material.

Many national cataloguing codes have based the rules for description on the general framework of ISBD. Also most national bibliographies are prepared according to this standard. Adherence to these descriptive standards by many cataloguing agencies, whether working in a manual or an automated environment, has provided greater uniformity in the communication and understanding of bibliographical information within countries and between countries. This is essential to Universal Bibliographic Control.

In respond to the requirements of automated systems, which were developing rapidly in the early 1970s, ISBD was designed in a way to facilitate the conversion of bibliographic records into machine-readable form, or as Gorman points out, "to maximize the interchange and processibility of data in the machine environment." This was done through the systematisation of the order of data elements and the punctuation that is used to separate these elements in a record.

Although ISBD is a computer compatible format, many automated systems do not use the ISBD order and/or punctuation, especially when displaying bibliographic records. This is in contrast to the primary aim of the standard. Many online catalogues rearrange the data elements, causing confusion from one system to the next. Much of the criticism of ISBD has been in relation to problems other than automation. Ricard, Lubetzky, Ayres criticised ISBD mostly for the punctuation, the redundancies and repetitive author statement.

ANGLO-AMERICAN CATALOGUING RULES, SECOND EDITION (AACR2 1978)

The second edition of AACR was the result of four years' work by the Joint Steering Committee for Revision of AACR (JSC) which had been set up in 1974 by the American Library Association, the [British] Library Association and the Canadian Committee on Cataloguing, with the support and cooperation of the British Library and the Library of Congress.

Tikku, AACR2 was "the result of the culmination of several factors, which appeared in the 1970's and thus necessitated the production of a revised edition of cataloguing rules".

These factors were: piecemeal revision of AACR1. the development of the International Standard Bibliographic Description (ISBD). LC's interest in 'desuperimposition', *i.e.*, allowing for changes to headings established under pre-AACR rules. and the use of computers in libraries.

During the period between the publication of the first and second editions of AACR many changes had taken place, such as the development of MARC formats, the development of computerised catalogues, the growth of centralised and cooperative bibliographic services and the proliferation of new media and nonbook materials, which had significant effects on cataloguing and bibliographic control.

Also, the introduction of ISBD (M), which was incorporated in AACR2, was considered to be a major factor in the move towards Universal Bibliographic Control (UBC). In spite of these factors, AACR2 maintained the same principles and objectives as AACR1 and was based on the work of those who created the first edition.

Gorman, coeditor of the code:

* "AACR2 should be judged not just on its own merits but also as part of a continuum, as part of the 'great tradition' in Anglo-American cataloguing which stretches back to Panizzi, Jewett, and Cutter."

The aims of the second edition of AACR as set out by JSC were:

* To incorporate already agreed revisions to AACR1.
* To harmonize the British and North American texts of AACR1.
* To incorporate international standards and international agreements.
* To take developments in library automation into account. and
* To incorporate changes arising from proposals for change coming from any source.

In comparison to AACR1, the second edition had the following features:

* AACR2 maintained a more logical and consistent structure than AACR1. In order to provide ease of use for cataloguers, it followed the sequence of the cataloguing process. The rules were divided into two parts: bibliographic description coming as the first part and choice and form of headings as the second. Also the wording, order, and method of construction of the rules were different.
* AACR2 incorporated fully the General International Standard Bibliographic Description in the rules for description, in that it prescribed the same order of elements and punctuation. As "an instrument for the international communication of bibliographical information", this standard is an important factor in achieving bibliographic standardisation and, at a higher level, Universal Bibliographic Control.
* AACR2 was designed for use in the construction of catalogues and other lists in general libraries of all sizes. With regard to the varying requirements of detail in bibliographic records in different libraries, three levels of description have been provided. These levels, *viz.*, minimum, medium or standard, and detailed or maximum were, in fact, a revival of Cutter's short, medium, and long entries and are applicable to all types of materials. The choice of a level of description was based on "the purpose of the catalogue or catalogues for which the entry is constructed".
* Unlike AACR1, the rules for entry and heading were applicable to all types of library materials. Gorman, the rules and the examples in AACR2 Chapter 21, unlike the book-oriented rules in AACR1, presented an integrated approach to all library materials.
* In AACR2 the concept of authorship was shrinking. This is apparent in the following aspects:
  - In some cases the code replaced the term 'authorship' with the term 'responsibility', which is more

comprehensive. A 'statement of responsibility' appeared after the title to indicate the type of responsibility of any one involved in the creation of the item. Also the terms 'Mixed authorship' and 'Shared authorship' that were used in AACR1 were replaced by 'Mixed responsibility' and 'Shared responsibility' respectively.

- A major difference of AACR2 from the older Anglo-American codes was that editors of collections were no longer regarded as authors. The decision was made in accordance to Statement 10.3 in the Paris Principles. This shrinking of the concept of authorship was a new trend in the family of the Anglo-American codes.
- In AACR2 the concept of corporate authorship was no longer prevalent, as can be seen in the restriction of cases where main entry was to be under the names of corporate bodies and the increase in the number of cases where serials were given title main entry. In terms of serials, all special rules for entry of serials were removed from the code with AACR2. Thus, rule 6 is not based on authorship. This approach has been criticised by some serials librarians and others on the grounds that it was hard to create relationships among the different publications of a corporate body.

* In accordance with the requirements of the MARC format, AACR2 abolished the dash entry. This was done by prescribing separate entry or multi-level description for items such as supplements, indexes, detached copies and offprints. The dash entry had been used in book and card catalogues and, once the MARC format was introduced, it was abandoned.

AACR2 followed its predecessors, mainly CCR and AACR1, in that the rules for choice and form of access points "apply to works and not generally to physical manifestations of those works, though the characteristics of an individual item are taken into account in some instances".

In spite of the fact that a computer catalogue permits a number of equal access points, the concept of main entry was retained in AACR2. The reasons for this, as presented by the proponents of the main entry concept in JSC's arguments, were on the basis that it is a central principle in conventional cataloguing theory and that it has practical utility in printed book catalogues, in shelf-listing, and in single-entry listings.

However, for those catalogues which are not based on the main entry principle, AACR2 instructed the cataloguer to use the rules in chapter 21 as a guidance for making necessary entries. Although AACR2 deemphasised the traditional concept of main entry and encouraged the use of 'access point' for any entry, it did not ignore its usefulness and states that:

It will be necessary, however, for all libraries to distinguish the main entry from the others when:

* Making a single entry listing
* Making a single citation for a work.

In addition, the concept of main entry is considered to be useful in assigning uniform titles and in promoting the standardization of bibliographic citation. Despite its flaws in a number of aspects, such as not being based on coherent principles, a lack of defined objectives and a lack of integrity, a lack of separate rules for deciding on serials publications access points and inconsistent treatment of the various media, ambiguities which make the rules open to misinterpretations, irrelevance to computerised catalogues, AACR2 obtained overall support among cataloguers and cataloguing educators.

It undoubtedly went further towards achieving standardisation and internationalisation than AACR1 and even more than any other code. Smiraglia, "AACR2 is an important partner in the international effort to share bibliographic data". The code was considered by *UNISIST Guide to Standards for Information Handling* as one of the standard codes to be used in a multinational context.

The declaration of 'desuperimposition' and the new policy of the Library of Congress towards the closing of its card catalogues beginning from 1980, which later was postponed to 1 January, 1981 was considered an important issue for American libraries. There was a great deal of frustration about the extent to which headings in existing catalogues constructed under older codes would be affected.

At the same time, the advent of online catalogues, as well as the difficulties of maintaining manual systems, encouraged many libraries of different sizes to close or freeze their card catalogues, to adapt themselves to the Library of Congress' policy, and to adopt fully AACR2.

ANGLO-AMERICAN CATALOGUING RULES, SECOND EDITION, 1988 REVISION (AACR2R)

The implementation of AACR2 engendered frustration in many types of library and generated a large amount of literature concerning its problems, shortcomings and flaws. To many cataloguers, the code did not fulfil their cataloguing requirements in a time of rapid movement towards information networks and the international exchange of bibliographic records.

Based on these criticisms and recommendations, the JSC published three separate groups of rule revisions in 1982, 1983, and 1985. These revisions and the complete revision of chapter, published in 1987, made it necessary to provide the profession with a new revision of the code. Thus, the *Anglo-American Cataloguing Rules, Second Edition, 1988 Revision* (AACR2R) was published under the editorship of Michael Gorman and Paul Winkler.

The appearance of the 1988 revision of the *Anglo-American Cataloguing Rules* did not arouse as much enthusiasm as its predecessor (AACR2) had in 1978. Although AACR2R is the result of ongoing revisions, it maintains the same principles and guidelines as AACR2. The major differences relate to the rules for description of some types of materials, notably computer files. Part II has some changes, of which the most important are in the areas of pseudonyms and geographic names as well as the headings for some subordinate corporate bodies and uniform titles for music.

Two major changes in the authorship concept have been addressed in AACR2R. Separate bibliographic identities are to go under their own headings in the catalogue. AACR2R rule

22.2B2 instructs the cataloguer to choose two or more headings for a person who uses a form of his or her name for one type of work and another name for another type of work.

Rule 22.2B3 takes the same approach: the heading for contemporary authors is to be chosen according to the name which appears in the manifestation of the work being catalogued. The aim is to simplify the cataloguer's task and to provide convenient access for the catalogue user.

As the fact that the direct name of a corporate body is more convenient to the catalogue user, AACR2R has taken this approach and suggests that the direct forms of heading be preferred. Rules for geographic names have also been drastically simplified to identify geographic names through addition to the name of the state, province, region, etc. in certain countries

The framers of AACR2R have tried to prepare a set of rules that could be applicable to all types of library materials in all formats and all languages. Thus, in comparison to its predecessors, the code moves further towards internationalism. The code has been adopted by many countries as their national cataloguing standard. It has also been translated into Arabic, Finnish, French, Japanese, Korean, Malaysian, Norwegian, Portuguese, Spanish, Swedish, Urdu and into Afrikaans, Chinese, Italian, Russian and Persian.

NON-ANGLO-AMERICAN CATALOGUING CODES

A number of national cataloguing codes have either been independently written or contain some major departures from the Paris Principles. In this part two non Anglo-American cataloguing codes, *i.e.*, the German cataloguing code will be briefly studied to acknowledge some of the basic concepts underlying cataloguing traditions outside the Anglo-American context.

The German Cataloguing Code

The *Instruktionen fr die alphabetischen Kataloge in der preussischen Bibliotheken* [Instructions for alphabetic catalogues in Prussian libraries, the PI or The Prussian Instructions], which had been in use since 1899, no longer satisfied the requirements of descriptive cataloguing in the second half of the twentieth century.

There was a strong need to adapt, as far as possible, to international cataloguing practice and to take into consideration a more precise treatment of publications, for example, to comply with modern forms and titles of publications and to take into consideration the impact of electronic data processing.

After the Paris Conference and in moving towards an international consistency of cataloguing codes, a new code began to be prepared by the Verein Deutscher Bibliotekare of the Federal Republic of Germany. Among the concepts covered by the new code, two concepts were new to the German cataloguing tradition: entry under corporate name and the filing of entries by computers.

In 1965 cooperation began with the Bibliotheksverband der D D R which was working along the same lines. In 1969 two parts of the code were published as preliminary editions. RAK was produced jointly by commissions of the Verein Deutscher Bibliothekare, of the Deutscher Bibliotheksverb and, and of the Vereinigung Osterreichischer Bibliothekare in 1969. The Rules in RAK apply to libraries of every size and of varying functions. They contain many alternatives for different cases.

RAK is based on the Paris Principles and ISBD. It is said that the code is closer to international recommendations than other cataloguing codes. Johnson reports some of the major differences between RAK and AACR. In terms of authorship, however, RAK continues the German tradition of attributing this concept only to persons.

For corporate bodies, it introduces the concept of 'Urheber' to identify such bodies as either creators or sponsors of anonymous works. The term 'Urheber' came with the introduction of the concept of corporate authorship and was taken over from legal theory and adapted for cataloguing purposes. In this context, the main entry is made under the 'Urheber' only when no personal author is named in the work and only when the title of the work is explicitly related to the corporate body as the originator.

The filing principle in the Prussian Instruction was different from that of other codes in that it was grammatical and not mechanical. In RAK this approach was changed to take advantage of electronic data processing in the filing of large groups of entries in automated catalogues. It is claimed that the RAK filing rules are the first filing rules for catalogues with the application of automation in mind.

To adapt the German code to the online environment and to consider possible changes to RAK, an expert committee was established in 1994 to continue the work of a special Online Expert Group. It is said that the Expert Group is working on possible modification of RAK with radical ideas and concepts which may be challenging the Anglo-American cataloguing tradition.

Among the issues for possible development for online catalogues are:

* The abandonment of the concept of main entry and the relegation of its function to rules for output format. In their present structures the rules for determining main and added entries are said to be too restrictive for online catalogues. For the online catalogue, none of the classic access points such as corporate names, personal names and titles need to be weighted as primary or secondary by means of tags or indicators.
* Indexing for online catalogues, for example, to avoid redundancies in title in the bibliographic description and in the tracing. It should be ensured that rules do not hamper existing data structures, as the many present redundancies do.
* Formatting possibilities and display of bibliographic description. The desired form of lists can be prepared according to the needs of the clientele for whom they are intended and not according to academic citation methods which are not consistent with OPAC displays

It remains to be seen what would be the consequences of such changes for the international exchange of bibliographic data and how far such new rules affect online retrieval of records in a global online environment.

The Japanese Cataloguing Code

The Japanese code, *i.e., Nippon Cataloguing Rules* (NCR), which was compiled in 1977, is not based on the Paris Principles. It is basically for publications in the Japanese and Chinese languages and is based on a *description unit card system* (DUCS) and does not conform to the principle of main entry.

In a catalogue constructed according to this system, multiple entries are created for an item by reproducing the unit card made for it. There are no main entry headings and as many headings as are needed are recorded in the tracing. The descriptive part of the record is created independently of the headings.

Four revisions were carried out in the 1980s and it was revised to be compatible with both the ISBDs and UNIMARC. The last edition, the 1987 edition, is still based on the no main-entry principle.

A most notable feature of NCR is in its treatment of bibliographic hierarchy. This novel feature has been incorporated in preparation for online catalogues. Based on the concept of bibliographic hierarchy as derived from the *Reference Manual for Machine-Readable Bibliographic Description* and unlike its 1977 edition, in which the 'physical unit' was taken as the basis for description, this edition has taken the 'work' as the basic unit for description.

In this situation, the physical manifestations of a work are considered subordinate to it. With this approach there is much flexibility for the treatment of bibliographic relationships through a multi-level record.

SUMMARY AND CONCLUSIONS

In studying the historical development of modern catalogues and cataloguing codes, particularly with respect to the physical form of the catalogue, a range of factors and elements have been highlighted as the most important concepts. The development of these concepts, which form the underlying principles of descriptive cataloguing and the design of cataloguing codes, has been substantially based on two fundamental factors: the form of the catalogue and the nature of bibliographic entities.

These concepts have been subject to constant assessment, reassess-ment and change throughout the history of modern cataloguing:

* *The Alphabetical Catalogue*: The classified catalogue of the early nineteenth century gradually gave way to the alphabetical catalogue, particularly the dictionary catalogue, which has been one of the most popular forms of the catalogue throughout the twentieth century. The development of cataloguing rules in the Anglo-American context for choice and form of entry has been influenced by this type of catalogue.
* *Objectives and Functions of the Catalogue:* The principles on which modern cataloguing codes have been formulated have developed in accordance with the objectives and functions of the catalogue. The older inventory function of the catalogue evolved into a finding function in the early nineteenth century and later also included an assembling function in Cutter's Rules and afterwards. Provisions for the choice of entry in cataloguing codes are based on the objectives and functions of the catalogue and how they should be discharged.
* *The Concept of a Work*: The controversial concept of 'work', as opposed to the concept of 'book' has had significant influence on other concepts and principles in descriptive cataloguing. By giving priority to one concept, other concepts such as the concept of authorship, choice and form of entries and uniform titles are influenced. Inconsistencies are present in some cataloguing codes due to the confusion between 'work' and 'book'.
* *The Concept of Entry:* As the most important means of approaching surrogates of library materials, the concept of entry has become fixed in bibliographic practice. Thus, a significant portion of any cataloguing code is devoted to rules for the construction of entries, which discuss what constitutes the entry and the choice of entry words and access points as well as the

form of entry words. Thus, this concept implies the significant notion that there is more than one approach for finding an item in a catalogue.

- *The Concept of Main Entry*: The question of determining principal responsibility, *i.e.*, the concept of main entry under which the complete catalogue record of an item is entered, has been one of the most important themes in Anglo-American cataloguing codes. With the advent of online catalogues, the value of the main entry has been challenged but with no satisfactory resolution of how to fulfil its functions in its absence.
- *Number of Access Points Per Work and the Reference Structure of the Catalogue*: As the medium through which the bibliographic record is accessible to the user and the technology of catalogue production has developed from the book catalogue to the card catalogue to the computerised catalogue, there has been more potential for increasing the number of access points by which the complete record is accessible. The author, main entry catalogue, with references, that Panizzi and Jewett found to be the most usable and reasonable eventually evolved into the dictionary catalogue. Development in the application of main and added entries is an indication of better, more flexible and more comprehensive ways of access to bibliographic information.

* *The Concept of Authorship*: This concept is one of the most important organising elements in catalogues and bibliographic lists. A considerable portion of most codes has been devoted to the concept of authorship and to addressing its numerous conditions and problems. Due to the various conditions and complexities of attribution what constitutes authorship in cataloguing is a controversial issue with no satisfactory and comprehensive definition having been established.

- *Personal Authorship*: Although there has not been consensus as to the definition of what constitutes authorship, this concept has been accepted as one of the most important organising and identifying attributes of a work in the Anglo-American cataloguing tradition, as opposed to oriental traditions. Throughout the evolution of types of authorship, the term has been extended to persons other than writers of works such as editors, compilers of collections, artists, photographers, cartographers and composers of music. There have, however, been changes in the last two decades so that editors and compilers no longer have the same authorship status as previously.
- *Corporate Authorship*: It was the Anglo-American tradition that extended the concept of authorship to corporate bodies. The concept, though sometimes controversial in definition, was retained for more than a century through the work of Panizzi, Jewett, Cutter, AA, ALA, ALA, ICCP, and AACR1. Although not completely agreed upon, the concept was included in ICCP. The concept has since lost some of its force and, in AACR2, the term 'corporate authorship' has been changed to 'corporate responsibility'.

* *Forms of Heading*: A major portion of each cataloguing code is concerned with the form of the name chosen as heading. This has been a significant contribution, in most codes over the past one hundred and fifty years, towards the achievement of uniformity in bibliographic description and access. In most modern cataloguing codes, it is suggested that a single form of name be used for all the works of an author. Uniform titles are another approach to bringing uniformity in the treatment of the various manifestations of a work.
* *The Principle of Standardisation*: A major aim of modern cataloguing codes has been the achievement of standardisation in bibliographic information. This

concept has been embodied in different codes in the provision of rules for transcription of cataloguing data from uniform sources, standardisation of bibliographic description, and uniform rules for different types of material. Standardisation has evolved from an internal uniformity within individual catalogues into an international context.

* *Form of the Catalogue*: In relation to the impact of the physical form of the catalogue on the design of cataloguing codes, it can be concluded that, in most cases, the form of the catalogue is either explicitly indicated in the code or can be implied from the predominant form of the catalogue at the time a code was being prepared.

In conclusion, while there have been considerable changes and revisions in rules, cataloguing principles have changed little. Most of the principles formulated in the nineteenth century by Panizzi, Jewett and Cutter have been adopted in our present codes. How does the online environment differ from the manual environment and what are the capabilities of the online catalogue which, as many writers claim in the literature, demand changes in both cataloguing principles and rules?

Such questions and concepts require that, in the first place, a thorough comparison of the two environments be carried out to reveal how far the process of input, storage and output of bibliographic data is different in the new electronic environment. The study of these differences will help to understand better the possible influence of the catalogue environment on cataloguing principles and rules.

9

Online Catalogues and Card Catalogues: Identification of Areas of Similarities and Differences

INTRODUCTION

This chapter is prerequisite to the following chapters, in that it provides the background for the study of the possible influences of online catalogues on both the bibliographic record and on cataloguing principles.

A major aim is to explore the development of online catalogues, their basic features and capabilities and also to reveal the major differences that exist between them and manual catalogues.

This comparison will help identify the differences and similarities in the processes by which a bibliographic record and, on a larger scale, a catalogue, is created, manipulated and made accessible to the catalogue user for searching and retrieval.

In this context, the requirements of online systems which may influence cataloguing rules will also be discussed. A thorough understanding of the conceptual as well as the practical and technical differences and similarities between the online catalogue and the card catalogue will then help in an investigation of the relevance of current cataloguing principles and rules to the online catalogue. It is not the intention of the present chapter to discuss the influence of the features and capabilities of online catalogues on individual cataloguing principles or concepts..

In any comparison between the online catalogue and the manual catalogue, it seems appropriate to choose the card catalogue among the other forms of catalogues as an appropriate approach, because:

* The card catalogue has been and still is one of the most important manual systems in use for more than a century,
* It is the basis from which the present cataloguing standards have been developed, and
* It is the basis on which the structure and contents of online catalogues have been developed, *i.e.,* online catalogues are the logical successors to card catalogues.

It is not the intention of this chapter to reject the merits of the card catalogue. A realistic approach in comparing the online catalogue with the card catalogue should reveal advantages and disadvantages in both catalogues.

Although there is overall support among librarians for online catalogues, most librarians consider having knowledge about the card catalogue to be very useful for an understanding of the origins of the present online system, particularly the structure of the MARC format and how individual records fit into the idea of a catalogue system.

This was clearly the case in the general discussions about the card catalogue on the AUTOCAT list, 20 November 1994 to 3 December 1994, commenting on the need to teach the card catalogue in library schools. In fact, an understanding of the origins and underlying concepts from which the present environment has evolved will help us develop catalogue systems based on substantive assumptions. In short, this understanding and comparison of the two environments will help us to reassess, refine and redesign our standards for the construction of catalogues.

John Hickey states:

> "Even if nobody still uses catalogue cards, more of our professional assumptions that we recognize are based upon unit cards and card displays. it helps to

have some acquaintance with the previous technology."

It should be noted that online catalogues and card catalogues can be compared from different perspectives and according to different criteria. However, this study will compare them with regard to the processes by which bibliographic records and files are created, manipulated and organised on the one hand and searched, retrieved and displayed on the other. The differences between the online catalogue and the card catalogue will be explored in terms of the input, manipulation and output processes of bibliographic data.

ONLINE CATALOGUES: WHAT THEY ARE

Online catalogues are a norm today. they are not static. they have developed rapidly and will continue to evolve further. By utilising the various capabilities of computers and telecommunications, online catalogues are adding new features that make them totally different from traditional catalogues. Online catalogues are now gateways to larger information systems or, as Hopkins says, they are the 'one-stop information store'.

The online environment is an environment encompassing a wide range of information tools, both bibliographic and non-bibliographic. Library catalogues are now a small but very important component of the evolving online environment and are accessible through different tools in the networked environment, the *public access computer system* (PACS).

The global network is the Internet including various PACS components such as Gopher, WAIS (Wide Area Information Servers), Netscape and Mosaic and other access modes such as Archie and FTP (File Transfer Protocol) tools. The Webpages created by libraries and other information providers are becoming very pervasive and are often used both by librarians and endusers as linking sources for library information.

The same workstation serves as a means of navigating the whole world of the Internet. In the online environment not only are the information tools different from the traditional tools but also the whole concept of access to bibliographic information has changed. Time and location are irrelevant in searching the online environment.

DEVELOPMENTS AND DIRECTIONS OF ONLINE CATALOGUES

As a result of a significant growth in scientific and technological information after the second world war and a resulting expansion in library collections, manual systems could no longer respond effectively to the ever-growing information needs of society.

In terms of fast and effective retrieval of bibliographic information, the card catalogue had many disadvantages. Its large size, complexity and high costs of maintenance made it more and more difficult for libraries to maintain as an up to date searching tool. It became obvious that a more flexible tool was needed to cope with the new conditions of libraries.

It was thus necessary to think of alternative ways of constructing library catalogues that could be cost-effective, manageable and easy to use. Following on the application of computers in other fields, librarians became assured that the computer's theoretical capability to control library operations constituted adequate grounds for embracing a mechanised approach. As Weihs and Howarth point out, "It was necessary to investigate the computer as a relatively cost-effective tool to provide library catalogs."

Computer applications, however, first occurred in library activities other than the provision of public access to the catalogue. Computers were used in libraries mainly for house-keeping types of activities such as circulation control, acquisitions and serial control. This did not directly affect patrons' access to the library catalogue. Library automation began in the early 1960s with the rationale that "If a job could be done by computer, then the number of staff required to work at a defined level of expertise could be reduced".

Although some evidence of automation of library operations other than cataloguing is reported from the 1950s and 1960s, it is the MARC (Machine-Readable Cataloguing) project that has been considered as one of the most important factors in the development of automated catalogues.

With the beginning of the MARC Distribution Service in 1969, large libraries began to utilise MARC magnetic tapes mainly for automated cataloguing in the standard form provided by the Library of Congress. The usefulness of MARC services in cataloguing, along with the increasing availability of computer technology in the late 1960s, led to more developments in automated catalogues.

In response to the needs of small and medium-sized libraries without access to a mainframe computer, centralised cataloguing services gave way to the establishment of bibliographic utilities in the early 1970s.

The Online Computer Library Center, established in 1971, has been considered to be a significant factor in the development of automated catalogues. With the standard cataloguing services of such bibliographic utilities, libraries were able to utilise the power of computer technology in a cost-effective way.

The proliferation of MARC-based cataloguing led to the realisation of the importance of uniform, standardised bibliographic description as the nucleus of bibliographic services at national and international levels. The growth of bibliographic utilities in the early 1980s as well as developments in telecommunication technology accelerated the move towards centralised MARC-based cataloguing and the need for standardised descriptive cataloguing.

A significant factor further affecting the development of online catalogues was that some libraries began to use MARC bibliographic information for their circulation systems in an online mode. Using short bibliographic records rather than full MARC records for circulation operations, a number of libraries tried to help their patrons in checking whether an item was on loan, on order, or at binding.

This was a form of public enquiry module, which later developed into the online public access catalogue (OPAC). However, as Seal pointed out "The public enquiry module will often replicate the structure of a card or COM [Computer Output Microform] catalogue."

Another major factor leading to the rapid development of online public access catalogues was the contribution, by some library system vendors, of designing and developing public access modules as an important part of their turnkey systems. These vendors tried to incorporate a more sophisticated structure for the public enquiry module with more searching facilities. It should be noted that the early public enquiry systems were not integrated with other library modules, such as acquisitions and serials control.

Due to both the relative success and acceptability of online public enquiry modules, and pressures from patrons and librarians, libraries began to consider developing online public access catalogues (OPACs) with more bibliographic information, *i.e.*, full MARC records and more searching capabilities, such as keyword access and Boolean searching.

The possibility of utilising MARC records as the foundation of bibliographic databases led to the development of the concept of the Integrated Online Library Systems (IOLS) in which "The information that was input at the acquisitions stage would form a basis for the catalogue record which, in turn, would support all library functions. Thus, a number of integrated systems, such as GEAC, ULISYS, ATLAS, DOBIS, NOTIS and VTLS, were established incorporating this modular design.

The overall factors relating to the growing interest in online catalogues have been numerous. It is generally agreed that the most important factors that led to the rapid proliferation and development of online catalogues in the early 1980s were those related to their search, retrieval and display capabilities. Moreover, the opportunity of feedback from librarians and library patrons has provided a continuing momentum for upgrading the structure, contents and capabilities of online catalogues.

Tracing the historical development of online public access catalogues, Hildreth and Matthews identify three generations of OPACs. This categorisation is based on the features and capabilities of online catalogues in the processes of input, storage and output of bibliographic information.

Matthews claims that most of the existing online catalogues are still in the first or second generations and only a few systems have moved beyond first-generation. Added to the three generations identified by Hildreth and Matthews, recent advances in OPACs using graphical user interfaces (GUIs) have introduced a fourth generation to online catalogues.

FIRST-GENERATION ONLINE CATALOGUES

Derived from circulation or cataloguing systems, first-generation online catalogues were in fact computerised card catalogues with almost the same traditional features. In contrast to the patrons' expectations from their use of computerised database systems, these new library catalogues provided limited author, title and controlled vocabulary subject heading access points. For this reason, first-generation online catalogues have been criticised as having no advantages over the card catalogue.

Searching in first-generation online catalogues was essentially based upon pre-coordinated information retrieval principles and was possible only through inputting the exact form of words or phrases. In contrast to searching in card catalogues, the patron had great difficulties as he/she had to input something into the system so that it could respond to his/her query.

As this was possible only through inputting the exact form of words or phrases, which was difficult to remember, searching was not as successful as the searcher expected. Keyword access was not available and refining a search by further limiting it to elements such as date of publication, language or country of publication was not possible. The interfaces, which were usually menu-driven, replicated traditional catalogues in their form of access by providing mainly phrase access to separate subject headings, title, and author indexes. Output and display of search results generally had a single format.

SECOND-GENERATION ONLINE CATALOGUES

With further developments in information technology, it was possible to provide a more sophisticated system for input, storage and output of bibliographic information. Second-generation online catalogues are a departure from traditional card catalogues and incorporate many new features for the provision of effective access.

In contrast to the limited input, storage and output capabilities of first-generation online catalogues, second-generation online catalogues are characterised as being powerful tools for the searching of bibliographic information. Keyword search, Boolean keyword search, cross index search and increasing or reducing of search results are among the features of second-generation online catalogues. Hildreth writes:

Today's second-generation online catalogs represent a marriage of the library catalogue and conventional online information retrieval (IR) systems familiar to librarians who search online abstracting and indexing databases via DIALOG, BRS, ORBIT, MEDLINE, etc.

Improved card catalogue-like searching and browsing capabilities have been joined with the conventional IR keyword and Boolean searching approaches. Many online catalogs support the ability to restrict searches to specified record fields, to perform character masking and/or right-hand truncation, and to limit the results by date, language, place of publication, etc. Also, bibliographic records may be viewed and printed in a number of different display formats.

However, it should be noted that there are a number of major differences between online catalogues and these IR systems that make second-generation online catalogues easier searching tools. With a combination of different search methods, the user is offered possibilities that were not available in first generation online catalogues.

Due to improvements in the design of database management softwares, the structure and content of bibliographic records in second-generation online catalogues may be enhanced by incorporating full records augmented by information such as tables of contents, summaries, content notes, abstracts and links to full electronic texts. Considerable increase in the length of fields was another improvement in second-generation systems.

Interfaces are usually in two modes, menu-driven and command-driven. this makes the interaction between the user and the catalogue more flexible. In terms of user assistance, these catalogues provide more options including, for example, help screens, error messages and suggestive prompts. Ease of use and user-friendliness are two major features of today's second-generation online catalogues.

THIRD-GENERATION ONLINE CATALOGUES

Only a few systems have moved beyond second-generation online catalogues into third-generation online catalogues with enhanced or more sophisticated features. Due to the growing sophistication and availability of technology, new capabilities are being added to online catalogues making them more adaptive to the needs of library patrons. Free text search, enriched database search and simultaneous journal citation searching are among the retrieval capabilities in third generation online catalogues. Furthermore, the mode of interaction has been developed to the point of conversational, adaptive dialogue and the bibliographic format can be tailored according to user preference. Operational assistance such as automatic, context-based correction is also available.

FOURTH-GENERATION ONLINE CATALOGUES

Beginning from the late 1980s, a most recent development in online public access catalogues has been achieved in providing easy access to bibliographic information by using graphical user interfaces (GUIs) such as Windows. These systems, which can be considered as fourth-generation catalogues, have moved away from the traditional menu-type interfaces and are more associated with client server and graphical user interface.

They use WIMP (windows, icons, mouse and pointers) interfaces to speed and simplify searching. With the Windows-style user interface available through PCs (personal computers, *i.e.*, intelligent, and not dumb terminals), there is much more functionality. In these systems the user has the flexibility to click on various buttons, each of which carries a special function.

Nevertheless, these systems do not eliminate but augment the keystroke access. There is also the possibility of using function keys for different purposes when keyboards are involved. In general, access is via mouse or keyboard or a combination of both. Searching capabilities in the Windows version of OPACs are greater than those found in other generations of online catalogues. Pointer capabilities allow the searcher to select exactly the term he/she is looking for, while pull-down menus provide additional options to make searching even more useful. By using scroll bars and pull-down menus, browsing in different indexes is very simple.

With the capability of post-Boolean searching, the search software also attempts to interpret users' search requests in order to present matches of greater or lesser interest to the user. This is called relevance ranking of the search terms. Similar to second and third generation online catalogues, these systems search for terms through using an implicit Boolean 'AND'.

Other Boolean operators such as 'OR' and 'NOT' can also be used to narrow down search results or such search strings can be constructed using the mouse alone. In addition, access has been enhanced by text retrieval qualifiers such as 'language', 'date' and 'form' of the text.

With this feature, it is possible to include new data elements that help in the better identification of the sought item. Integral or add-on text retrieval modules to provide range searching, related term searching, wild card features, adjacency and proximity are supplied by some systems.

One of the recent additional advanced features of fourth-generation OPACs is the 'hypertext' function. Through this function, any word that the user selects or highlights can be used to search all the fields and subfields in all the records in the database for any occurrence of that word. This dynamic feature helps the searcher to navigate the database to find more relevant sources of information.

ONLINE CATALOGUES: HOW THEY DIFFER FROM MANUAL CATALOGUES

There have been some general attempts in the literature of the past decade to briefly compare different types of library catalogues. However, these comparisons have not been concerned with the concepts that underlie the nature and structure of the catalogue. In the following parts, the two types of catalogue will be compared in terms of the creation, manipulation and search/retrieval/display of bibliographic records.

CREATION AND MANIPULATION OF BIBLIOGRAPHIC RECORDS

Structure and Content of Bibliographic Records

By 'structure of the record' is meant the bibliographic description consisting of data elements arranged and presented in a given order, such as card catalogue formats and MARC formats. It is generally understood that the medium, via which bibliographic records are created, manipulated and made accessible to the searcher, influences their structure and content.

The computer has made possible the enriching of the structure and contents of bibliographic records. While the space limitations of 3" x 5" cards generally restrict the level of data elements to be entered in a record, the content of a bibliographic record in an online catalogue makes it possible and desirable to include more data elements such as those fixed-length data elements indexed in field 008 in the USMARC bibliographic format and even data such as summaries, tables of content, and full texts. This issue has been of major interest to librarians and system designers during the past decade and there have been some proposals in this regard.

User studies of the early 1980s showed that most users of online catalogues would like to have access to tables of contents, back-of-the-book indexes and summaries. Other suggestions have included the titles of essays in collected works or festschriften, book introductions, book jacket material, and the assignment of more subject headings. With the advent and further development of online catalogues it has become possible to assign a larger number of access points to bibliographic records. In comparison to the conventional main and added entries in the card catalogue, any data element in a bibliographic record may be designated as an access point.

MARC Format and Categorisation of Data Elements

As a set of standards for the identifying, storing and communicating of cataloguing information, MARC has significantly contributed to the growth of library automation and to the development of online catalogues. Although the MARC record was conceived as an automated version of the catalogue card, the structure is flexible enough to store bibliographic information in more detailed fields and subfields due to the requirements of automated systems for separate identification of data elements.

While the medium for the card catalogue is the 3" x 5 " card with a fixed, less flexible format, most online catalogues use MARC as a communication format for the exchange of bibliographic information. In this regard, MARC communicates bibliographic information with more flexibility than the card catalogue.

With the machine-readable format, in which the bibliographic information on a record has been broken down into fields and subfields, it is possible to separately identify each data element. This approach also allows for inclusion or exclusion of data elements for output as desired.

Based on the MARC format, bibliographic records can be created and tailored according to the specific needs of the library without either discarding standardisation or diminishing the quality of cataloguing.

In the card environment, cataloguing depends on a longer process of manual checking against other catalogues, the ordering of card sets and receiving and interfiling them in the catalogue. This process in online catalogues is done more comprehensively and easily by subscribing to bibliographic utilities or by purchasing MARC products and downloading the needed records into the library's automated system.

MARC records permit a fuller level of description. more data elements to be included in the description and many more data elements to be assigned as access points for retrieval. A MARC record also includes other data, including non-bibliographic data that are used for catalogue maintenance. There is now a trend towards preserving detailed bibliographic records in machine-readable form.

The amount and type of information that constitute a 'full bibliographic record' is certainly open to debate, but since the late 1960s the accepted standard has been the MARC format. The data that can be contained in a MARC record include the entire spectrum of information normally presented on catalogue cards plus a great deal of other potentially valuable categorizing information that can be encoded in fixed elements and elsewhere on record.

However, MARC format has been criticised for being an electronic version of the catalogue card and for its limited accommodation of hierarchically structured information. There are also some problems with the MARC tagging and indexing of data elements that influence retrieval in online databases. Systems may differ from one another in the indexing of fields and it is often difficult to find out what fields are indexed by a given system. This results in retrieval and display problems, leading to user confusion.

Bibliographic Standardization

In comparison to manual systems, the online environment gives much more emphasis to the concept of standardisation. Although the idea of standardised bibliographic description seems to have first appeared with derived cataloguing and the sale of Library of Congress cards in 1898 and later with the introduction of the *National Union Catalogue* (NUC), it was not until the 1970s that the application of computers to library operations and the advent of online catalogues gave to standardisation a much more significant role.

With regard to the description, choice and form of data elements to be included in a bibliographic record, conformity to standards, *e.g.*, cataloguing codes, ISBDs and MARC formats, are vital to online catalogues.

Unlike libraries of two decades ago with their independent card catalogues, libraries of today often create their own catalogue records according to national and/or international standards for the purposes of easy communication of and access to bibliographic information. Now, it is common for libraries of any size to participate in networks. One result of this, as Wajenberg points out, is an ever-increasing pressure to conform to national and international standards.

Uniformity and consistency are basic requirements for effective bibliographical control. The rapid growth of shared cataloguing systems, developments in bibliographic utilities and the need for bibliographic exchange between databases in the last decade has led to a stronger reaffirmation of the value of standardisation in bibliographic records. Standardisation helps bibliographic records to be uniformly created, manipulated, exchanged and retrieved.

As the cataloguing community moves closer to making the ideal of universal bibliographic control a reality through local, regional, provincial, national, continental and international networks, all libraries assume the responsibility of maintaining standards requisite to maintaining the network. Integration and standar-dization are the keywords in the increasing move-ments towards, and promotion of, interconnected telecommunicating automated systems.

Despite this emphasis on the significance of standardisation in the online catalogue, this concept has been considered only in the inputting of data elements in bibliographic description and not in the output and display, whereas in the card catalogue both input and output are standardised.

For example, both the card catalogue and the online catalogue conform to the ISBD standard for the input format, *i.e.*, the order of areas, punctuation and levels of description. However, in online catalogues the output format is not fixed as in card catalogues and may be flexible.

As Gorman and associates state, the standardisation and formalisation of description and access points is crucial to the online environment and to the effective exchange of bibliographic records. As an important concept that has developed over the last hundred years to meet the changing forms of the catalogue and the needs of the profession, standardisation will continue in the future and as Wajenberg points out, at an accelerated pace.

Input Inconsistencies and Level of Tolerance

A major difference between a manual and an automated catalogue lies in the fact that the creation of bibliographic records for online catalogues demands more precision and logic in terms of typography, spelling, punctuation, spacing, coding of fields and subfields.

This is a critical requirement for computerised systems, since such errors can result in a serious separation or an improper sequencing of entries and therefore can lead to the irretrievability of records. In other words, any errors, even if very small, for instance a faulty keystroke, will be magnified in the online catalogue.

However, in a manual system, when filing catalogue cards or when retrieving information, the human brain can often ignore such minor errors and treat them as if they are correct and file them in the right place.

Errors and inconsistencies can be corrected in the process of filing cards, whereas in the automated catalogue there is a lower level of tolerance towards such errors as variations in format, filing and indexing, and literal and logical inconsistencies within the catalogue. In general, the online catalogue is far less forgiving of cataloguing and typographical errors than is the card catalogue.

CONSTRUCTION AND MAINTENANCE OF THE CATALOGUE

Structure and Content of the Catalogue

By 'structure of the catalogue' is meant how the catalogue is built up, the kinds and content of files and indexes constituting it and the relationships of these files and indexes to one another.

For example, a card catalogue, whether in dictionary or divided form, may include different files such as:

* Authors
* References
* Titles
* Subject headings and
* Shelflists

The advent of the online catalogue has given new dimensions to the catalogue's structure. It is generally maintained that the online catalogue can support a more complex yet more dynamic structure than that of the card catalogue. The online file may be independent and self-contained, it may be related to files of similar scope and structure or it may be integrated with other files such as holdings, circulations, acquisitions and authority files.

The online catalogue provides services that were not part of the traditional library catalogue. Access to circulation information, status information, holding information, indexing of special collections, serials and so on have become possible through the development of the contents and structure of the catalogue.

While the structure of the card catalogue is based on the concept of several discrete entries for a single item, the online catalogue maintains a single-entry structure for a single item but with several indexes as access points to records in the master file.

Emphasising what constitutes the structure of an online catalogue, Svenonius states that:

* In its general sense *structure* refers to an aggregate of elements related, or arranged with respect, to each other . . . The structure of a catalogue or catalogue database consists of bibliographic, authority, and holdings records arranged in a given order and referencing one another through a variety of syndetic relationships. Thus, filing rules, together with ordering devices, such as the main entry and see and see also references, define a catalogue structure....The structure of biblio-graphic descriptions consists of data elements arranged and presented in a given order. Thus, card catalogue formats and MARC format represent different but related bibliographic structures, the former intended for display and the latter for communication.

In terms of addition to the contents of the catalogue, the online catalogue has a growing ability to enlarge its own scope. Results of a nationwide survey on the use of online catalogues in the United States revealed that respondents were enthusiastic about accessing journal articles, newspaper articles, encyclopaedias, dissertations, films and government documents through online catalogues.

Other studies showed that users wanted the catalogue to be expanded to include journal titles, government publications and dissertations and journal citations, indexes to collections, content services, abstracts and book reviews. Thus, it can be concluded that the contents of the online catalogue will be expanded in parallel with developments in the technology of catalogue construction.

Integration of the Catalogue

Integration has been considered as an important feature of the recent online catalogue in the sense that different parts of the library automated system are integrated through the use and manipulation of the same record as the basis for different library operations. In such an integration, a single master bibliographic record is tagged and can be manipulated for different library operations, such as acquisitions, cataloguing and circulation. A consequence of integration of the online catalogue, as pointed out by Buckland is that bibliographic information in different parts of a library system, as well as other useful information, can be accessible to users and to other libraries. Such a concept indicates the impor-tance of uniformity and standardisation of bibliographic records in the online environment.

Another interpretation of integration in the online environment is related to various methods of access to bibliographic information. In such an integration, different files and databases can be accessible via the same terminal. This concept has opened up a new era in bibliographic services and is considered as a significant factor in the enhancement of the catalogue. There are increasing attempts to build information systems with integrated access to different types of information services. The trend towards the integration of book trade bibliographic databases and A and I services with the online public access catalogue is an approach which makes the library catalogue a window to the whole bibliographic apparatus, a concept not feasible in the manual catalogue. These different kinds of integration have implications for cataloguing principles.

Authority Control

Authority control ensures the consistent use of names, series and subjects. No bibliographic record can be entered into the system until all assigned headings under which it can be searched are verifiable against the approved authority file. In a manual system, it is a time-consuming and costly operation and requires the services of skilled staff.

There are many advantages to authority control in an online catalogue: in terms of maintaining cataloguing operations, it is particularly advantageous when major revisions to name and subject headings have to be done.

In terms of searching, the actual search that the user does is via an authority control file. What the user inputs to the system is automatically switched through the index to the correct form. In the online environment, the authority records are usually linked with bibliographic records.

There are a number of reasons for the resurgent interest in authority control in the online environment. The various difficulties that users have had with searching names and, as Potter points out, the inconsistencies and errors in the records used to build the databases for online catalogues have led to new attention being given to the concept of authority control. For example, the ability to search personal names in either direct order or through initials has led to the enhancement of the scope and structure of authority files.

Another major difference in the process of authority control between a manual system and an automated system is that correction or change of any heading in the card catalogue is a time consuming operation, whereas this task in some automated systems is to a great extent facilitated through a 'global change' which automatically generates a correction or change in all relevant records. Although authority control in the online environment is at an early stage of development and, at present, only a few systems have operational authority control modules, the online catalogue's features and capabilities have given a new dimension to the notion of authority control.

Much work needs to be done into the need for authority control in online catalogues. access by name will decrease and the concept of name references will change and the need for authority files in the traditional sense may become less important.

In making the concept of authority control in the online environment clearer, Gorman points out that:

* It is evident that traditional reference structure was designed for premachine catalogues. The ideas that underlie references have been taken over in machine systems and incorporated into the notion of authority files. An authority file consists, very simply, of the approved form of access point for a person, body, or title, together with the references to that approved form and links to other related authority records. We have already seen that, in the computer catalogue environment, the distinction between a main and added entry access point no longer has meaning. The authority record takes this progress a step further. It, in effect, abolishes the distinction between an access point and a reference.... In other words, two of the basic assumptions of traditional catalogue codes—the main entry and the distinction between a heading and a reference—have survived.

Filing Rules and Problems

In any library catalogue, access points are usually filed according to alphanumeric order, which is a conventional arrangement applicable to most information systems accessed by human beings. However, filing is different in the manual catalogue and the automated catalogue.

The arrangement of access points has always been of particular interest to librarians and there have been a number of specific filing rules published to date. The *ALA Filing Rules,* The *Library of Congress Filing Rules* developed by John Rather, and the rules developed by the British Library Filing Committee are among the most important. Although developments in filing rules have been strongly in the direction of commonsense and are oriented towards the intelligent user, users actually have major problems in identifying the exact location of a heading in the sequential order of a large card catalogue.

In a manual system, filing is flexible and can be executed according to the order which seems desirable to the catalogue user, whereas, in a computer catalogue, it must follow the logic of the computer.

Filing in a manual system follows the principle of *file as if*: that is, the form and order in which access points are arranged is according to the interpretation of the librarian with the supposition that the arrangement would be the most desirable to the user. For instance, the number *3* can be filed as if it were the word *three*.

The use of the computer has influenced filing practices and it is generally agreed that the principle of *file as is,* which is necessitated by the introduction of computer filing, has more validity in the computer environment. This principle states that characters or words should be filed as they are and not as if they were something else. for example, the number '3' as *3,* and 'three' as *three.* This realisation of the logical as well as the practical differences between filing in a manual catalogue and a computer catalogue came with the earliest attempts in the application of computers to bibliographical work. Current filing rules, which were developed for manual systems, proved not to be effective in a computer environment.

Users of online catalogues can encounter many problems when searching for bibliographic information. Due to different software specifications, computer-based filing has not been entirely standardised and the burden of thinking, for example, about the exact form of access points and the way punctuation and non alphabetic symbols are treated is left to the user.

In manual filing it is possible, by a simple convention, to ignore stop words such as 'the', 'and', 'of', 'a', 'an', etc. at the beginning of titles whereas, in the computer catalogue, this issue demands special programming and in some cases they are difficult to handle. The treatment of punctuation poses another problem for the computer catalogue. while symbols, such as commas, apostro-phes, periods and hyphens, may cause problems in the manual catalogue, they are considered as characters and are located in their 'logical' places by the computer unless software is created to overcome these difficulties.

While the presence or absence of punctuation may be important in access points, they may or may not be important for online display. Diacritics and extended character sets to accommodate non-roman scripts are other important issues in computer filing of entries.

In sum, the logical arrangement of data elements in the computer has implications for the form of access points in the online catalogue. As an example, see the treatment of "Sir," which comes before forenames and thus interferes with filing. This can be seen in the change of some rules for the form of headings in the second edition of the Anglo-American Cataloguing Rules.

In fact, the incorporation/modification of some rules in AACR2 concerning the filing of data elements has arisen in response to the requirements of filing in the computer catalogue. For example, the inclusion of given names in parentheses in cases where the initials are not adequate for identification of authors with identical surnames is to respond to computer filing.

In terms of conference headings the form and order of the number, the date and the location of a conference in parentheses is an illustration of filing relevant to a computer. The place of numeric identifying elements in music uniform titles, *e.g.*, "Pianos (2)" rather than "2 Pianos", is another example of this issue.

SEARCHING, RETRIEVAL, AND DISPLAY OF BIBLIOGRAPHIC RECORDS

User Interfaces

A significant difference between the online catalogue and the card catalogue comes at the stage in which the user interacts with the catalogue, *i.e.*, bibliographic records can be searched, retrieved and displayed. Online catalogues are here considered to be a great departure from card catalogues and it seems that there will be more developments in this regard in the near future.

While the card catalogue is a self-evident medium with a clear physical existence, the online catalogue is not revealed to the users and is not easy to grasp in their first interactions with it. In an online environment, the user cannot immediately understand the catalogue or its structure, coverage and searching mechanisms unless he/she interacts with the system and tries different options for searching and displaying of bibliographic information.

Despite these limitations of the online catalogue, users show a high degree of satisfaction with the variety of features and capabilities it has at the output stage. *Graphical user interfaces* (GUIs) have made interaction with and use of online systems easier and more desirable. It seems likely that, in the near future, new generations of online catalogues will incorporate intelligent interfaces and sophisticated search/retrieval/display facilities.

Interactivity

Online catalogues have often been defined in the literature as 'interactive' catalogues. In the *Dictionary of Information Technology, 'interactivity'* is defined as "system or piece of software that allows communication between the user and the computer in a conversational mode." Interactivity is considered as a major advantage of online catalogues over card catalogues. "It is this interaction between the user and the computer system that really sets apart the online catalogue from the other types of library catalogs"

Unlike in the card environment, if the user does not input a query in the system, the system will not respond to him/her. This process, namely the action of inputting a query by the user and responding by the computer, occurs quickly in real time and in a dynamic and progressive way.

In sum, the concept of interactivity in the online catalogue is well defined below:

> "Online catalogues can be reactive and able to respond to the user in an intelligent way. This can be used to indicate what searching options are available, to correct operational errors, to suggest alternative items which might particularly match the search criteria and to guide the user through a long search. The reader can then be given help and feedback from the system itself, without needing to consult library staff. This approach is impossible in a card or a COM catalogue".

With the introduction of the online interactive catalogue, it has also become possible to record how users interact with the system and search the catalogue. In this way, *i.e.*, through 'transaction log' analysis, librarians are able to check how users approach the catalogue and how frequently search terms appear, as well as to examine other aspects of search/retrieval problems, *e.g.*, users' errors and unsuccessful searches. Many catalogue use studies have been and are being done using transaction logs as a means of data collection.

User's Input Errors and the Catalogue's Level of to Lerance

As pointed out earlier, online catalogues are less forgiving than card catalogues in terms of any kind of error, either in the input stage by the cataloguer, or in the searching stage by the user. A general problem with computers is that they are usually unforgiving of errors. if the user makes the smallest of mistakes, they will not necessarily recognise it as a mistake, and even if they do they will often not offer help in correcting the mistake. However, there are systems being developed that recognise errors, display the type of error, and offer help to the searcher.

User Assistance

In comparison to card catalogues, online catalogues have the ability to provide user assistance in a variety of ways and at different levels. Mitev classifies such aids in four categories as 'retrieval aids', 'linguistic aids', 'navigational aids', and 'semantic aids'. This is a major advantage over the card catalogue in that the system can respond to the user's problems and help him/her as to what the next move to achieve the result would be. Online catalogues have developed, over the past decade, different devices for providing help to their users in the different stages of searching the system.

Most online catalogues have the ability to customise help messages, screen displays and system prompts according to the needs of the user. Online assistance enables the user to influence the dialogue at all times in a clear way. This is not possible in manual systems.

User Satisfaction

It is generally stated that there is a higher level of satisfaction with online catalogues than with card catalogues and that users prefer this new form of the catalogue to the traditional card catalogue. Matthews, Lawrence, and Ferguson, over 90% of users like the online catalogue and almost 75% of users rate the online catalogue as being better than the card, book or microform catalogue.

It is also interesting to note that this high level of satisfaction is consistent across all types of libraries. Lewis, in reporting the results of different user studies, states that: "Users have a strong preference for online catalogs over card catalogs, and they very much want the new technology to succeed". Balaam and Burton and Hawkins report user satisfaction with OPACs despite their shortcomings.

A reason for preference of the online catalogue, even in its primitive form, to the card catalogue is related to its search and retrieval capabilities. It is also safe to assume that, as online catalogues continue to mature in terms of user interface, enhanced content and access, the level of satisfaction will be even greater.

Another point worth mentioning is that the result of different online use studies show that use of the catalogue and use of the collection have increased with the introduction of online interactive catalogues. This, in turn, leads to higher user satisfaction as he/she becomes able to fulfil his/her information needs in easier, faster and more effective ways.

A major group of OPAC users are librarians themselves who are among the strong supporters of such systems. In a series of discussions in the electronic mail discussion group PACS-L@UHUPVM1.UH.EDU, 7-20 April 1994 and in response to Nicholson Baker's "Annals of Scholarship: Discards" published in the *New Yorker*, 4 April 1994, concerning the closing or storing of card catalogues, most librarians supported online catalogues as being superior to card catalogues.

Charles Hildreth considers Baker's article to be a nostalgic approach to the historical value of card catalogues. For Hildreth card catalogues represent a dead-end technology and their maintaining would be very expensive. Instead, online catalogues are open-ended, with a pure potentiality that will never reach its 'final' form.

Walt Crawford asserts that online catalogues are ever-evolving systems that, when reasonably well designed, offer substantially better access and, unlike card catalogues, can be maintained as well as improved.

Robin Alston supports online catalogues for their advantages over card catalogues in many ways and states that a major advantage is that most of the key elements on a record in an online catalogue are searchable, while massive amount of information on catalogue cards are not retrievable. Although there are deficiencies in OPACs, as Baker expresses very well from the point of view of a scholar, online catalogues will keep improving, while card catalogues have not any potential for improvement.

Searching and Retrieval Capabilities

With regard to searching capabilities, the online catalogue is a significant departure from traditional library catalogues. One of its most interesting features and a major advantage over the card catalogue, is the ability of the user to search for the needed item in a variety of ways that are not available in the manual catalogue.

Online catalogues are able to generate both a greater number of access points as well as new searching capabilities that enable the user to search the catalogue with little information to hand. In addition to controlled-vocabulary searches by author, title and subject headings, for which relevant indexes have been created and maintained in the online catalogue, it is possible to search bibliographic records through access points such as other title information, series, standard numbers and any other significant data through keyword searching.

In general, although there are still shortcomings in the searching capabilities of online catalogues, particularly in subject searching, the findings of various studies indicate that users show much enthusiasm in online catalogues' searching capabilities. The following types of searches in the online catalogue are not available in the manual catalogue and can help the user to execute a greater variety of searches:

Keyword Searching

Keyword access is a very powerful search tool and can create much greater flexibility for the user to search item(s) of which he/she has not exact information. This is extremely difficult in the card catalogue.

Keywords, *i.e.,* every indexed word in the bibliographic description, mainly headings, titles, other title information, contents notes and subjects, are appropriate alternatives for the catalogue user who cannot match the exact bibliographic information in the catalogue.

When searching the catalogue, it is not necessary for the user to enter the exact form and order of words. while keyword searching is an alternative to controlled-vocabulary searching, it can also act as a complement to it. The potential value of keyword searching has often been highlighted in the literature. For example, reporting the result of a transaction log analysis of the Colorado University Library OPAC, Wallace found that 53% of searches were keyword searches.

In many online catalogues, there are options for limiting keyword searching to fields such as author, title, subject, or cross index. Among these options, title keyword searching provides a useful tool both as a substitute for subject access and for specific items when the exact or full title is not known.

Some online catalogues provide keyword searching of abstracts and a number of systems extend this capability to the entire text of a document, a trend that is becoming common in many online search services.

It is extremely difficult to search authors under their forenames in manual catalogues, whereas in online catalogues with keyword access it has become possible to execute such searches. The same capability is available in the online catalogue for searching compound words of which the exact, full form is not known. However, keyword searching has its disadvantages: in some cases too many records may be retrieved and some records may be irrelevant to the searcher's need.

Boolean Searching

Influenced by A&I (*Abstracting and Indexing*) services, many online catalogues have the ability to run Boolean searches. With the use of Boolean operators, such as AND, OR, NOT, it is possible to define subsets of the desired subject or concept when two or more sets are combined.

Specificity is what Boolean searching offers: the user can combine two or more terms in a search statement and narrow or broaden the parameters of the subject of his/her interest. Matthews points out that:

"In most OPACs, a Boolean 'and' is assumed when two or more terms are entered in a search statement, especially if the search is conducted on a single field or type of information, such as author, title, or subject".

Truncation

As in A&I services, some online catalogues permit the user to broaden the set of records to be retrieved by shortening the search word through entering a special truncation symbol immediately after the shortened search word, or before it, or within the word. Most online catalogues perform right-hand truncation implicitly rather than explicitly. This feature of online catalogues provides greater flexibility for the user to broaden access to the necessary information when character-by-character exact match does not help. It should be noted, however, that users have difficulty in understanding and using this type of searching in online catalogues. In some cases, truncation also results in either too many hits or irrelevant records. This has implications for cataloguing principles and rules.

Browse Searching

When the search aim is not specific, the desired results are not precisely known in advance or the correct terms for representing the user's query are not known at the outset, "browse searching is the most useful and preferred approach". Browsing, which is a good feature of the card catalogue, is becoming available in the form of browsable indexes in more and more online catalogues.

The natural searchability that browsing offers satisfies users. In this type of searching, lists of index terms are usually presented in alphabetical order and the searcher can navigate the database by going forward or backward through the desired index until he/she finds the index term which may lead him/her to relevant records.

A novel interface for browsing, which can improve access and the effectiveness of end-user searching, has been developed very recently. Using a GUI, some advanced online systems offer improved searching functionality by providing a multi-windowed view of data stored on a relational database management system.

This novel interface can help the user to search bibliographic databases in a multi-windowed environment, each of which represents an index of the catalogue with scrollable windows. This approach has the advantage that the user can browse different indexes on the same screen to filter their content and find the most relevant items.

Among the indexes are: author, title, publication date, document type, language and subject headings. It would be possible, therefore, to match different indexes and find related documents which have the same values, *i.e.*, identical data elements. This facility helps the user in appreciating the actual contents of the database through its different indexes and removes the problem of search specification using values that are not present.

Hypertext Searching

A most recent addition to searching capabilities in information retrieval systems, including advanced online catalogues, is hypertext searching or 'hypersearch'. Non linear, associative hypertext systems offer a search approach that attempts to more closely mimic human thought processes. It is stated that hypertext, when used with bibliographic records, could overcome the static nature of existing catalogues.

The hypersearch facility, such as that one offered by GoPAC from Data trek, can simply be applied by highlighting a term or clicking on a highlighted term in the record. The system will search for any occurrences of the highlighted term in all fields and subfields or all authority-controlled fields in all records in the database.

The number of postings associated with the term will be indicated or the system will show a brief display of those related records which contain the same term. The term is highlighted in the retrieved records so that the searcher can see in which field it is located and can decide on the relevance of the record to his/her information need.

During the display of related records, the possibility exists for the user to shift his/her focus and to continue a hypertext search on new and more relevant data elements. In this way, the hypertext facility helps users to navigate throughout the catalogue to find possible related works.

Author-title Search

In most online catalogues, there is an option for searching a known item through the author's surname combined with any keyword from the title. This is the clearest way to execute known-item searches. However, in those systems which restrict the search to author surname and the first word of the title, this type of search has the disadvantage of retrieving too many records when the author's surname is a common name, such as 'Smith', 'Johnson', and so on, or the title of the item begins with common words, such as 'Introduction', 'History', and so on.

Another disadvantage is that, in most cases, users do not remember the first word of titles and thus fail to use this type of search in online catalogues. Nevertheless, it is very useful, for example, for searching titles on reading lists and it emphasises the importance of surname field.

ID Numbers

Another type of search in some online catalogues is possible through ID numbers. Among possible ID numbers are: call number. *International Standard Book Number* (ISBN). International Standard Serial Number (ISSN). document number. computer system number, *e.g.,* OCLC (Online Computer Library Center), RLIN (Research Libraries Information Network) or WLN

(Western Library Network). local system number, *e.g.*, accession number. These types of search are usually performed by library staff.

Other Searching Sapabilities

Other types of searches in online catalogues include full-text searching, proximity searching, adjacency searching which are available only in a few online catalogues. These new searching capabilities in the online catalogue have revolutionised the way in which users search the library catalogue. The results of different use studies indicate that the searching patterns of users in online catalogues have changed. In other words, the online catalogue has affected the ways in which users search for bibliographic information in library catalogues.

Output and Display

Display of bibliographic information is another major aspect in which the online catalogue departs greatly from the card catalogue. Surveying OPACs in a number of Canadian academic libraries, Cherry report that screen display is the best developed area in online catalogues.

The last step at the catalogue, viewing a search result through the display of the bibliographic record(s), is what the user actually gains from the system. The quality of such a display affects the overall usefulness of the catalogue. While the form and content of bibliographic records in the input/output format in the card catalogue are fixed, the online catalogue permits a flexible format, with the possibility of displaying bibliographic information in a variety of ways and at different levels.

The ways in which bibliographic information is presented in the online catalogue in response to searches vary from system to system. Each system has its own techniques for manipulation of a search result. This is impossible in the card technology where space limitations and the fixed form of bibliographic description do not permit any flexibility or manipulation of search results.

The level of bibliographic description is usually flexible and can be designed according to the user's needs. On the other hand

and from a system perspective, as Boll points out, there is a range of display formats suitable for a computer screen or a page printout rather than a three by five inch card.

Online display formats usually include:

* 'Brief-listing display' which shows, on one or more screens, the overall results of a search through 'author', 'title' and 'date' of publication,
* 'Medium-level display' containing the standard bibliographic description, access points and status and location information, and
* 'Full bibliographic display' which shows full description with all access points, including added entries, and may contain summary and/or table of contents of the item.

Another major difference between the online catalogue and the card catalogue is the way in which data elements in a record make up and represent a bibliographic record. Reynolds points out three functions in this regard: the labelling of data elements, the sequence in which data elements appear and the spacing between them.

The online catalogue can include identifying labels before data elements for distinguishing the bibliographic text in a record. Labels may be highlighted, or displayed in uppercase characters or in a different colour. In relation to the sequence of data elements appearing in a bibliographic record, there is a fairly high degree of uniformity among online catalogues.

As in the card catalogue, the arrangement usually follows the numerical sequence of MARC tags or the ISBD order. Some online catalogues do not incorporate ISBD punctuation on the basis that users do not comprehend such 'secret punctuation'.

However, it should be noted that a number of problems may arise from the differences in the input and output formats in the online catalogue. A problem which would be difficult for the user to understand is that the relationships of headings to bibliographic data may not be clear to him/her.

For example, the role of persons associated with the work or manifestations of a work may not be distinguished in the way these names are displayed on the screen in conjunction with the title of the work. Therefore, the user may miss what he/she is seeking. In short, output in online catalogues is not controlled by cataloguing standards.

Limiting Search Results

Limiting or restricting the search results is a good feature of online catalogues and seems to have been copied from A&I services. Crawford, this capability of online catalogues should be offered or performed only when the search yields a large result. Matthews points out that assisting the searcher in refining or expanding a search shows the powerful capability of the online information retrieval system over the card or COM catalogue.

In terms of refining the search results, the online catalogue has a great advantage over the card catalogue. When many records are retrieved in response to a search, the user may want to restrict them to certain aspects that might seem more relevant to his/her need.

This is not possible in the card catalogue whereas, in most online catalogues, due to the assigning of some subfields in the MARC format as active and searchable, the user has the opportunity of further restricting, reducing or narrowing the search results. For example, the searcher can limit all the search results to works in a particular language, in a particular type of material or all the works published prior to, during or after a given date, or even works of a certain level of difficulty. This is done by specifying certain control fields and other MARC elements that can be used for limiting search results.

With further developments in online catalogues it is expected that the limiting of search results will become more sophisticated and more flexible for the user. In addition to the usual access points available in the card catalogue, more data elements are being indexed and more indexes are likely to be created in the online catalogue.

Sorting Search Results

Another feature of online catalogues is the opportunity offered to the user to sort the search results in the way that will best fulfil his/her need. Most online catalogues can sort the retrieved records according to such data elements as the author, the title and the date. This sorting capability requires that, in addition to usual access points, more data elements be indexed in MARC records in the database.

Some systems, such as OKAPI (Online Keyword Access to Public Information) the experimental OPAC developed at the Polytechnic of Central London, SMART, the US National Library of Medicine catalogue CITE (Current Information Transfer in English), STATUS/IQ, CANSEARCH, PLEXUS provide ranked output and relevance feedback.

They sort and display results of a search in order of highest occurrence of keywords. Given the searcher's judgments of retrieved items as either relevant or irrelevant, some of these systems can be asked to perform another search modified automatically by relevance feedback to provide a new ranked output list.

Status, Holdings and Location Information

A major feature of the online catalogue is its ability to link circulation information to bibliographic and holdings information and to show to the searcher the status and location of the sought item(s). The user of the online catalogue is able to see the status of any volume and/or copy of the item and whether the item he/she is looking for is available on the shelf or it is on loan, on order, at binding, missing or is not for loan.

The status information also displays the 'date due' of an item on loan. The online catalogue can also show the location of the item in the library, *e.g.*, on which level and/or in which part it is located. All such information is useful also for stock taking and check-in purposes. These features help the patron, particularly the remote user, saving his/her time in knowing the status and location of the needed item(s).

Access and Availability

Unlike in a manual system, the user of the online catalogue has access to bibliographic, circulation, acquisition, holdings and location information at the same terminal, whether within the library or in other libraries through remote access. Again, this capability may be an indication of the need for uniformity and standardisation of data elements and also the importance of integrity in the structure of different files in the system.

In contrast to the possibilities for online consultation, card technology is a strictly localised medium with many physical restrictions to its use. Almost all libraries have a single set of catalogue cards for a document. To some extent a book catalogue or a COM catalogue might help in making the library catalogue available in different locations but these catalogues are costly to update at regular intervals, particularly when the collection is very large.

Unlike the card catalogue, the online catalogue is accessible through terminals located in different places in the library and outside the library via local area networks (LANs) and wide area networks (WANs). In the online environment it is possible for different users, whether inside the library building or outside it, to use the catalogue online and to even search the same record simultaneously. In terms of access to library catalogues, distance has now become irrelevant. Technology has enabled us to have decentralised access to bibliographic information.

Interconnectivity is one of the most important goals of libraries today and can take different forms. Many library catalogues are now accessible through the different tools in the Internet such as Netscape, Gopher, Mosaic and Telnet. This is a great advantage over the manual system and will continue to expand with further developments in telecommunication allied to a decrease in telecommunication costs.

There is also more flexibility with interconnectivity for the searcher to go from one catalogue to another. This is done through the same catalogue or other catalogues which have a WWW forms-based interface. These developments have brought with them new concepts such as globalisation of catalogues and the 'library without walls'.

With the availability of different types of OPAC systems to remote users over networks, for example, over the Internet, libraries need to conform to a new standard known as Z39.50. This standard is a protocol for information search and retrieval in a client-server environment, and is now moving from a standard to an operational reality. Z39.50 is used by libraries to access and search remote databases.

The WAIS system has implemented the standard to provide a consistent environment with consistent user interface, search and retrieval services. In environments supporting Z39.50 connectivity, the user sees remote catalogues as though they were additional databases available from the local system.

The standard is also being used in different library operations such as technical services, acquisitions and interlibrary loans. In this context, Z39.50 encompasses bibliographic databases, full-text documents, even numeric databases. For example, for bibliographic databases, a list of fields needed to exchange information and support those functions has been developed.

With advances in telecommunications and the rapid development of different facilities in the Internet it is now also possible to have access to electronic texts and files stored anywhere in the world. As we move to the end of the twentieth century, more full text services will become accessible through remote databases.

10

Guidelines for Standardized Cataloguing for Children

The library community has long recognized that children have their own unique characteristics and requirements as library users. They are considered a different enough audience, as users of both print and nonprint materials, that special bibliographic treatment of library materials is warranted to meet their developmental needs.

Many adult users of libraries—especially parents, teachers, and other caregivers—will also benefit from this treatment when they are using catalogs created to provide simple and full information about the content of library materials for younger and less sophisticated readers.

Adults using catalogs created for adult or general use will already have discovered that such catalogs distinguish children's materials in a library by such mechanisms as subject heading subdivisions indicating that a given work is "juvenile fiction" or "juvenile literature" as well as through differences in location.

BACKGROUND

In recognition of the unique nature of juvenile library users and in response to their needs, the *Library of Congress* (LC) established the *Annotated Card* (AC) programme in 1966. Currently administered by the Children's Literature Section, U.S. and Publisher Liaison Division, the programme has adapted the Library's cataloguing policies and practices to include annotations, modified subject heading use, and some special classification options.

The headings LC developed for use with children's materials are now known as Children's Subject Headings (CSH). The AC programme was originally accessed through catalogue cards that included annotations from the Library of Congress. it is now available through MARC (*Machine-Readable Cataloguing*) records and LC's Cataloguing-in-Publication (CIP) programme.

During the 1960s, as libraries found it cheaper or more convenient to rely on commercial or centralized processing services, it became apparent that standardization of cataloguing practices was necessary. More recently, many libraries began contributing records to shared databases, lending further weight to the need for standardization.

A study by the Cataloguing of Children's Materials Committee of the Resources and Technical Services Division (RTSD) of the American Library Association (ALA) found that the lack of a uniform standard meant that many libraries developed customised cataloguing according to their own perceived needs or that they accepted nonstandard cataloguing from other sources.

The cost of customised cataloguing, however, cuts into other services, and if the source of cataloguing changes, so do the style and standard of cataloguing. The Cataloguing of Children's Materials Committee also foresaw that the development of MARC standards and widely used bibliographic utilities offered potential for the wider dissemination of standardized cataloguing if guidelines for standardization could be developed and followed.

In response, the committee recommended in 1969 that LC's practices for cataloguing children's materials be adopted as a national standard. This recommendation was subsequently adopted by the Cataloguing and Classification Section of the Resources and Technical Services Division (RTSD. in 1989 renamed *Association for Library Collections and Technical Services* [ALCTS]).

Since the original guidelines were developed, many more libraries have benefited from shared cataloguing efforts, either through bibliographic utilities or commercial processors using MARC records, so that it is now even more advantageous in terms of cost and data compatibility to accept this standardization. The creation and exchange of bibliographic data at an international level, and access to these data by commercial processors as well as by libraries, have led the ALA to accept LC's cataloguing for children's materials as a standard.

In 1982, the Cataloguing of Children's Materials Committee, with the cooperation of the Children's Literature Section (recently renamed the Children's Literature Team, History and Literature Cataloguing Division) at LC, developed the "Guidelines for Standardized Cataloguing of Children's Materials," which were accepted by the RTSD board of directors on July 14, 1982.

Widespread use of MARC records has made it possible for many smaller libraries to automate their catalogs, converting retrospectively from card catalogs to online and World Wide Web (Web) catalogs and acquiring current machine-readable records from LC, materials vendors, and specialized vendors of cataloguing data for use in online computer systems. International developments in content and MARC standards in turn suggest the need for again updating the guidelines for policies and practices for cataloguing library materials for children, which were last revised in 2005.

SCOPE

The guidelines are intended for use in cataloguing all materials deemed intellectually suitable for children and young people. Although the matter of deciding what materials are suitable for inclusion in a given juvenile collection may be difficult and subjective, these guidelines address the needs of catalogue users through ninth grade, or approximately age 15. However, although application of these guidelines to materials for grades ten through twelve is optional, that choice may be convenient in high school libraries to provide uniformity.

LC considers materials to be "juvenile" works when they are intended by the author or publisher, or deemed suitable by the cataloger, for use by children and young people in these age and grade ranges. Catalogers in libraries with juvenile collections are encouraged to consider implementing the LC standard for all grade levels and ages newborn through 18, if their collections include materials for teens at all levels.

Agencies that contribute cataloguing to a shared database using the MARC format place an appropriate code in the fixed-field character position for target audience, indicating the intended level of the material.

Code j indicates the item is intended for general use by children and young people through the age of 15 or the ninth grade. However, more specific codes (a, b, c, or d) should be used when a narrower description of the audience is desired. If an item is appropriate for more than one audience, the code for the principal target audience is assigned.

The audience codes are defined as follows:

* a Preschool (up to, but not including, kindergarten)
* b Primary (kindergarten through grade 3)
* c Preadolescent (grades 4 through 8)
* d Adolescent (grades 9 through 12)
* g General (any audience level, including the general adult population)
* j Juvenile (all through age 15 or grade 9)

These guidelines are compatible with national cataloguing tools and should be used in conjunction with them. Currently these tools include the following:

* *Anglo-American Cataloguing Rules:* current edition (AACR2) with its latest revision and amendments, or finalized rules of Resource Description and Access (RDA) when that becomes available to the individual library
* *Library of Congress Rule Interpretations:* (LCRI)—LC policies and interpretations of AACR2 if they are applied by the individual library
* *Cataloger's Desktop:* A CD-ROM and web subscription product that includes the most-used cataloguing documentation resources in electronic form, if that product is used by the individual library in lieu of printed documentation
* *Library of Congress Subject Headings:* (LCSH), including AC/CSH modifications and principles for applying them, as issued annually and published daily on the Web when AC/CSH modifications and principles differ

from instructions published in *Subject Headings Manual* (intended for application of subject headings in non-juvenile catalogs)

* *Abridged Dewey Decimal Classification and Relative Index:* (Current edition), or *Library of Congress Classification* schedules, if those are applied at the individual library

These guidelines are based on the practices of the Library of Congress for cataloguing children's material, and they note or expand on certain rules and options in AACR2 or RDA. Rules, options, and practices that are not touched on are not meant to be excluded. References within this text to individual rules are to rules in the current (second) edition of AACR2.

Although some MARC 21 field numbers and subfield codes are identified in the guidelines, complete instructions and further information about MARC 21 and in the printed documentation for *MARC 21 Format for Bibliographic Data* and some local system manuals. Some commonly used MARC 21 fields are listed in table.

Table. 10.1 Marc 21 Bibliographic Fields Commonly Used in Juvenile Records

010	Library of Congress Control Number (LCCN)	538	System details note
		546	Language note
020	International Standard Book Number (ISBN)	600	Subject added entry Personal name
050	Library of Congress Call Number	650	Subject added entry-Topical term
082	Dewey Decimal Classification	651	Subject added entry-Geographic name
100	Main entry-Personal name		
110	Main entry-Corporate name	655	Index term-Genre/form term
130	Main entry-Uniform title		
245	Title statement	658	Index term-Curriculum objetive
246	Varying form of title		
250	Edition statement	700	Added entry-Personal name
260	Publication, distribution, etc, (Imprint)		
		710	Added entry Corporate name
300	Physical description		
490	Series statement	730	Added entry-Uniform

Table Contd...

500 General note	title
505 Formatted contents note	800 Series added entry-Personal name
508 Creation/Production creadits note	830 Series added entry-Uniform title
511 Partcipant or performer note	826 Electronic location and access
520 Summary note	
521 Target Audience Note	
526 Study Programme information note	

GUIDELINES FOR DESCRIPTION AND ACCESS

These guidelines address the following:

* Description of print and nonprint—including electronic —materials and resources
* Name, title, and series access points for various types of materials
* Subject heading use for juvenile catalogs
* Classification of juvenile collections

DESCRIPTION

Level of Description

The description of the material to be cataloged must follow the second level of description as found in rule 1.0D2 in AACR2 unless there is a special need for third-level (very detailed) description. Although many libraries have previously used abbreviated cataloguing similar to the first level of description, the first level of description does not provide for elements that are considered important by many libraries and, therefore, are required by the guidelines.

These elements include statements of responsibility (including subsequent statements of responsibility such as "illustrated by..."), dimensions, and series information. Elements that require clarification, or for which specific treatment is suggested, are discussed more fully in the following parts.

General Material Designation

The general material designation (GMD), or general material designation (rule 1.1C. subfield h of MARC field 245), though optional in AACR2 and selectively applied in LCRI, is strongly recommended in these guidelines for *all* nonbook formats of materials in List 2.

The GMD should appear in square brackets immediately following the title proper, because its purposes are to identify the broad class of material to which an item belongs and to distinguish between different forms of the same work early in the description. It precedes any other title information, such as a subtitle. Use of the GMD "text" is optional. however, most agencies do not use it for books.

Table 10.2: Example of an Annotated Catalogue Card for a Book

Fic Kerby, Mona, Owney, the mail-pouch pooch/Mona Kerby; Pictures by Lynne Barasch.— 1st ed.—New York: Farrar, Straus and Giroux, 2008. [42] p.: col. ill., map; 21 cm. *Summary:* In 1988, Owney, a stray terrier puppy, finds a home a in the Albany, New York post office and becomes its official mascot as he rides the mail train through the Adirondacks and beyond, criss-crossing the United States, into Canada and Mexico, and eventually travelling around the world by mail boat in 132 days. *ISBN-13:* 978.0-374-35685-9 *ISBN-10*: 0-374-35685-8 1. Owney (Dog)—Juvenile fiction. [Oweny (Dog)-Fiction. 2. Terriers—Fiction. 3. Dogs—Fiction. 4. Mascots-Fiction. 5. Postal service—Fiction. 6. Vogages and Travels—Fiction.] I. Barasch, Lynne, ill. II. Title. PZ10.3.K4845 Own 2008 [Fic]—dc 22 2006047605

Notes

AACR2 provides for many optional elements. The note area of the catalogue record has the widest range of options. Notes may be provided if the cataloger or cataloguing agency deems them necessary. they may be accepted or revised as part of a record from a vendor, with special attention to appropriate language for the potential user of the material.

These guidelines strongly encourage use of the summary or annotation note (MARC field 520), which is part of most Annotated Card programme records. It consists of an objective statement of the most important elements of the plot, theme, or topic of the work. A summary, or annotation, should describe the unique aspects of the work and generally justify, whenever possible, the assigned subject headings, but it should not praise or criticize the item's content nor be so vague as to be useless in making a selection.

Words in the summary should be chosen to facilitate keyword searching in online catalogs, using synonyms for words found in the title and subject headings, for example. Users of nonbook items are especially dependent on summary notes because of the greater difficulty of browsing such materials. However, a summary note is not required if a contents note (MARC field 505) that describes the nature and the scope of the work is used. A contents note is used to record the titles of individual selections contained in an item such as a book, sound recording, or videorecording. AACR2 specifies the order in which notes are to be given. If both the summary note (MARC 520) and the contents note (MARC 505) are present, the contents note will often be the last note in the record.

Table 10.3. Example of a Marc 21 Record for a Book

Leader 01776cam a2200385 a 450			the Adirondacks and
001	14374812		beyond, criss-crossing
055	20081124130439.0		the United States, into
008	060512s2008nyuab		Canada and Maxico,
	j b 000 1 eng		and eventually traveling
010 _	Ia 2006047605		around the world by
020 _	Ia 0374357858		mail boat in 132 days.
020 _	Ia 97803743568559	650 0_	Ia Owney (Dog) Iv
040 _	Ia DLC Ic DLC Id		Juvenile fiction.
	TxGeoBT	650 1_	Ia Owney (Dog) Iv
042 _	Ia lcac		Fiction.
05000	Ia PZ10.3K4845	650 1_	Ia Terriers Iv Fiction.
	Ib Own 2008	650 1_	Ia Dogs Iv Fiction.

Table Contd...

082 00	Ia [Fic] I2 22
1001_	Ia Kerby, Mona.
245 10	Ia Owney, the mail-pouch pooch/Ic Mona Kerby; pictures by Lynne Barasch.
250_	Ia 1st ed.
260_	Ia New York: Ib Farrar, Straus and Giroux, Ic 2008
300_	Ia [42]p.: col. ill., map ; Ic 21 cm.
520_	Ia In 1888, Owney, a stray terrier puppy, finds a home in the Albany, New York post office and becomes its official mascot as he rides the mail train through
650 1_	Ia Mascots Iv Fiction.
650 1_	Ia Postal service Iv. Fiction
650 1_	Ia Voyages and travels Iv Fiction.
85642	I3 Contributor biographical Information: Iu http://www.loc.gov/ catdir/enhacements/ fy0804/2006047605.b.html
85642	I3 Publisher description: Iu http://www.loc.gov/ catdir/enhancements /fy0804/ 2006047605.d.html

Information about system requirements should be provided for videorecordings, electronic resources, and some sound recordings. One may use or include such common terms as *CD* or *DVD* in notes. The participant or performer note (MARC field 511) is used to list names of performers or cast members on sound recordings and videorecordings. The cataloger may optionally provide name added entries for any or all names in 511 notes.

Two other notes are especially applicable to juvenile materials. Target audience notes (MARC field 521) contain information about reading grade level, interest age level, or interest grade level of the intended audience of an item. Because more than one may be provided, and measures and opinions often do not agree, the source of the statement of level must be included. The awards note (MARC field 586) contains information about awards associated with an item, such as the Newbery Medal and Academy Awards, along with the date (year) of the award.

ISBN

The International Standard Book Number (ISBN. MARC field 020) is required when available. If there are two or more ISBNs, they should all be included in separate 020 fields. In a

MARC record, the ISBN is given near the beginning of the record, before the rest of the description. On cards, the area for standard number and terms of availability (price) follows the area for notes.

NAME, TITLE, AND SERIES ACCESS POINTS

There is no variation from AACR2 in either choice or form of main entry for children's materials. The form of added entries for names and titles also remains the same. However, for names used as subject access points follow the guidelines in the part "Subject Headings." The choice of added entries for names and titles and the choice and form of series added entries are discussed here.

Table 10.4: Example of an Annotated Catalogue Card for a Nonbook Item

636.752 Grogan, John, 1957–
Marley and me [sound recording]/written and read by John Grogan.—
[New York]: Harper Audio, p2005.—
5 sound discs: digitl; 43/4 in.—
Compact discs.
Subtitle on Container: Life and love with the world's worst dog.
Abridged reading of the book, published New York: Morrow, 2005.
Summary: Auther John Grogan's vivid description of how Marley, a wriggly yellow furball, grew into a large Labradoe retriever and changed his family's life.
ISBN-13: 978.0-167132-6
1. Grogan, John, 1957-. 2. Labrador retriever—Florida—Biogaphy. [1. Grogan, John, 1957-. 2. Labrador retriever.] I. Title. II. Title: Marley and me
SF429.L3G76 2005x 636.752'7'092-dc22

Name Access Points

The LC maintains an electronic file of the authorized form of each name in its bibliographic records. The authorized form is established according to the rules in AACR2 Part 2, along with various rule interpretations (LCRIs) and options that appear there. As part of the name authority component (NACO) of the Programme for Cooperative Cataloguing (PCC), many non-LC participants contribute records to the Name Authority File (NAF). The file is more broadly known as the LC/NACO Authority File.

Currently, the file contains over six million authority records. Of this total, names, series titles, uniform titles, and name/title combinations are found in the LC/NACO file. These include topical subjects as well as the names of fictitious characters. These authority records are freely available for consultation, copying and pasting, and downloading. Librarians developing catalogs for young and other readers should always verify and use the form of names and titles in the LC/NACO file so that searchers are not confused by multiple forms representing the same person or body.

In bibliographic records, added entries for individuals (MARC field 700) and groups (corporate bodies, MARC field 710) are provided to improve access to names other than those used as main entries, which are authorized forms of entry for the individual or first-named author of a work:

* Added name entries should be made for all authors if two or three individuals or bodies collaborated on the work. If four or more collaborated, an added entry (called a "tracing" in card catalogs) is made only for the first author named.
* Added entries for illustrators are required, as their contribution to a work may equal or overshadow that of a writer. Access to the record by illustrators' names is important not only for the artistic content but also for collocating works of artists. If the illustrator is also the author of the work, a separate added entry is not made. For illustrators whose contribution consists only of the cover, frontispiece, or incidental or repeating chapter-head decorations, or for designers who are not also the illustrators, added entries are optional.
* Added entries should be made for principal performers on sound recordings and for producers,

directors, and writers of videorecordings unless there are more than three of each. If there are four or more, make an added entry only under the one named first in each category. However, the cataloger may exercise judgment in the number of added entries, limiting these to those deemed useful for a young audience.

* Although AACR2 allows the optional use of function designations for editors, compilers, and the like (subfield e of MARC field 700), only the designation ill. (for illustrator) is required by these guidelines.

Title Access Points

Generally, make a title entry for all items in the library. Specifically:

* Make an added entry for the title even if the title proper (MARC field 245, subfield a) is the same as an assigned subject heading. Even in a catalogue in which name-title and subject entries are interfiled, this added access is important for younger catalogue users. It is also essential for divided card catalogs and online catalogues, as the title must appear as an entry in the title index itself, thus allowing for retrieval by title alone.
* Make an added entry for the title even if the title proper is the same as the main entry heading for a personal or corporate name.

In MARC records, the first indicator setting will be 1 in field 245. this indicates that title entry is made for the title proper. Added title entries (MARC field 246) should be made for other versions of a title under which users are likely to search, whether these actually appear on the item or not. Varying forms of titles are recorded in MARC field 246 with the first indicator set to 3 so that these titles will be indexed and retrievable in a title search. The authorized forms of many names (personal, corporate, etc.) as well as series and uniform titles may be easily verified in the LC/NACO file.

Series Access Points

Series access is particularly important for children's materials because the series title is a source of information about the content and approach of a work. Make a series added entry for each work in the series that is cataloged if it provides a useful access point. Add the number of the individual work within the series if there is a number.

The series added entry (MARC field 490) should use the title as it appears on the item. If the series title is deemed unimportant for searching purposes, as in the case of an imprint name used as a series title, the title is given in MARC field 490. The first indicator in the 490 field specifies whether there will be an added series entry and whether it will be indexed. A first indicator of 0 specifies that the series title will not be indexed.

For example,

* 490 1_ ‡a Pelican books

If, as is most often the case, that title is useful in searching, it is then searched in the LC/NACO authority file. the authorized form of the series is then recorded in field 8XX of the MARC record, whether it is the same as or different from the title that appears on the item. The first indicator setting of 1 in field 490 specifies that the series will be indexed. the second indicator of 0 in field 830 specifies that the authorized form of the title has no nonfiling characters.

For example,

* 490 1_ ‡a Sports stars
* 830 _0 ‡a Sports stars
* 490 1_ ‡a A series of unfortunate events. ‡v bk. 1
* 830 _0 ‡a Lemony Snicket's A series of unfortunate events
* 490 1 ‡a Kids make a difference
* 830 _0 ‡a Reading expeditions series. ‡p Kids make a difference

When the authorized form of the series has a personal name as the first element, it is entered in an 800 field. The name in subfield a is used as in the LC/NACO authority file followed by a t subfield containing the series title. The entire name-title entry must be used. The first indicator is set to 1 when the first element of the author's name is a surname.

For example,

* 490 1 ‡a Alphabet books
* 800 1 ‡a Moncure, Jane Belk. ‡t Alphabet books

Series added entries can be uniform titles, including collective uniform titles, although few of this type are encountered in juvenile collections. For example,

* 800 1_ ‡a Shakespeare, William, ‡d 1564-1616. ‡t Works. ‡f 2008

SUBJECT HEADINGS

Until the Library of Congress's Subject Authority File was made available on the Web, the best print source for subject headings was the most recent edition of *Library of Congress Subject Headings* (LCSH) with its list of Children's Subject Headings (CSH). The online version, which contains records contributed by participants in the Subject Authority Cooperative programme (SACO), is now part of the LC/NACO authority file.

Although the online version is more current, CSH terms are rarely changed, and the printed version is usually entirely satisfactory. The printed version includes the usage guidelines—including subdivision practice—in addition to the list, so this version is still invaluable. The list is also available on Classification Web, a subscription product.

The CSH list contains terms created as alternatives to terms in the main list. these replacement terms are designed to offer more appropriate subject headings for juvenile catalogue users and to afford them easier subject access to materials. Each term includes references to the unused term(s)—that is, those found in the main list and which have been replaced by the bold-font terms.

Any heading chosen from a printed copy of the multivolume LCSH ("big red") books should be checked against the exception list of CSH (in the front of the first volume or in the supplementary volume) or online to see if there is a replacement term.

Records created under the CSH programme are updated online daily and are distributed weekly and daily via subscription on the MARC Distribution Service. Although record and card printing programmes may be coded to delete or keep the bracketed information, CSH records may be identified easily by the presence of a subject heading with a second-indicator value of 1.

For example:

* 600 11 ‡a Lincoln, Abraham, ‡d 1809-1865 ‡x Childhood and youth
* 650 _1 ‡a Holiday cooking
* 651 _1 ‡a Virginia ‡x History

CSH headings are identified in Cataloguing-in-Publication (CIP) data and on catalogue cards by brackets.

For example,

* [1. Family life—Fiction. 2. Christmas—Fiction.]

Subject headings may also be added from the *Sears List of Subject Headings,* either by a vendor or local cataloguing agency, with the second indicator set to 7 and the code "sears" provided in subfield 2 to identify the source of the term.

For example,

* 650 _7 ‡a Glass manufacture. ‡2 sears

If the cataloger is using OCLC's standards, the second indicator in the 6XX field should be set to 8 for Sears subject headings.

* 650 _8 ‡a Glass manufacture

APPLICATION OF CHILDREN'S SUBJECT HEADINGS AND SUBDIVISIONS

Some CSH headings are simplified forms of standard LC headings, but the chief difference between CSH and LC heading use is in the rules for application of subject headings.

Review the full details, found in the front matter in LCSH volume 1. only a brief summary is provided here:

* *Omit the subdivision*—Juvenile literature, and related subdivisions such as—Juvenile films and—Juvenile fiction.
* Avoid special juvenile form headings, such as Children's poetry and Children's plays.
* Avoid the term *American* and the subdivision—United States when the subject is universal in nature. Use other geographic terms normally, such as the names of states or provinces and other nations.
* Delete words in topical headings that would be superfluous in a juvenile catalogue. For example, use Parties instead of Children's parties.

* Assign subject headings to fiction as well as nonfiction to bring out the most important subject-oriented aspects of the work. For example, use the subdivision —Fiction for all fictional material.
* Assign both specific and broader, general headings (*e.g.*, Turtles and Sea turtles) to a work if both provide useful subject access.
* Assign headings designating the literary form (*e.g.*, Jokes. Stories in rhyme) whenever access by form of material appears helpful.
* Assign both popular and scientific terms (*e.g.*, Cats and Felidae) for the same work if that appears helpful, especially for older children. Note, however, that the CSH list customarily substitutes common names of animals and plants for scientific ones in the LC standard list.
* Assign CSH replacement subdivisions, such as—Cartoons and comics, in juvenile catalogs.

CREATION OF NEW SUBJECT HEADINGS

The CSH list and LCSH do not provide suitable terminology for the children's materials at hand, the following steps may be taken:

* Contact LC to suggest new subject headings for the CSH list or LCSH
* Create a term to be used locally, and give it in MARC fields 690 or 653 if your automated system allows searches on these fields.
* If using the Sears list, create a term to be used locally, and write the term at its alphabetical place in the book.

USE OF MARC FIELD 658 FOR CURRICULAR OBJECTIVES

If it is the policy of the local library or is deemed important to list index terms denoting curriculum or course-study objectives applicable to the materials being described, use terms found in published local or state sources in subfield a and identify the source in subfield 2 of the MARC 658 field. Other subfields in this field, such as subfield c (Curriculum code), are optional.

For example:

* 658 _ _ ‡a Earth and space ‡c 1211(b)(7-8) ‡2 txac
* 658 _ _ ‡a Community history ‡2 local

CLASSIFICATION

The following guidelines require the choice of either the Dewey Decimal Classification (MARC field 082) or the Library of Congress Classification (MARC field 050).

Dewey Decimal Classification

* For fiction for preschool through second grade (K–2) or through age 8, assign the letter E.
* For fiction for third grade (age 9) and up, assign the classification Fic or F.
* For nonfiction materials, assign a number from the current abridged edition of the Dewey Decimal Classification (DDC). Treatment of biography is described in item 4 of this list.
* For biography, assign the class number representing the subject of the person's most noted contribution, as instructed in the current abridged edition of the Dewey Decimal Classification. The Cutter should be based on the subject entry for the individual. For collective biography, assign 920. the Cutter is based on the main entry. Other options included in the Abridged DDC are also appropriate, such as B for individual biographies. LC provides full and abridged DDC numbers for both individual and collective biographies, as well as the B option, in its MARC records.

Library of Congress Classification

* For fiction, assign numbers from the PZ schedule.
* For nonfiction materials, assign numbers from the appropriate nonfiction schedule.

Classification of Folklore

Under either Dewey or Library of Congress classification, use the following guidelines to determine whether an item is folklore:

* Folklore is defined as those items of culture that are

learned orally, by imitation or by observation, including narratives (tales, legends, proverbs, etc.). A story about fairies is not folklore unless it meets the criterion of having been handed down orally from generation to generation. It might be a modern piece of fantasy instead.

* Regard relatively faithful retellings and adaptations of folk material as folklore.
* Do not consider religious mythology, stories from the Bible or other religious scriptures, modern fantasies, or drastic alterations of folk material as folklore, but class them elsewhere.

LOCAL IMPLEMENTATION

Adopting this standard does not require libraries or catalogers to use records created by LC or to accept all elements of records available online or through commercial vendors. Data manipulation and design of local cataloguing profiles are provided by most commercial vendors and utilities and are accommodated by most machine-readable formats.

However, libraries that contribute to shared databases and vendors that supply MARC records are expected to conform to those database or union catalogue standards. Libraries that do not use computer services now, or that are not currently involved in shared catalogs, may well do so in the future.

It is thus to the advantage of all libraries to have and follow a recommended standard for cataloguing juvenile materials. As a further benefit, by making children's cataloguing compatible with that for adult materials—without sacrificing its unique characteristics—this standard enables the young user to understand the adult catalogue, whether it is in a public or academic setting.

These guidelines give sufficient latitude for the individual cataloger or library to meet local needs while remaining within the standard. The recommendations in these guidelines are intended to meet the requirements of young library users, in accordance with the purpose of the catalogue record.

Bibliography

Balagopal, K.: *"A Manual of MARC Practice for Libraries"*, Andhra Pradesh: *Economic and Political Weekly*, 2001.

Bandhu, P.: *Authority Work: The Creation, Use, Maintenance, and Evaluation of Authority Records and Files*, New Delhi: Long Life Publications, 2003.

Bapat, Gururao V.: *MARC Manual: Understanding and Using MARC Records*, Karnataka: Regional Resources Centre for Folk Performing Arts, 2002.

Bhargav, G.: *Cataloging the Web: Metadata, AACR, and MARC*, Hyderabad: Self Publications, 2005.

Bhat, Chandrashekhar: *Authority Control: Principles, Applications, and Instructions*, New Delhi: Concept Publishing Company, 2003.

Charsley, Simon R.: *The Conceptual Foundations of Descriptive Cataloging*,New Delhi: Sage Publications, 2006.

Charsley, Simon: *"Cataloging Non-print Materials: Blitz Cataloging Workbook"*, Hyderabad: *Economic and Political Weekly*, 2005.

Chitnis, V.: *Foundations of Cataloging: A Sourcebook*, Pune: Futuristic Digital, 2005.

Clough, John E.: *Media Access and Organization: A Cataloging and Reference Sources Guide for Nonbook Materials*, New York: The Macmillan Company, 2001.

Coburn, Thomas B.: *The Future of Cataloging*, Delhi, Motilal Banarsidas, 2000.

Deliege, Robert: *The Future of the Descriptive Cataloging Rules, Man*, London: Cambridge University, 2003.

Jogdand Mahipal, *The Bibliographic Record and Information Technology*, Mumbai: College of Social Work, 2001.

Jogdand, P.: *Minimal Level Cataloging by National Bibliographic Agencies*, New York: Cambridge University Press, 2000.

Kale, R.: *Learn Descriptive Cataloging*, London: Cambridge MA: Perseus Publishing, 2006.

Kumar, N.: *Origins, Content, and Future of AACR2 Revised*, Shipra Publications, Banglore, 2004.

Michael, S.: *Policy and Practice in Bibliographic Control of Non-book Media*, Toronto: Thomson Nelson, 2008.

Omvedt, G.: *Manheimer's Cataloging and Classification: A Workbook*, Hyderabad: Self Publications, 2007.

Pal, R.: *The Nature of "A Work": Implications for the Organization of Knowledge*, Hyderabad: Self Publications, 2000.

Pandit, V.: *The Intellectual Foundation of Information Organization, Maharashtra: Vidnayak Sansod Prakashan, Ujgaon*, Maharashtra: Pune University, 2002.

Paswan, S.: *Encyclopedia of Library Cataloguing*, Kolkotta: Kolkotta University, 2002.

Punalekar, S.: *The Intellectual Foundation of Information Organization*, New Delhi: Gyan Prakashan, 2001.

Raj, M.: *The Organization of Information*, New York: Institute of Modern Studies. 2006.

Tirmare, P.: *Library Cataloging: Issues and Facts*, Maharashtra: Pune University, 2000.

Webstar, J.: *Library Cataloging in Modern Indian Libraries*, New Delhi: Vistar Publications, 2001.

Zelliot, E.: *Dr. Wynar's Introduction to Cataloging and Classification*, New Delhi: Jain Publications, 2003.